Longing, Intimacy and Loneliness

This book examines the very basic human need to belong. It looks at the intimacy that is a cornerstone of such belonging and closeness, romantic relationships, which signify belonging in the Western world, and loneliness and love, which are inextricably linked to the subject. The book examines these constructs and considers other issues such as the basic human need to belong; the different love styles and how they are expressed; empathy, social support and humour and their influence on looseness and romantic elations; loneliness and marital adjustment; the influence of culture on relationships and the loneliness felt by the partner.

This book is based on papers that were originally published in *The Journal of Psychology*.

Ami Rokach, PhD is Executive Editor of *The Journal of Psychology*. He is a clinical psychologist, and a member of the Departments of Psychology at York University, Toronto, Canada; The Centre for Academic Studies, Or Yehuda Israel; and Walden University, USA.

Longing, Intimacy and Loneliness

Edited by
Ami Rokach

LONDON AND NEW YORK

First published 2014 by Routledge

2 Park Square, Milton Park, Abingdon, Oxfordshire OX14 4RN
711 Third Avenue, New York, NY 10017

Routledge is an imprint of the Taylor & Francis Group, an informa business

First issued in paperback 2018

Copyright © 2014 Taylor & Francis

All rights reserved. No part of this book may be reprinted or reproduced or utilised in any form or by any electronic, mechanical, or other means, now known or hereafter invented, including photocopying and recording, or in any information storage or retrieval system, without permission in writing from the publishers.

Notice:
Product or corporate names may be trademarks or registered trademarks, and are used only for identification and explanation without intent to infringe.

British Library Cataloguing in Publication Data
A catalogue record for this book is available from the British Library

ISBN 13: 978-0-415-84218-1 (hbk)
ISBN 13: 978-1-138-37786-8 (pbk)

Typeset in Times New Roman
by Taylor & Francis Books

Publisher's Note
The publisher accepts responsibility for any inconsistencies that may have arisen during the conversion of this book from journal articles to book chapters, namely the possible inclusion of journal terminology.

Disclaimer
Every effort has been made to contact copyright holders for their permission to reprint material in this book. The publishers would be grateful to hear from any copyright holder who is not here acknowledged and will undertake to rectify any errors or omissions in future editions of this book.

Dedication

To Natalie, the love of my life, who has been the source of happiness, grace, and love for me and those who know her.

Contents

Citation Information   ix

Longing, Intimacy and Loneliness: *The Interplay Between Romance, Love and Alienation* – An Introduction
Ami Rokach   1

Part I: What Contributes to a Good Intimate Relationship   7

1. Dimensions and Aspects of Longing: Age and Gender Differences in Swedish 9-, 12-, and 15-Year-Old Children
   Olle Holm   9

2. Processes Through Which Adolescents Believe Romantic Relationships Influence Friendship Quality
   Jennifer. J. Thomas   26

3. How Do Romantic Relationship Satisfaction, Gender Stereotypes, and Gender Relate to Future Time Orientation In Romantic Relationships?
   Nuray Sakalli-Ugurlu   48

4. Empathy and Social Support Provision in Couples: Social Support and the Need to Study the Underlying Processes
   Inge Devoldre, Mark H. Davis, Lesley L. Verhofstadt, and Anne Buysse   58

5. Relationship Satisfaction and Conflict Over Minor and Major Issues In Romantic Relationships
   Duncan Cramer   84

6. Socially Desirable Responding and Impression Management in the Endorsement of Love Styles
   Martin F. Davies   91

7. Humor Use in Romantic Relationships: The Effects of Relationship Satisfaction and Pleasant Versus Conflict Situations
   Bethany Butzer and Nicholas A. Kuiper   100

CONTENTS

8. Words as Environmental Cues: The Effect of the Word "Loving" on Compliance to a Blood Donation Request
   Virginie Charles-Sire, Nicolas Guéguen, Alexandre Pascual and Sébastien Meineri — 116

Part II: Loneliness and Intimate Relationships — 133

9. Loneliness and Marital Adjustment of Turkish Couples
   Ayhan Demir and Hürol Fişiloğlu — 135

10. How Does Culture Influence the Degree of Romantic Loneliness and Closeness?
    Sean Seepersad, Mi-Kyung Choi and Nana Shin — 146

11. Longing, Love, and Loneliness
    Ami Rokach — 154

    Index — 165

Citation Information

The following chapters in this book were originally published in various issues of *The Journal of Psychology*. When citing this material, please use the original page numbering for each article, as follows:

Chapter 1
Dimensions and Aspects of Longing: Age and Gender Differences in Swedish 9-, 12-, and 15-Year-Old Children
Olle Holm
The Journal of Psychology, volume 135, issue 4 (2001)
pp. 381–397

Chapter 2
Processes Through Which Adolescents Believe Romantic Relationships Influence Friendship Quality
Jennifer. J. Thomas
The Journal of Psychology, volume 146, issue 6 (2012)
pp. 595–616

Chapter 3
How Do Romantic Relationship Satisfaction, Gender Stereotypes, and Gender Relate to Future Time Orientation In Romantic Relationships?
Nuray Sakalli-Ugurlu
The Journal of Psychology, volume 137, issue 3 (2003)
pp. 294–303

Chapter 4
Empathy and Social Support Provision in Couples: Social Support and the Need to Study the Underlying Processes
Inge Devoldre, Mark H. Davis, Lesley L. Verhofstadt, and Anne Buysse
The Journal of Psychology, volume 144, issue 3 (2010)
pp. 259–284

Chapter 5
Relationship Satisfaction and Conflict Over Minor and Major Issues In Romantic Relationships

CITATION INFORMATION

Duncan Cramer
The Journal of Psychology, volume 136, issue 1 (2002)
pp. 75–81

Chapter 6
Socially Desirable Responding and Impression Management in the Endorsement of Love Styles
Martin F. Davies
The Journal of Psychology, volume 135, issue 5 (2001)
pp. 562–570

Chapter 7
Humor Use in Romantic Relationships: The Effects of Relationship Satisfaction and Pleasant Versus Conflict Situations
Bethany Butzer and Nicholas A. Kuiper
The Journal of Psychology, volume 142, issue 3 (2008)
pp. 245–260

Chapter 8
Words as Environmental Cues: The Effect of the Word "Loving" on Compliance to a Blood Donation Request
Virginie Charles-Sire, Nicolas Guéguen, Alexandre Pascual and Sébastien Meineri
The Journal of Psychology, volume 145, issue 5 (2012)
pp. 455–470

Chapter 9
Loneliness and Marital Adjustment of Turkish Couples
Ayhan Demir and Hürol Fişiloğlu
The Journal of Psychology, volume 133, issue 2 (1999)
pp. 230–240

Chapter 10
How Does Culture Influence the Degree of Romantic Loneliness and Closeness?
Sean Seepersad, Mi-Kyung Choi and Nana Shin
The Journal of Psychology, volume 142, issue 2 (2008)
pp. 209–216

Please direct any queries you may have about the citations to
clsuk.permissions@cengage.com

Longing, Intimacy and Loneliness: *The Interplay between Romance, Love and Alienation* - An Introduction

AMI ROKACH

"The whole conviction of my life now rests upon the belief that loneliness, far from being a rare and curious phenomenon, peculiar to myself and to a few other solitary men, is the central and inevitable fact of human existence." [Thomas Wolfe]

Ours is the age of relationships. We, in the Western world, believe in the uniqueness, importance and availability of relating to others, thinking that we know how to conquer the barriers against closeness that we erect. Whereas in the past, work was seen as the valued solution to self-fulfillment, today it is relationships which appear to be the main, if not the only means by which self-esteem can be affirmed. A paradox is thus created, whereas on one hand we yearn for close intimate relationships, on the other hand our social conditions are not conducive to the development of close, intimate human relations. Our Western life style, in the dawn of the twenty first century, both enhance interpersonal alienation and makes it more difficult to cope with (Rokach, 2000). Everyone is seeking companionship and many seem to be having trouble finding it. Good, close, intimate relationships have become scarce (Gordon, 1976; Meer, 1985).

Loneliness has become a familiar way of life to millions of North Americans; to adolescents, the single, divorced, house wives, and the scores of people who call hot lines and suicide prevention centers. It is so widespread and aversive, that a billion-dollar loneliness industry has been developed to meet the desire of those who don't know what to do about their loneliness (Rokach, 1988). We are tempted with an array of relational possibilities, social skills upgrading, and semi-forced joined activities. Many lonely people join the ride in an attempt to become un-lonely, and frequently end up more hopeless than they were when they started. Dating online and the explosive growth of Facebook, are but two attempts at creating virtual communities, that may replace, for many, flesh-and-blood friends (see also Cacioppo & Patrick, 2008).

Humans are fundamentally social creatures. Our quality of life, even our survival, depend on others. We thrive on social intercourse and consequently, when we become socially disconnected our psychological, physiological and even spiritual well-being may be negatively affected (Pond, Brey & DeWall, 2011). As Distel (2010) noted, the average person spends nearly 80% of his or her waking hours in the company or others. People's survival depends on their collective abilities, rather than on their individual might.

Psychology, while showing growing interest in loneliness, has not devoted much attention to the need to belong. And as Doherty (1995) so poignantly observed, our very sophisticated microscopes make the heavens (and the bigger picture) invisible. "As social beings most humans live in a matrix of relationships that, to a larger extent, define their identity ... and our personality" (Mellor et al., 2008, p. 213). Such reliance on belongingness explains the resultant loneliness and psychological health issues which may arise when those needs remain unfulfilled. People in relationships which are mutually nurturing, report higher satisfaction than reported by those who are not in such relationships (Baumeister, Wottman & Stillwell, 1993). Pond et al. (2011) asserted that the desire for social acceptance is universal and instinctive. In fact, contends Baumeister and colleagues (1995), there may be an "internal gauge" which they termed the 'Socio-meter' and which helps us constantly monitor the environment for clues to changes in our inclusionary status. For it is so important to us, that as we become aware of it, we may endeavour to improve it (see also Leary, Rogers, Canfield & Coe, 1986).

Dean Ornish (2007), in his recent book *The Spectrum* observed that "Medicine today focuses primarily on drugs and surgery, genes and germs, microbes and molecules. Yet love and intimacy are at the root of what makes us sick and what makes us well. If a new medication had the same impact, failure to prescribe it would be malpractice" (p. 30). Many studies, Ornish maintained, that were conducted throughout the world have shown that those who feel lonely and depressed are many times more likely to die prematurely than those who have a strong sense of love and intimacy, connection and community. He further believes (and I join him in it) that the most powerful motivating force in the world is Love. Love is even more powerful than survival. For instance, almost all parents would suffer, or even sacrifice their lives, to help or keep their children safe and away from harm's way.

So what is love? That is a question that is probably as old as humanity. Writers, philosophers, poets and sculptors have attempted to describe and capture its meaning for centuries, but it is only relatively recently that social scientists have shown interest in researching and writing about it (Fehr, 2006). An eloquent definition of love was offered by Gottschall and Nordlund (2006) who observed that "To love someone romantically is ... to experience a strong desire for union with someone who is deemed entirely unique. It is to idealize this person, to think constantly about him or her, and to discover that one's own life priorities have changed dramatically. It is to care deeply for the person's well being, and to feel pain or emptiness when he or she is absent" (p. 450).

It is, thus, obvious that humans yearn to belong, that their survival depends on it, and that if they do not receive it, loneliness is the result. Loneliness may act as pain does for our bodies. It alerts us to the need to connect, belong and be part of a group or community, and better yet – to be loved. Love is not a panacea to loneliness, but can nourish our souls, introduce a sense of belonging into our lives, and adds what some may call, "salt and pepper" to our existence.

The present book is a compilation of articles that have addressed those issues: loneliness, belonging, and the intimacy of love. The first part *'What Contributes to a Good Intimate Relationship'* deals with what contributes to good intimate relations. The following articles form this section:

Holm (2001) viewed longing as a "blend" between love and sadness, or as others suggested a blend between depression and happiness. In researching the effects of age and gender on longing, as experienced by adolescents of both genders, this study's results indicated that 15 year old female adolescents experienced longing significantly more than males of the same age. Holmes concluded that those differences were found since girls not only are more aware than boys of their feelings, but experience more deeply and more frequently the longing to belong and be loved.

Still addressing adolescents, Thomas (2012) explored how romantic relationships influence their (adolescents') friendships. Three hundred and forty students, of both genders from grades nine and eleven, indicated that they believed that in romantic relationships one can find intimate exchange, co-rumination, encouragement, and conflict resolution on a frequent basis. Additionally, gender differences indicated that romantic relationships may exert stronger influence over friendships of females than over the ones developed by males. Thus concluded Thomas, the process which he investigated influences friendships either positively or negatively.

Sakalli-Ugurlu (2003) was intrigued to explore intimate relationship satisfaction, and whether and how it relates to the structural set of beliefs about men and women in romantic relationships. Results indicated that *women's* attitudes towards men's assertive mode of behaviour, and *men's* dominance in relationships, were important predictors of their future time orientation towards romantic relationships, more so than actual relationship satisfaction. Men, on the other hand, in forming their future time orientation towards romantic relationships, were influenced by men's assertiveness and romantic relationship satisfaction and less by men's dominance. Women, as may be intuitively expected, were more future oriented in their ongoing romantic relationships than men were.

Develdore, Davis, Verhofstadt & Buysee (2010) attempted to find out what are the antecedents of social support provision within close relationships. Social support, while of utmost importance to all of us, is particularly poignant in marital and intimate relationships. Research, generally, did address that issue, but there is not much exploration of the factors that contribute to provision of such support. The authors addressed cognitive and affective empathy of the support provider and how it influences the actual level of support provision in romantic relationships. Results clearly indicated that spousal support provision was affected by the emotional depth of the relationship, and that individual differences in empathy, beyond relational variables, were a significant factor in spousal empathy provision.

Cramer (2002) examined the romantic relational quality from a different perspective. Since all relationships are punctuated by disagreements and arguments, he explored how conflicts – over minor or major issues – affect the couple's relationship satisfaction. Sixty four women and twenty nine men completed scales measuring their satisfaction from the relationship, and the conflicts they had to address. Results indicated, as we could expect to find in couples who are doing well, that most conflicts involved minor rather than major conflicts. This study found that conflicts, whether minor or major ones, affected relationship satisfaction in a similar manner. Consequently, suggested Cramer, it is not so much the importance of the issue that the couple is facing or are in conflict about, but the way they handle it.

Love was viewed by theoreticians as composed of six different styles: Eros, Ludus, Storge, Pragma, Mania and Agape. Davies (2001) investigated the social desirability of the various styles as related to the gender of those displaying them. His results could be summarized as follows:

a. Men, but not women, associate Eros (romantic, passionate love) with social desirability.
b. Men associate Ludus (game-playing love) with social desirability, while women associate it with social undesirability.
c. Agape (selfless love) is associated with social desirability in women, but with social undesirability in men.

Since romantic relational satisfaction is so central for intimately involved couples, Butzer & Kuiper (2008) examined the effects of positive, negative, and avoiding type humour on romantic relationships. They wanted to explore how those types of humour were related to the degree of relational satisfaction and to the type of situation involved: a conflict vs. a pleasant encounter. Results indicated that couples used, mostly, positive humour with their partner; they utilized less frequently avoiding humour, and tried to stay away from negative humour. That provides support to previous findings that positive humour is often used to reduce tension in romantic relationships, though occasionally, couples use humour to also change the topic of conversation or to put their partner down. In general, it was found, that degree of relational satisfaction is related to the use of humour in intimate romantic relationships.

Love and loving words can do wonders, we know it. We all yearn for love, and rejoice in being loved. Charles-Sire, Guéguen, Pascual & Meineri (2012) went beyond what makes us feel good, and wondered whether utilizing the words 'love' and 'loving' when asking for something, like soliciting blood donations, would actually increase the number of people who are ready to donate blood. A large number of participants (N = 3600) took part in a study where solicitors of blood donations wore t-shirts with the words "Loving = Helping" or "Donating = Helping." Results confirmed the authors' hypothesis. Using the word 'Love' increased blood donations as compared to a control condition. The authors noted that their results support previous research that showed the influence of the cognition of love on helping behaviour. While they did not investigate it, may I suggest that these results may provide a basis for research that explores loving words and their affect on enriching intimate relationships, support and giving in the community.

The second part of the book, '*Loneliness and Intimate Relationships*', includes articles that address intimacy, love, and loneliness. Demir & Fişiloğlu (1999) explored the relationship between loneliness and marital adjustment in Turkish couples. They contend that while research has demonstrated that married people are less lonely than unmarried ones, a single question as may often be asked about one's marital status (i.e., "What is your marital status") is not sufficient to determine a person's satisfaction or loneliness as related to his most intimate relationship. More information is needed, they contend, such as about her relational quality to supplement the question about marital status. Fifty eight married couples were given questionnaires to determine their loneliness and to assess the *quality* of their relationship. Results indicated an inverse relation between loneliness and marital adjustment, meaning good marital adjustment was associated with low level of loneliness. Hence, they concluded, it is not simply the fact that one is married that may shield one from loneliness, but it is the relationship quality that contributes to it.

While Demir et al., explored how marital adjustment may be related to loneliness, Seepersad, Choi & Shin (2008) suggested that culture influences romantic loneliness as well. In the U.S. and most Western countries, love is an acceptable basis for marriage. Couples look, in their union, for mutual responsiveness, a strong connection, and interdependence. In non–Western countries, such as in Korea contend the authors, the situation is different; the importance of love in choosing a marital partner is much less important, and the main sources of intimacy are one's parents and siblings. Participants from both countries, the U.S. and Korea took part in this study which explored the association between romantic relationships, the degree of closeness within those relationships, and romantic loneliness. Results revealed that culture, indeed, influences not only romantic loneliness, but the degree of closeness they experience as well. Romantic relationships, it was found, have greater importance and influence on romantic loneliness in the U.S. than in Korea. More specifically, U.S. participants, in comparison to Korean participants, reported a higher level of romantic loneliness when a romantic partner was absent and lower romantic loneliness when their partner was present. Additionally, American participants reported a higher level of closeness in their romantic relationship than did the Koreans. One more interesting result should be mentioned: in both countries, loneliness is decreased for those who are in a romantic relationship.

Rokach, in a review first published in this book, examined the concepts of belonging, love, and loneliness and the interrelationships between them. While we all yearn to belong and be loved (even if we, as humanity, cannot even properly define that concept), love can bring bliss, joy, and togetherness. However, when things don't go the way we hoped for, when the couple grows away, love can be tinged with disappointment, hurt, alienation from our loved one, and loneliness.

To conclude, aside from expressing a resounding thank you to the authors who wrote the articles that this book is composed of, I would like to whole heartedly thank Marlene Almeida of York University in Toronto, for her tireless and diligent help in creating this edited book. Marlene was part of developing the idea for the book, assembling the very enlightening articles from which some ended up in this book, and developing a list of contact addresses so that I was able to communicate with the authors of these articles. And last, but not least, many thanks to Routledge's (U.K.) Emily Ross for her guidance, assistance, and good advice in bringing this project to fruition.

REFERENCES

Baumeister, R.F., & Leary, M.R. (1995). The need to belong: Desire for interpersonal attachments as a fundamental human motivation. *Psychological Bulletin, 117*(3), 497–529.

Baumeister, R.F., Wotman, S.R., & Stillwell, A.M. (1993). Unrequited love: On heartbreak, anger, guilt, and scriptlessness, and humiliation. *Journal of Personality and Social Psychology, 64*, 377–394.

Cacioppo, J.T., & Patrick, W. (2008). *Loneliness: Human nature and the need for social connection.* New York: W.W. Norton.

Distel, M.A., Rebollo-Mesa, I., Abdellaoui, A., Derom, C.A., Willemsen, G., Cacioppo, J.T., & Boomsma, D.I. (2010). Familial resemblance for loneliness. *Behavioural Genetics, 40*, 480–494.

Doherty, W.J. (1995). *Soul searching: Why psychotherapy must promote moral responsibility.* New York: Basic Books.

Fehr, B. (2006). A prototype approach to studying love. In R.J. Sternberg & K. Weis, (Eds.), *The new psychology of love* (pp. 225–246). New Haven, CT: Yale University Press.

Gordon, S. (1976). *Lonely in America*. NY: Simon & Schuster.

Gottschall, J., & Nordlund, M. (2006). Romantic love: A literary universal? *Philosophy and Literature, 30*, 450–470.

Leary, M., Rogers, P., Canfield, R., & Coe, C. (1986). Boredom in interpersonal encounters: Antecedents and social implications. *Journal of Personality and Social Psychology, 51*, 968–975. doi:10.1037/0022-3514.51.5.968.

Meer, J. (1985, July). Loneliness. *Psychology Today*, 28–33.

Mellor, D., Stokes, M., Firth, L., Hayashi, Y., & Cummins, R. (2008). Need for belonging, relationship satisfaction, loneliness, and life satisfaction. *Personality and Individual Differences, 45*, 213–218.

Ornish, D. (2007). *The spectrum*. NY: Balantine Books.

Pond, R.S., Brey, J., & DeWall, C.N. (2011). Denying the need to belong: How social exclusion impairs human functioning and how people can protect against it. In S.J. Bevinn, (Ed.), *Psychology of loneliness* (pp. 107–122). NY: Nova SciencePub.

Rokach, A. (1988). The experience of loneliness: A tri-level model. *Journal of Psychology, 122*, 531–544.

Rokach, A. (2000). Loneliness and the life cycle. *Psychological Reports, 86*, 629–642.

PART I: WHAT CONTRIBUTES TO A GOOD INTIMATE RELATIONSHIP

Dimensions and Aspects of Longing: Age and Gender Differences in Swedish 9-, 12-, and 15-Year-Old Children

OLLE HOLM

ABSTRACT. Longing can be defined as a secondary emotion, as a blend of the primary emotions of love and sadness. There are several possible dimensions and aspects of longing (O. Holm, 1999). Both age and gender differences are well documented in earlier research on other emotions. In the present investigation, 122 girls and 120 boys, ages 9, 12, and 15 years, in compulsory school in Sweden, answered a questionnaire about dimensions and aspects of their own longing. The results showed both age and gender differences. Girls, especially in the 15-year-old group, experienced longing significantly more than boys. The results were interpreted as generally in accordance with what is known from earlier research on other emotions.

IN RESEARCH ON EMOTIONS, some, such as love and sadness, have attracted the interest of several investigators and theorists, and others have received almost no attention at all. Longing is one of these unnoticed emotions. Although most human beings have experienced longing, it is seldom mentioned in the scientific emotion literature. In everyday language the word is well known and understood, and if one listens to the lyrics of popular music, for example, one often hears the expression of longing for someone or something that isn't present at the moment.

Longing can be considered a blend of love and sadness (Shaver, Schwartz, Kirson, & O'Connor, 1987), and its synonym, yearning, was described by Kemper (1987) as a blend of depression and happiness. *Longing* was defined by Holm (1999) as a blend of love and sadness, sometimes with some other emotion involved. It is possible that the kinship with such powerful emotions as love, happiness, sadness, and depression has led to the relative neglect of longing in scientific research.

Longing and the terms that seem to be most related to it—yearning and desire—are defined in *Oxford Advanced Learner's Dictionary* (1994) as the following: Longing is an "intense desire" (p. 735), yearning is described as either a "strong desire or tender longing" (p. 1485), and desire is described as "strong sexual longing" or "desire for something/to do something" (p. 325).

Desire has been used as a key concept in a number of studies and books in different fields, most recently as an educational motivational concept—the desire to learn—by Oldfather, West, White, and Wilmarth (1999), and as the most basic of all human motives—an instinctive desire for continued life—by Pyszczynski, Greenberg, and Solomon (1997). In a developmental psychological study by Lee, Eskritt, Symons, and Muir (1998), 2-year-old children were shown to use eye gaze for desire inference; and in feminist psychology, adolescent girls' experiences of sexual desire were studied by Tolman and Szalacha (1999). In a psychoanalytical article by Meissner (1999), desire and sexual desire are grouped with other motivational concepts for discussion purposes. Thus, desire can have quite different meaning in different contexts.

Yearning is often used in psychoanalytical writings as a concept in connection with object losses (often parents) (Frankiel, 1994; Freudenberger & Gallagher, 1995; Lifton, 1990) or with grief (Melges & DeMaso, 1980). Other kinds of yearning are found in romantic love (Person, 1991), in yearning for intimacy (McAdams, 1989), and in yearning for things that are past (Davis, 1979). Thus, yearning is also used with somewhat different meanings in different contexts. But both yearning and desire are found more often than longing, at least in scientific writings.

Because longing, as a concept, has not been treated more than marginally by researchers, in the literature review for this study I focused mainly on what can be found for emotions generally, and with respect to age and gender differences, because the participants in this investigation were boys and girls aged 9 to 15 years. The literature shows that development from initial innate reactions to a multiplicity of emotions takes place early in life. From general reactions that show distress, contentment, and interest (Lewis, 1993), infants at 3 months of age already show a dozen emotions (Emde, 1980; Izard & Buechler, 1979; Sroufe, 1984).

Schemas of objects, events, and persons also appear early (Jacobs, 1993; Stern, 1985), and affect experiences (Harrison, 1986). During the first 3 years, the majority of adult emotions emerge and develop in a child (Lewis, 1993), and there is continous development past 3 years of age (Lewis; Michalson & Lewis, 1985). The so-called child's theory of mind (Astington, Harris, & Olson, 1988; Harris, 1991, 1993; Wellman, 1990) describes the development of children's understanding of emotions from age 1 (intentionality) over the preschool years (belief and desire) to the school years (external expression of an internal state).

The development of emotions has been described from a general perspective by Fisher, Shaver, and Carnochan (1990), who described the developmental process as gradually moving from basic to culture-specific, subordinate category emotions; and as developing through stages: three (Reissland, 1985) or five (Harter & Buddin, 1987). Harris (1993) and Whitesell and Harter (1989) have also given descriptions of specialized emotion development. At about 8 years old, children realize that their actions ought to meet moral and social standards if they wish to be proud of what they have done. At about the age of 9, they acknowledge that the same situation can provoke two opposite emotions, whereas younger children usually do not admit that more than one emotion can be experienced at a time. Similar results are reported by Olthof, Terwogt, van Eck, and Koops (1987), and Terwogt, Koops, Oosterhoff, and Olthof (1986). Age effects in training children to acknowledge mixed emotions have also been reported. Six- to 7-year-olds were found to benefit more from such training than 4- to 5-year-olds (Peng, Johnson, Pollock, & Glasspool, 1992).

In the preschool years, children already seem to understand that a perspective or belief partly determines how a person feels (Nannis & Cowan, 1987; Saarni, 1993). In middle childhood they also start to use mental strategies to change emotional experiences. Whereas younger children may try to change a situation (externally), older children may look inward to see if the internal experience can be changed, for example, by a reinterpretation of the situation or by focusing on something positive (Saarni, 1993). Cognitive self-control strategies such as redirecting thoughts have been found to be more common among 9-year-olds than among 7-year-old children (Tsukamoto, 1997). Such strategies mature gradually and also depend on cognitive and verbal skills. Compared with adults, neither 8- nor 11-year-olds were able to produce vocabulary that expressed emotion concepts described by adults (Aldridge & Wood, 1997).

Age differences in the development of emotions have been found in many studies. Glasberg and Aboud (1982) found that kindergartners and second graders differed regarding sadness. The younger children denied sad experiences more than the older children and were also less likely to see sadness as part of their personal disposition. Age differences between preschoolers and third and fourth graders have been reported regarding the ability to match and generate affective labels for emotionally laden situations, among them sadness (Brody & Harrison, 1987). In an investigation of children from Grades 1, 3, 5, and 7 who described situations in which they were sad and assessed the intensity of sadness, the younger children tended to report lower levels of sadness than the older children (Rotenberg, Mars, & Crick, 1987).

In a study of anger and sadness, children in Grades 5, 8, and 11 expressed greater self-efficacy and regulation of sadness than of anger (Zeman & Shipman, 1997). Age differences in understanding and expressing emotions may disappear as individuals grow older.

In a study of experiences of sorrow with two groups, ages 15 to 16.5 and 20 to 25 years old, no differences were found (Magen, Birenbaum, & Pery, 1996). In a study by Russell and Ridgeway (1983), the same dimensional structure in data for both third graders and college students was reported. Thus, age differences or lack of them may depend on experiences rather than on cognitive maturation beyond a certain level. In a study comparing young children (from 4 years old) with older ones (up to 12 years), Harter and Buddin (1987) found that the younger children used a more basic set of emotions than the older children did.

Knowledge of how and when to control emotional displays increases between Grades 1 and 5, but then levels off (Gnepp & Hess, 1986). Children in four age groups (first, third, fifth, and seventh graders) who were asked about their anger, experienced similar causes and intensities for anger but differed in their motives and in the consequences. The older children showed increases most clearly in the constructive motive of making others see their point of view and in verbal insult and indirect retaliation as consequences. Physical assault decreased with age (Rotenberg, 1985). Research on children's perceptions of the perceived controllability of negative events showed systematic relations between pity and uncontrollability and between anger and controllability for age groups 6 to 7, 8 to 9, and 11 years old. A developmental increase in the linkage of guilt to controllable events was also found (Graham, Doubleday, & Guarino, 1984).

Age differences in self-attributed embarrassment were reported in a study by Bennett (1989) in which three different situations—no audience, a passive audience, or an active (i.e., deriding) audience—were described. For 5- and 8-year-old children, embarrassment was significantly greater in the active audience condition than in the passive audience condition. For older children, of 11 and 13 years, any audience was potentially embarrassing. That is, there was a shift from concern with others' manifest reactions to subjective evaluations of the self with age.

That audiences are important for both embarrassment and pride was also shown in a study by Seidner, Stipek, and Feshbach (1988). They found that references to social comparison increased with age in children 5, 7, 9, and 11 years old. Cognitive structural development influences emotional understanding, which, in turn, influences how emotional experiences are internalized and conceptualized (Nannis, 1988).

Gender differences in emotion have also attracted many investigators, who seem to have concentrated more of their research on somewhat older children, but gender differences in younger children have also been shown. Birnbaum (1983) showed that children 3 to 5 years old believed that adult men showed anger more than adult women and that fear, sadness, and happiness were shown more by women. Older boys increasingly inhibit most emotions, whereas girls inhibit socially unacceptable ones such as anger (Brody, 1985). This fact does not necessarily imply that boys do not notice emotions. In a study of emotion identification in others, girls were better than boys in correctly identifying emotions at 3 years of age, but at age 5 boys were significantly better than girls (Adams, Summers, & Christopherson, 1993); and in a study of humane attitudes toward peers, boys showed more humane attitudes than girls did (Abramenkova, 1983).

But in a longitudinal study of continuities in emotion understanding by

Brown and Dunn (1996), girls outperformed boys. Girls also had higher average scores than boys in a study of facial and verbal measures of empathy with children 5, 9, and 13 years old (Strayer & Roberts, 1997). Anger is shown more by boys, according to findings by Buntaine and Costenbader (1997). Boys in Grades 4 and 5 reported significantly higher levels of aggressive responses than girls in a self-report anger questionnaire; in this study, differences in the locations of the schools was also found to play a role. As a group, the children in urban settings reported significantly higher levels of anger than children in rural and suburban settings (Buntaine & Costenbader).

Adults can be expected to pass on their conceptions to children. Some studies of gender differences in emotion have had adult participants. In a sample of individuals between the ages of 17 and 88 years, Malatesta and Kalnok (1984) found that emotion was more important in the lives of women and that individuals of both sexes monitor and inhibit the expressions of feelings in different ways over the adult years. Timmers, Fisher, and Manstead (1998) investigated gender differences in motives for regulating emotions and found that women are more concerned with relationships, whereas men are more motivated to stay in control and express power.

Parents' effects on their children's emotional development was discussed by Brody and Hall (1993), who in their review of mother–child and father–child interaction research found that both parents discuss emotions more with daughters than with sons and also display a wider range of emotions to daughters than to sons. Brody and Hall also concluded from the studies reviewed that girls are encouraged to learn to express feelings through words and facial expressions, whereas, with the exception of anger, boys are disencouraged from doing so. Boys learn to act on their feelings rather than to talk about them. Evidence that negative emotions might be easier learned in families was presented by Denham, Zoller, and Couchoud (1994), who also found that children with the least understanding of emotion had mothers who showed more anger. Dunsmore and Halberstadt (1997) proposed a model for how a family's way of expressing emotion might influence children's formation of schemas.

Garner, Robertson, and Smith (1997) found that mother's and father's emotion socialization practices differed and in some cases depended on the child's gender. In a study of 5th, 8th, and 11th graders, Zeman and Shipman (1997) found that 8th graders reported regulating emotion most and expected the least interpersonal support from mothers. In a study of maternal expressiveness and its effects on children, children of less expressive mothers were more positively expressive than children of more expressive mothers, who were more negatively expressive (Halberstadt, Fox, & Jones, 1993).

In a study of emotional expressivity in undergraduates and their parents, Heinhold, Kerr, and Palladino (1998) found that both parents were more in agreement with their daughters' ratings than with their sons' ratings. For both male and female children, mothers' ratings of positive, but not negative, emotion were correlated with children's ratings. Fathers' ratings of negative, but not positive, emotion in the family were correlated with childrens' ratings.

Higher expressivity of emotions in women was found in a study of sex role orientation using Bem's Sex Role Inventory (Bem, 1981). Individuals of either sex who were androgynous and feminine were more expressive of all emotions but hate. Masculine subjects of either sex ranked below them on love, sadness, and happiness (Ganong & Coleman, 1985). In a study on attractiveness of gender types by Green and Kenrick (1994) all the participants preferred androgenous partners, with the highly expressive female-type rated second by all.

In a study by Diener, Sandvik, and Larsen (1985) women had higher scores for emotional intensity. In another, by Dosser, Balswick, and Halverson (1983), women were more expressive than men. Major and Heslin (1982) reported that women rated actors involved in touch interactions as more attractive than actors in no-touch interactions, whereas men did the reverse. In two studies reported in an article by Jussim, Milburn, and Nelson (1991), results showed that women were regarded stereotypically as more emotionally open than are men.

Other studies have also found gender differences in emotionality. In a study of childhood memories of emotionality, significant differences in activity and emotionality between men and women were reported. Men's memories were more active and women's more emotional (Friedman & Pines, 1991). A study by Fujita, Diener, and Sandvik (1991) showed that women were as happy as, and more intense than, men. Mirowsky and Ross (1995) found that men keep emotions to themselves more than women do and that women express emotions more freely than men.

Sprecher and Sedikides (1993) found that women reported several emotions more frequently than men did and that women believed themselves to be more emotional in general, whereas men believed women to be more emotional in the experience of negative but not of positive emotions. Thus, higher emotionality in women has been repeatedly documented. Brody (1993) concluded in her review that the influence of socialization, hormonal factors, genetic factors, and neuropsychological factors may all contribute to individual differences in gender roles.

In sum, studies of emotions and their development show both age and gender differences. Regardless of the origins of these differences—biology, maturation, or socialization—the emotion of longing should also show differences between age and gender groups. My aim in this study was to describe such differences in children 9, 12, and 15 years old. The following are my predictions: Most children in these age groups, even the youngest, will regard longing as consisting of mixed emotions and will answer questions about them. They can also be expected to use internal strategies for changing their experiences such as focusing on something positive or trying to find some kind of distraction.

The two younger age groups will not be expected to be able to produce vocabulary expressing emotion concepts as adults do.

I expected that older boys would show less of their longing, whereas girls would show more and be more expressive about it. Girls will also be longing more for relationships than will boys.

Method

Participants

Participants were 242 children (122 girls and 120 boys) from the Swedish compulsory school: 37 girls and 31 boys from Grade 3 (9 years old), 45 girls and 47 boys from Grade 6 (12 years old), and 40 girls and 42 boys from Grade 9 (15 years old). They all responded individually and anonymously in class to a questionnaire about longing that was presented to them by student practice teachers. The student teachers explained how they should respond to questions with alternatives, answered children's questions about the procedure, and supervised and collected the completed questionnaires.

The questions (see Appendix) were built on the dimensions suggested by Holm (1999) and aspects of those dimensions. The word *love* was not used in the questionnaire, because it is not a common word among children. The word *happy* was chosen instead in the questions in which primary emotions were mentioned. The children answered the questions on a Likert-type scale with the points *often* (4), *sometimes* (3), *seldom* (2), and *never* (1). The children could add examples or comments to their answers.

One question was about the focus of longing. Because nothing is empirically known about children's longings, it was important to find out what they long for—persons, events, things, or something else—and how frequently such longings occur. What kind of feeling is their longing—happy, sad, both, or some other feeling? Are the definitions given at the beginning of this article useful in studying children's longings? Do children of different ages feel longing as one of opposite emotions, happy or sad, or do they sometime regard it as a mixture of these two? Are there ever other emotions present? A question about when longing occurs was aimed at finding out if there are some situations or times of day that trigger longing.

I posed the question about what children usually do when longing is present to find out if reactions are active or passive, and if active, to determine the way in which they are active. Are some cognitive self-control strategies involved? Another question concerned the direction: Do children long to get away from something, or can longing be considered as longing for something? How frequently is longing the desire to be with someone, and how frequently is it the desire not to be with someone? Questions about positive or negative expectations were posed to see how common hope or disappointment are as ingredients in longing.

Longing also has a direction in time. Is it more common to long for something from the past or for something that might happen in the future? These are different kinds of longing (nostalgia vs. hope). I wanted to see whether there were age or gender differences in the groups in this investigation. In longing there could be agent—oneself or someone else—and it was interesting to see whether there were some differences in that respect.

Longing can also be of different intensities. The children were asked about the respective frequencies of these varying intensities. They were also asked how often they experienced longing. To avoid the possibility that they would not be represented from the researcher's perspective only, I asked the children to describe in their own words what longing feels like and to give any comments that occurred to them about longing

Results

The ratings were tested for statistical significance between gender and age groups for each question (seeTables 1–3). Answers to open questions and comments were categorized (see Tables 4–6). Almost all ratings from the older groups in the comparisons were higher than from the younger groups, and the girls' ratings were also almost always higher than the boys' ratings. Exceptions are marked in the tables. (For question numbers, see Appendix.)

The girls' ratings were higher in 12 of 14 comparisons; 9-year-old boys had somewhat higher ratings for activity, and 15-year-old boys longed for things somewhat more often than did girls in the same age group. The 15-year-old girls showed significant differences from same-aged boys in intensity and frequency

TABLE 1
Significant Differences Between Girls' and Boys' Ratings of Different Aspects of Their Own Longing

Question	Age 9	Age 12	Age 15	Aspect
4a		$p < .001$	$p < .01$	Person
4b	$p < .05$			Event
4c			$p < .05$[b]	Thing
5c		$p < .05$	$p < .05$	Mixed emotion
7b	$p < .05$[b]			Activity
9a		$p < .05$	$p < .05$	Positive relation
9b			$p < .05$	Negative relation
11b			$p < .01$	Future
13a			$p < .001$	High intensity
13b			$p < .001$	Medium intensity
14			$p < .001$	Frequency

Note. See the Appendix for wording of the questions. The superscript [b] indicates that boys had the higher mean.

TABLE 2
Significant Differences Between Age Groups in Boys' Ratings of Different Aspects of Longing

Question	Ages 9 and 12	Ages 12 and 15	Ages 9 and 15	Aspect
4b			$p < .05$	Event
4c		$p < .05$		Thing
7b		$p < .01^y$	$p < .01^y$	Activity
8		$p < .01$		Direction
10b			$p < .05$	Negative expectation
12a	$p < .05$			Self
13b	$p < .05$			Medium intensity

Note. See the Appendix for wording of the questions. The superscript y indicates that the younger group had the higher mean.

TABLE 3
Significant Differences Between Age Groups in Girls' Ratings of Different Aspects of Longing

Question	Ages 9 and 12	Ages 12 and 15	Ages 9 and 15	Aspect
4b	$p < .05^y$	$p < .001$		Event
4c		$p < .05$		Thing
4d			$p < .05$	Else
5c			$p < .05$	Mixed emotion
8			$p < .05$	Direction
9a	$p < .05$		$p < .001$	Positive relation
9b			$p < .05$	Negative relation
10a		$p < .05$	$p < .001$	Positive expectation
10b			$p < .01$	Negative expectation
11a			$p < .05$	Past
11b		$p < .05$	$p < .01$	Future
12a	$p < .01$		$p < .001$	Self
13b		$p < .05$	$p < .001$	Medium intensity
14			$p < .01$	Frequency

Note. See the Appendix for wording of the questions. The superscript y indicates that the younger group had the higher mean.

of longing, and their longings were also significantly more often directed toward something in the future, and for some person(s). The 12-year-old girls longed for persons more often than did the same aged boys, and 9-year-old girls longed for events more often than the boys of the same age. At age 15, the differences between boys and girls become more pronounced than at earlier ages.

TABLE 4
Categories and Number of Answers, by Gender and Age Group
Question: When Are You Longing?

Gender/ age	Depends on mood	It differs	Before the event happens	Different times of the day	When away from home	Memories	In school	Total
Girls, 9	4	6	2	3	7	3	3	28
Boys, 9	4	4	11	3	3	3	2	30
Girls, 12	6	1	10	13	4	4	6	44
Boys, 12	9	6	11	3	4	3		36
Girls, 15	20	11	4	6		4		45
Boys, 15	9	14	2	4	1	1	2	33
Total	52	42	40	32	19	18	13	216

Note. The number of answers differed among participants.

TABLE 5
Categories and Number of Answers, by Gender and Age Group
Question: What Do You Do When You Are Longing?

Gender/ age	Something distracting	Unspecified	Working with it	Talking with someone	Trying to forget it	Total
Girls, 9	26	4	9	3	1	43
Boys, 9	16	2	2	1	4	25
Girls, 12	26	16	7	4	4	57
Boys, 12	18	10	3	2	2	35
Girls, 15	14	8	9	7	2	40
Boys, 15	14	6	6	4		30
Total	114	46	36	21	13	230

Note. The number of answers differed among participants.

There was a significant difference between the age groups 9 and 15 in longing for some event, and between the age groups 12 and 15 in longing for some thing. Younger boys reported themselves to be more active when they were longing than did the 15-year-old boys. There was a significant difference in negative expectation between the age groups 9 and 15; 9- and 12-year-old boys differed in their answers to the question of whether they had been longing for something with themselves as agents, and the same age groups also differed in their answers on the question about intensity of longing. In both cases, older boys longed more often than younger ones. Exceptions from this were found for activity.

TABLE 6
Categories and Number of Answers, by Gender and Age Group
Question: Describe What It Feels Like When You Are Longing

Gender/age	Exciting	Positive	Negative	Joyful	Sad	Miscellaneous	Total
Girls, 9	9	7	10	1	7	5	39
Boys, 9	4	3	13	1	1	5	27
Girls, 12	10	14	12	11	11	15	73
Boys, 12	2	17	8	7	5	13	52
Girls, 15	7	21	10	13	8	15	74
Boys, 15		13	8	4		10	35
Total	32	75	61	37	32	63	300

Note. The number of answers differed among participants.

Younger girls rated highest in longing for some event. Between ages 12 and 15, there were significant differences between the age groups in all facets of longing. However, overall, girls' longing increased with age in every aspect but one. Age differences in emotion become more obvious as girls reached adolescence (see Table 4).

The most frequent answer to the question "When are you longing?" was that it depends on mood; that answer was especially common among the 15-year-old girls. The unspecified "It differs" was more used among 15-year-olds than in the younger groups. "Before the event happens" was more common in the younger groups, and the answer "Different times of the day" was most used by 12-year-old girls. The frequencies for the remaining categories were low.

The most frequent answer in every group to the question "What do you do when you are longing?" was something that distracted them from feeling the emotion. The 12-year-olds used the highest number of unspecified answers. Although all frequencies in the categories "Working with it" and "Talking to someone" were low, the pattern showed that girls use these strategies somewhat more often than boys do. In each age group, the boys gave fewer answers than the girls (see Table 5).

In response to the question regarding what longing feels like, there were few answers in the category "Exciting," although girls used this answer more often than boys. Longing was experienced as a positive emotion more often among the older children than among the younger children, for whom it was more often negative. But the low frequencies makes this very tentative. The girls seemed to experience longing both as joyful and sad more often than the boys did. The category "Miscellaneous" had higher frequencies among the older children. Overall, and in each age group, the girls gave more answers than the boys did (see Table 6).

In answer to the open question "Describe what it feels like to be longing," the 9-year-olds described it mostly as happy or sad. These young children also seemed to have some difficulty in expressing themselves in written language. The following are some answers from the 12-year-old students: "It feels like time is slowing down"; "I feel like I'm striving towards something"; "It is rather odd. I am happy and sad at the same time"; "Sometimes I am sad, sometimes happy, sometimes disappointed, and sometimes envious." No general pattern was found, except that girls in this age group gave more answers than the boys did.

Among the 15-year-old students, the girls generally were more verbal and gave more and longer answers than the boys did. Some examples of answers from girls in this group were: "Sometimes it feels like something is missing inside oneself"; "If you are longing for a person it can almost hurt"; "When I am thinking of my former boyfriend it is with sadness, melancholy, and love that I'm longing." Examples of answers from boys: "Nothing gets done, you just think"; "You don't want to do anything but that which you are longing for"; and "Darned good, really."

Answers to the question "Is there anything else that you want to say about longing?" were few and did not show any pattern at all.

Discussion

A result that is clearly visible with regard to both gender and age is that girls had higher ratings in most aspects for which significant differences appeared, especially in the 15-year-old group. From same-sex comparisons, I also found that most of the differences appeared among the girls in the 9- and 15-year-olds. Differences in same-sex comparisons among boys were fewer—7 aspects compared with 14 for the girls—and did not reach the levels of significance that were found for girls. This result indicates that girls experience more deeply, or at least are more aware of, the different aspects of their longing than boys and that they do so increasingly as they get older. The results are consistent with what could be expected from the literature on other emotions, (e.g., Brody 1993, 1995).

The differences in experiences of the intensities of longing between boys and girls were also considerable and present among all the age groups. Although the girls experienced longing more intensely as they got older, the boys seemed to do the reverse. However, research on groups older than those I used in this study is needed to see whether such trends continue.

There were also differences in the frequency of longing. Girls experienced longing more often than boys, and older girls more often than younger ones, that is, roughly the same pattern as for intensity. These findings about intensity and frequency are in accordance with the literature on other emotions, (Brody 1985; Diener et al., 1985; Sprecher & Sedikides, 1993).

Compared with boys, girls' longing was more often for persons, and there were also gender differences regarding positive and negative relations. Comparisions between age groups of girls showed that longing for positive relations increased with age, but longing to get out of some relation also increased with age. However, women have always been found to be more interested than men in relating to others, and the results are thus in accordance with earlier findings (e.g., Brody & Hall, 1993).

Regarding expectations of longing, no gender differences appeared, although differences were found in same-sex comparisons among age groups. Overall, expectations of longing among boys and girls increased with age, possibly because of the growing awareness and the amount of experience that come as one gets older.

Differences between the genders and between the girls' age groups regarding longing as a mixed emotion may reflect that girls are more observant of, and perhaps better at describing, emotions, which is also in accordance with earlier findings (Mirowsky & Ross, 1995). Differences in activity between the sexes show that younger boys are more likely than girls or older boys to do something active when they are longing, but this tendency decreases with age.

The only pattern that could be seen in the open questions at the end of the questionnaire was that the girls answered more often and gave longer answers than the boys did. This was more pronounced with age.

Generally, the results indicate that for girls, longing increases with age, whereas in boys, longing seem to level off or decrease. The girls also gave longer answers to the questions than the boys did and expressed more longing for relationship. These results are in accordance with earlier research findings—that is, that girls are more verbal and better at describing their emotions. Brody and Hall (1993) summarized their review of gender and emotion by saying that they were repeatedly surprised by the consistency of the literature across several types of data. The results reported here are also consistent with results from earlier research on other emotions.

One implication for socialization and education is that more systematic training in talking about emotions both at home and in preschool and school might make boys better equipped to interact with and understand girls, and other boys as well. More research is needed among groups older than the 15-year-olds I used in this investigation to find out whether the observed trends regarding longing continue. There is also a need for a close examination of the concepts mentioned at the beginning of this article. What are the similarities and differences among the concepts of longing, yearning, and desire?

REFERENCES

Abramenkova, V. V. (1983). Joint activity in the development of a humane attitude toward preschool peers. *Soviet Psychology, 22,* 38–55.

Adams, G. R., Summers, M., & Christopherson, V. A. (1993). Age and gender differences in preschool children's identification of the emotions in others: A brief report. *Canadian Journal of Behavioural Science, 25,* 97–107.

Aldridge, M., & Wood, J. (1997) Talking about feelings: Young children's ability to express emotions. *Child Abuse and Neglect, 21,* 1221–1233.

Astington, J. W., Harris, P. L., & Olson., D. R. (Eds.). (1988). *Developing theories of mind.* New York: Cambridge University Press.

Bem, S. L. (1981). *Bem Sex-Role Inventory.* Palo Alto, CA: Mind Garden.

Bennett, M. (1989). Children's self-attribution of embarrassment. *British Journal of Developmental Psychology, 7,* 207–217.

Birnbaum, D. W. (1983). Preschoolers' stereotypes about sex differences in emotionality: A reaffirmation. *The Journal of Genetic Psychology, 143,* 139–140.

Brody, L. R. (1985). Gender differences in emotional development: A review of theories and research. *Journal of Personality, 53,* 102–149.

Brody, L. R. (1993). On understanding gender differences in the expression of emotion. In S. L. Ablon, D. Brown, E. J. Khantzian, & J. E. Mack (Eds.), *Human feelings: Explorations in affect development and meaning,* Hillsdale, NJ: The Analytic Press.

Brody, L. R. (1995). Gender differences in emotional development: A review of theories and research. *Journal of Personality, 53,* 102–149.

Brody, L. R., & Hall, J. A. (1993). Gender and emotion. In M. Lewis & J. M. Haviland (Eds.), *Handbook of emotions* (pp. 447–460). New York: The Guilford Press.

Brody, L. R., & Harrison, R. H. (1987). Developmental changes in children's abilities to match and label emotionally laden situations. *Motivation and Emotion, 11,* 347–365.

Brown, J. R., & Dunn, J. (1996). Continuities in emotion understanding from 3–6 years. *Child Development, 67,* 789–802.

Buntaine, R. L., & Costenbader, V. K. (1997). Self-reported differences in the experience and expression of anger between girls and boys. *Sex Roles, 36*(9–10), 625–637.

Davis, F. (1979). *Yearning for yesterday. A sociology of nostalgia.* New York: The Free Press.

Denham, S. A., Zoller, D., & Couchoud, E. A. (1994). Socialization of preschoolers' emotion understanding. *Developmental Psychology, 30,* 928–936.

Dunsmore, J. C., & Halberstadt, A. G. (1997). How does family emotional expressiveness affect children's schemas? *New Directions for Child Development, 77,* 45–68.

Diener, E., Sandvik, E, & Larsen, R. J. (1985). Age and sex effects for emotional intensity. *Developmental Psychology, 21,* 542–546.

Dosser, D. A., Balswick, J. O., & Halverson, C. F. (1983). Situational context of emotional expressiveness. *Journal of Counseling Psychology, 30,* 375–387.

Emde, R. N. (1980). Levels of meaning for infant emotions: A biosocial view. In W. A. Collins (Ed.), *Development of cognition, affect, and social relations* (pp. 1–37). The Minnesota Symposia on Child Psychology, Vol. 13. Hillsdale, NJ: Erlbaum.

Fisher, K. W., Shaver, P. R., & Carnochan, P (1990). How emotions develop and how they organize development. *Cognition and Emotion, 4,* 81–127.

Frankiel, R. V. (Ed.). (1994). *Essential papers on object loss.* New York: New York University Press.

Freudenberger, H. J., & Gallagher, K. M. (1995). Emotional consequences of loss for our adolescents. *Psychotherapy, 32,* 150–153.

Friedman, A., & Pines, A. (1991). Sex differences in gender-related childhood memories. *Sex Roles, 25*(1–2), 25–32.

Fujita, F., Diener, E., & Sandvik, E. (1991). Gender differences in negative affect and well-being: The case for emotional intensity. *Journal of Personality and Social Psychology, 61,* 427–434.

Ganong, L. H., & Coleman, M. (1985). Sex, sex roles, and emotional expressiveness. *The Journal of Genetic Psychology, 146,* 405–411.

Garner, P. W., Robertson, S., & Smith, G. (1997). Preschool children's emotional expressions with peers: The roles of gender and emotion socialization. *Sex Roles, 36*(11–12), 675–691.

Glasberg, R., & Aboud, F. E. (1982). Keeping one's distance from sadness: Children's self-reports of emotional experience. *Developmental Psychology, 18,* 287–293.

Gnepp, J., & Hess, D. L. (1986). Children's understanding of verbal and facial display rules. *Developmental Psychology, 22,* 103–108.

Graham, S., Doubleday, C., & Guarino, P. A. (1984). The development of relations between perceived controllability and the emotions of pity, anger, and guilt. *Child Development, 55,* 561–565.

Green, B. L., & Kenrick, D. T. (1994). The attractiveness of gender-typed traits at different relationship levels: Androgynous characteristics may be desirable after all. *Personality and Social Psychology Bulletin, 20,* 244–253.

Halberstadt, A. G., Fox, N. A., & Jones, N. A. (1993). Do expressive mothers have expressive children? The role of socialization in children's affect expression. *Social Development, 2,* 48–65.

Harris, P. L. (1991). The work of the imagination. In A. Whiten (Ed.), *Natural theories of mind* (pp. 283–304). Oxford, England: Blackwell.

Harris, P. L. (1993). Understanding emotion. In M. Lewis & J. M. Haviland (Eds.), *Handbook of emotions* (pp. 237–246). New York: The Guilford Press.

Harrison, I. (1986). A note on the nature and the developmental origins of affects. In A. Richards & M. Willick (Eds.), *Psychoanalysis: The science of mental conflict* (pp. 191–206). Hillsdale, NJ: The Analytic Press.

Harter, S., & Buddin, B. J. (1987). Children's understanding of the simultaneity of two emotions: A five-stage developmental sequence. *Developmental Psychology, 23,* 388–399.

Heinhold, A. M., Kerr, S. L., & Palladino, L. (1998). Gender differences in parents' perceptions of their adult children's and their families' emotional expressivity. *Personality and Individual Differences, 24,* 559–564.

Holm, O. (1999). Analyses of longing: Origins, levels, and dimensions. *The Journal of Psychology, 133,* 621–630.

Izard, C. E., & Buechler, S. (1979). Emotion expression and personality integration in infancy. In C. E. Izard (Ed.), *Emotions in personality and psychopathology.* New York: Plenum Press.

Jacobs, D. (1993). Theory and its relation to early affective experience. In S. L. Ablon, D. Brown, E. J. Khantzian, & J. E. Mack (Eds.), *Human feelings: Explorations in affect development and meaning* (pp. 305–316). Hillsdale, NJ: The Analytic Press.

Jussim, L., Milburn, M., & Nelson, W. (1991). Emotional openness: Sex-role stereotypes and self-perceptions. *Representative Research in Social Psychology, 19,* 35–52.

Kemper, T. D. (1987). How many emotions are there? Wedding the social and the autonomic components. *American Journal of Sociology, 93,* 263–289.

Lee, K., Eskritt, M., Symons, L. A., & Muir, D. (1998). Children's use of triadic eye gaze information for "mind reading." *Developmental Psychology, 34,* 525–539.

Lewis, M. (1993). The emergence of human emotions. In M. Lewis & J. M. Haviland (Eds.), *Handbook of emotions* (pp. 223–235). New York: The Guilford Press.

Lifton, B. J. (1990). The formation of the adopted self. *Psychotherapy in Private Practice, 8,* 85–91.

Magen, Z., Birenbaum, M., & Pery, D. (1996). Experiencing joy and sorrow: An examination of intensity and shallowness. *International Forum for Logotherapy, 19,* 45–55.

Major, B., & Heslin, R. (1982). Perceptions of cross-sex and same-sex nonreciprocal touch: It is better to give than to receive. *Journal of Nonverbal Behavior, 6,* 148–162.

Malatesta, C. Z., & Kalnok, M. (1984). Emotional experience in younger and older adults. *Journal of Gerontology, 39,* 301–308.

McAdams, D. P. (1989). *Intimacy: The need to be close.* New York: Doubleday.

Meissner, W. W. (1999). The dynamic principle in psychoanalysis: II. Toward a revised theory of motivation. *Psychoanalysis and Contemporary Thought, 22,* 41–83.

Melges, F. T., & DeMaso, D. R. (1980). Grief resolution therapy: Reliving, revising, and revisiting. *American Journal of Psychotherapy, 34,* 51–61.

Michalson, L., & Lewis, M. (1985). What do children know about emotions and when do they know it? In M. Lewis & C. Saarni (Eds.), *The socialization of emotions* (pp. 117–139). New York: Plenum Press.

Mirowsky, J., & Ross, C. E. (1995). Sex differences in distress: Real or artifact? *American Sociological Review, 60,* 449–468.

Nannis, E. D. (1988). Cognitive–developmental differences in emotional understanding. *New Directions for Child Development, 39,* 31–49.

Nannis, E. D., & Cowan, P. A. (1987). Emotional understanding: A matter of age, dimension, and point of view. *Journal of Applied Developmental Psychology, 8,* 289–304.

Oldfather, P., West, J., White, J., & Wilmarth, J. (1999). *Learning through children's eyes: Social constructivism and the desire to learn.* Washington, DC: American Psychological Association.

Olthof, T., Terwogt, M. M., van Eck, O., & Koops, W. (1987). Children's knowledge of the integration of successive emotions. *Perceptual and Motor Skills, 65,* 407–414.

Oxford Advanced Learner's Dictionary (1994). Oxford, England: Oxford University Press

Person, E. S. (1991). Romantic love: At the intersection of the psyche and the cultural unconscious. *Journal of the American Psychoanalytic Association, 39,* 383–411.

Peng, M., Johnson, C., Pollock, J, & Glasspool, R. (1992). Training young children to acknowledge mixed emotions. *Cognition and Emotion, 6,* 387–401.

Pyszczynski, T., Greenberg, J., & Solomon, S. (1997). Why do we need what we need? A terror management perspective on the roots of human social motivation. *Psychological Inquiry, 8,* 1–20.

Reissland, N. (1985). The development of concepts of simultaneity in children's understanding of emotions. *Journal of Child Psychology and Psychiatry, 26,* 811–824.

Rotenberg, K. J. (1985). Causes, intensity, motives, and consequences of children's anger from self-reports. *The Journal of Genetic Psychology, 146,* 101–106.

Rotenberg, K. J., Mars, K., & Crick, N. (1987). Development of children's sadness. *Psychology and Human Development, 2:1,* 13–25.

Russell, J. A., & Ridgeway, D. (1983). Dimensions underlying children's emotional concepts. *Developmental Psychology, 19,* 795–804.

Saarni, C. (1993). Socialization of emotion. In M. Lewis & J. M. Haviland (Eds.), *Handbook of emotions* (pp. 435–446). New York: The Guilford Press.

Seidner, L. B., Stipek, D. J., & Feshbach, N. D. (1988). A developmental analysis of elementary school-aged children's concepts of pride and embarrassment. *Child Development, 59,* 367–377.

Shaver, P., Schwartz, J., Kirson, D., & O'Connor, C. (1987). Emotion knowledge: A further exploration of a prototype approach. *Journal of Personality and Social Psychology, 52,* 1061–1086.

Sprecher, S., & Sedikides, C. (1993). Gender differences in perceptions of emotionality: The case of close heterosexual relationships. *Sex Roles, 28*(9–10), 511–530.

Sroufe, L. A. (1984). The organization of emotional development. In K. R. Scherer & P. Ekman (Eds.), *Approaches to emotion.* (pp. 109–128). Hillsdale, NJ: Erlbaum.

Strayer, J., & Roberts, W. (1997). Facial and verbal measures of children's emotions and empathy. *International Journal of Behavioral Development, 20,* 627–649.

Stern, D. (1985). *The interpersonal world of the infant.* New York: Basic Books.

Terwogt, M. M., Koops, W., Oosterhoff, T., & Olthof, T. (1986) Development in processing multiple emotional situations. *The Journal of General Psychology, 113,* 109–119.

Timmers, M., Fisher, A., & Manstead, A. S. (1998). Gender differences in motives for regulating emotions. *Personality and Social Psychology Bulletin, 24,* 974–985.

Tolman, D. L., & Szalacha, L. A. (1999). Dimensions of desire: Bridging qualitative and quantitative methods in a study of female adolescent sexuality. *Psychology of Women Quarterly, 23,* 7–39.

Tsukamoto, S. (1997). A developmental study on children's understanding of emotion and emotional self-control. *Japanese Journal of Psychology, 68,* 111–119.

Wellman, H. M. (1990). *The child's theory of mind.* Cambridge, MA: MIT Press.

Whitesell, N. R., & Harter, S. (1989). Children's reports of conflict between simultaneous opposite-valence emotions. *Child Development, 60,* 673–682.

Zeman, J., & Shipman, K. (1997). Social-contextual influences of expectancies for managing anger and sadness: The transition from middle childhood to adolescence. *Developmental Psychology, 33,* 917–924.

APPENDIX
Questionaire About Dimensions and Aspects of Longing

All questions except 1, 2, 3, 5d, 6, 15, and 16 were answered with the alternatives of *often, sometimes, seldom,* and *never.* Comments could be added to all answers.

1. Sex.
2. Age.
3. Place of birth: a) Sweden. b) Other country.
4. Have you been longing for a) some person, b) some occasion, c) some thing, d) something else?
5. Is longing a) a happy feeling, b) a sad feeling, c) both happy and sad, d) something more than happy or sad? What?
6. When are you longing?
7. What do you do when you are longing? a) I am just waiting until it is over. b) I am doing something. What?
8. Have you been longing to get away from someone or something?
9. a) Have you been longing to be together with someone? b) Have you been longing to not have to be together with someone?
10. a) Have you been longing for something that you hope will be good? b) Have you been longing for something that might turn out to be disappointing?
11. a) Have you been longing for something from the past? b) Have you been longing for something in the future?
12. a) Have you been longing for something that you will do yourself? b) Have you been longing for something that you hope somebody else will do?
13. a) Have you ever been longing very much? b) Have you ever been longing rather much? c) Have you ever been longing just a little?
14. Do you think that you are longing a) often, b) sometimes, c) seldom, or d) never?
15. Describe what it feels like to be longing.
16. Is there anything else that you want to say about longing?

Processes Through Which Adolescents Believe Romantic Relationships Influence Friendship Quality

JENNIFER J. THOMAS
Wilkes University

ABSTRACT. Little is known about how romantic relationships influence adolescents' friendships. The purpose of this exploratory study was to identify behaviors through which adolescents believe romantic relationships influence friendship quality. Intimate exchange, co-rumination, encouragement, and conflict resolution were identified as processes through which romantic relationships influence friendship quality. Associations between these variables and friendship quality were investigated with 340 adolescents. Adolescents believed these processes occurred frequently within friendship. Gender differences suggest girls may be more sensitive to the influence of romantic partners on their friendships than are boys. Hierarchical regression analyses revealed that greater intimacy, encouragement, compromise, and less co-rumination were associated with more positive beliefs about friendship quality when one friend has a girlfriend or boyfriend. Greater co-rumination and less encouragement were predictive of negative friendship quality. Thus, these processes may represent avenues through which romantic relationships positively and negatively influence friendship quality. Findings highlight the need to understand friendships as part of a complex social network that includes romantic ties.

ADOLESCENTS' ROMANTIC RELATIONSHIPS are embedded within a rich network of peer relationships (Brown, 1999; Cavanagh, 2007). As such, researchers have investigated various ways in which peers, especially friends, affect romantic relationships. These studies show that friends have far reaching influence over one another's romantic lives, from providing information about who acceptable romantic partners are (Wood, Senn, Desmarais, Park, & Vernberg, 2002), to providing a context in which to learn social skills necessary for close

---

The author would like to thank the schools, teachers, and adolescents who participated in the study. Thanks are due to Thomas J. Berndt for insight into the design of the study and for comments on earlier versions of the article. Thanks also to Wesley K. Woo and Meridith Pease Selden for their comments on the article.

relationships (Connolly & Goldberg, 1999). Surprisingly, little attention has focused on the reverse of this relationship: how romantic relationships influence adolescents' pre-existing friendships. Thus, the purpose of this exploratory study was to identify behaviors, or interactional processes, through which adolescents believe romantic relationships may affect the quality of their friendships. The study had three overarching goals: First to identify interactional processes and second to determine whether there were gender differences in beliefs about these behaviors. The final aim was to ascertain whether these behaviors were associated with cognitive representations of friendship quality when a friend has a boyfriend or girlfriend.

This study has theoretical and practical significance. From a theoretical standpoint, researchers have highlighted the need to understand adolescents' friendships from a social network perspective (Rodkin & Hanish, 2007; Zimmer-Gembeck, & Kindermann, 2010); however, this network has rarely included the influence of romantic ties. A clearer understanding of the developmental significance of peer relationships and the processes of peer influence will be achieved by examining friendships within a context that includes romantic partners. Also, a gap in the literature exists concerning whether peer relationships affect boys and girls differently (Rubin, Bukowski, & Parker, 2006). By examining gender differences, this study will help further our understanding in this area. From a practical standpoint, romantic relationships may pose a problem for the maintenance of friendships during adolescence. In fact, adolescents report that having a boyfriend or girlfriend can cause them to exclude friends (Roth & Parker, 2001) and end friendships (Shulman, 1993). Because the ability to maintain multiple, supportive relationships requires skills that individuals will draw upon throughout their lifetime, it is important to understand how adolescents think about these relationships and the behaviors that enable them to simultaneously sustain both types of relationships.

Cognitive Representations of Relationships

As a first step in understanding how romantic relationships influence friendships, adolescents' cognitive representations of relationships and interactional processes were examined. Beliefs about relationships have been identified as an important level of analysis when investigating adolescent romantic experiences (Collins, 2003). In addition, social information processing theory (Crick & Dodge, 1994) and theories of social cognition (Fiske & Taylor, 1991) posit that an examination of relationship beliefs is a valid method for understanding relationships. Individuals have internal representations of the social world which guide their social interactions by shaping how they attend to, process, remember, and judge social information. As such, adolescents' responses to hypothetical situations are commonly used as a measure of how they would behave in a given situation and their responses correspond with their actual behavior (Chung & Asher, 1996). Research has shown that adolescents have cognitive representations of romantic relationships regardless of whether they are in a relationship (Brown, Feiring, &

Furman, 1999) and these beliefs may guide the relationships they develop. Indeed, cognitive representations of romantic relationships are related to the quality of adolescents' actual romantic relationships (Furman & Simon, 2006). To examine this assumption, cognitive representations of relationships were compared to reports of actual relationships.

Interactional Processes

The processes examined were intimate exchange, co-rumination, encouragement, and conflict resolution strategies. As elaborated upon in the following, they were selected due to their important theoretical implications for friendship quality during adolescence.

Intimate Exchange. Sullivan (1953) argued that during adolescence certain social needs, such as intimacy, could only be met within a friendship. Indeed, intimate self-disclosure emerges and becomes a defining feature of friendship quality in adolescence (Furman & Buhrmester, 1992). Intimate exchange that surrounds a friend's romantic partner may serve as an interactional process through which a romantic relationship influences the friendship. In fact, Connolly and Goldberg (1999) hypothesized that romantic relationships enhance the closeness of friendships during adolescence if these relationships serve as topics of conversation between friends. This hypothesis remains largely unexplored in part because the majority of investigations into intimacy have focused on the general content of the disclosure (e.g., "how often do you share secrets with your best friend?," see Furman, 1996). However, one study revealed that adolescent girls' discussions with friends often centered on issues related to romance (Simon, Eder, & Evans 1992). This study examined whether adolescents believe a friend's romantic partner serves as a topic of conversation between friends.

Co-rumination. Co-rumination refers to excessively discussing problems with another individual while focusing on the negative feelings associated with those problems (Rose, 2002) and may represent a special form of intimate exchange between friends. Indeed, friendships characterized by more intimate self-disclosure are also rated higher in co-rumination (Rose). And, the more emotionally intense or potentially negative a conversation topic, the more intimate the disclosure is considered (Reis & Patrick, 1996). As with intimacy, prior investigations of co-rumination have examined the frequency of general disclosures (e.g., "When one of us has a problem, we talk to each other about it for a long time;" Rose, 2002). However, just as friends may disclose thoughts and feelings about a romantic partner with one another, so too may they share problems concerning their romantic relationship. In fact, adolescent girls expect their friends to commiserate with them when their romantic relationships are not working out (Thompson, 1994).

Encouragement. Encouragement refers to expressing support for another's relationship. Researchers have not examined whether adolescents' boyfriends or girlfriends encourage them to maintain friendships. However, the reverse, encouragement by friends for a romantic relationship, has been assessed with college students. For example, individuals are more likely to continue in their romantic relationship when they believe their friends think the relationship should last (Etcheverry & Agnew, 2004). And romantic relationships persist longer when friends are perceived to be approving of the relationship (Felmlee, 2001). Thus, just as individuals perceive friends to be supportive of one another's romantic relationships, so too may romantic partners encourage friendships.

Conflict Resolution Strategies. Managing conflict is integral for maintaining close relationships during adolescence (Laursen, 1996). When friends begin dating, a friend's romantic relationship may become a source of tension between friends. According to interdependence theory, those in close relationships feel distressed and threatened when their relationship partner has others with whom he or she can spend time (Rusbult & Arriaga, 1997). In fact, many adolescents say they feel left out by friends who are romantically involved, and they ignore their friends when they have a boyfriend or girlfriend (Roth & Parker, 2001). Moreover, they describe strong, negative emotional reactions such as anger when thinking about being ignored by a friend for a romantic partner (Roth & Parker).

How adolescents resolve conflicts that result from a friend's romantic relationship represents a pathway through which romantic relationships may influence friendships. According to cognitive-developmental models of conflict, when adolescents experience conflict with friends they are most likely to engage in compromise and problem solving because of the emergence of abstract thought (Laursen & Collins, 1994; Laursen, Finkelstein, & Betts, 2001). Similarly, Rusbult, Verette, Whitney, Slovik, & Lipkus' (1991) theory of accommodative behaviors puts forth that individuals in close relationships are motivated to use accommodative behaviors such as problem solving for a partner who has behaved badly. Specifically, they identified voice or voicing concern (i.e., a constructive behavior that includes discussing the problem that resulted in the conflict and suggesting solutions; problem solving), withdrawing (i.e., behaviors associated with neglecting the relationship such as ignoring the partner and spending less time together), and threat of relationship termination (e.g., behaviors that indicate a partner will exit the relationship, such as telling the partner the relationship will end) as common responses to conflict within close relationships (Rusbult et al., 1991).

According to interdependence theory, those in close relationships are motivated to engage in behaviors that sustain the relationship (Rusbult & Arriaga, 1997). Thus, due to the more constructive nature of compromise and voice, it is expected that that adolescents will more strongly endorse these strategies compared to withdrawal and threat as behaviors they would employ to manage conflicts that that emerge between friends due to one friend's romantic partner.

Gender Differences. Theories of social-cognitive relationship style or relational orientation (Rose & Rudolph, 2006) suggest that gender differences should emerge for cognitions of interactional processes. Rose and Rudolph theorized that girls more strongly endorse connection-orientation goals while boys more strongly endorse status-orientation goals within their peer relationships. As such, girls should be more likely than boys to engage in activities with friends that foster a sense of connection and promote care and concern for each other. Indeed, girls report greater self-disclosure within friendships (Buhrmester & Prager, 1995), more emotionally intimate friendships (Rose & Rudolph), and they co-ruminate more than boys do (Rose, 2002). Similarly, gender differences in relational orientation have been revealed for the manner in which adolescents resolve conflicts: Girls rely on constructive strategies such as compromise more than boys (Laursen & Collins, 1994). Thus, when examining potential interactional processes through which romantic relationships influence friendship, gender differences should emerge that reflect the differing social-cognitive relational styles of girls and boys. Specifically, compared to boys, girls will more strongly endorse intimate exchange, co-rumination, encouragement, compromise, and voice and will less strongly endorse withdrawal and threat.

Associations With Friendship Quality

Beliefs about interactional processes should be meaningfully related to cognitive representations of friendship quality. Although romantic relationships may pose a problem for friendships during adolescence (Roth & Parker, 2001), the behaviors identified may enhance the positive quality of friendships and allow friends to remain close even when one friend has a boyfriend or girlfriend. According to interdependence theory, those in close relationships strive to maintain interactions that are rewarding (Rusbult & Arriaga, 1997). Intimate exchange, co-rumination, and constructive conflict resolution strategies represent interactions that are rewarding. Indeed, intimate self-disclosure results in increased understanding and trust within friendships (Buhrmester & Prager, 1995) and more time co-ruminating leads to increased positive friendship quality (Rose, Carlson, & Waller, 2007). In addition, adults resolve conflicts utilizing more constructive strategies when they are in relationships characterized by more positive features (Rusbult et al., 1991). And, adolescents with lower quality friendships engage in more destructive strategies such as threat in response to conflict (Rose & Asher, 1999).

The degree to which a romantic partner encourages a friendship represents an additional process through which romantic relationships may positively influence the quality of adolescents' friendships. The principle of transitivity derived from balance theory (Heider, 1946) posits that individuals are more likely to have a stable and satisfying relationship if they believe their own or their partner's social network approves of the relationship. In fact, individuals who perceive their friends to be encouraging of a boyfriend or girlfriend have more stable, intimate, and supportive romantic relationships than do those who perceive less support from friends for their romantic relationship (Sprecher & Felmlee, 2000).

Summary of the Current Study

The purpose of this study was to examine adolescents' cognitive representation of the interactional processes through which romantic relationships may influence friendship quality. The first goal was to establish whether adolescents believe intimate exchange and co-rumination about a romantic partner, encouragement of a friendship, and conflict resolution are behaviors that occur within friendships when friends are dating. The first hypothesis was based on interdependence theory: Compromise and voice would be more strongly endorsed than threat and withdrawal. The second aim was to examine gender differences in these processes. Based on theories of relationship orientation (Rose & Rudolph, 2006) the second hypothesis was that girls would more strongly endorse intimacy, co-rumination, encouragement, compromise, and voice and would less strongly endorse withdrawal and threat than boys. The final goal was to determine whether beliefs about interactional processes were associated with beliefs about friendship quality when a friend is dating. The final hypothesis was based on interdependence theory and the principle of transitivity: Adolescents would view friendships as higher in positive and lower in negative quality when they believe a friend's romantic relationship would serve as a source of intimacy and co-rumination, when there is greater encouragement of a friendship, and when conflicts are resolved with more compromise and voice and less withdrawal and threat.

Method

Participants and Procedure

The final sample included 340 students, 192 ninth graders (113 girls; M age = 14.98 years, SD = .41 years), and 148 eleventh graders (91 girls; M age = 16.93 years, SD = .43 years), from four high schools in the rural Midwest. Fifteen students were excluded because they did not complete the survey correctly or were missing too much data (for ethical purposes, it was emphasized that students could skip any questions they did not want to answer). To be included, complete data for cognitive representations of friendship, actual friendship quality, and at least one of the interactional processes was necessary. Data were more likely to be missing for conflict items (about 5%) because they were last on the questionnaire. The percentage of students receiving free or reduced lunch ranged from 16% to 33%. The ethnic composition of the sample was representative of the area. Most students (n = 320) were European American; one was African American; one was American Indian or an Alaskan Native; six were Hispanic; eight were multiracial, one selected "Other"; and three left this item blank. Consent forms were returned by 75% of the ninth graders and 84% of the eleventh graders.

A letter and a consent form were distributed to students to bring home to their parents. Parents were instructed to grant or deny their child's participation, and for each form that was returned, teachers received a $1 donation for classroom activities. Students completed the questionnaire in their classrooms. Although students read questionnaire items themselves, each section of the questionnaire was paced by a researcher so that students completed the questionnaire at a similar rate. The questionnaire was anonymous and wording of items corresponded with the sex of the adolescent (e.g., he vs. she).

Measures

Intimate Exchange. A 9-item measure was devised for the study. Guided by past research (e.g., Furman, 1996; Reis & Shaver, 1988), items measured the frequency of self-disclosure of emotions and feelings (i.e., evaluative intimacy), and activities and factual information (i.e., descriptive intimacy) concerning a friend's romantic partner. Students considered what is true for a typical best friendship between two individuals of the same age and sex as the student and in which one of the friends had a boyfriend or girlfriend (i.e., female version, "A girl your age named Sandra has a best friend named Janine and a boyfriend named Robbie. Janine does not have a boyfriend. How likely are Sandra and Janine to talk about ____?"). Sample items include, "... . Sandra being in love with her boyfriend?" and "... things Sandra would not tell anyone else about her boyfriend?" Cronbach's alpha was .86.

Co-rumination. Nine questions were adapted from the Co-Rumination Questionnaire (Rose, 2002). As with intimacy, students considered a typical friendship between two people the same age and sex as the students and in which one of the friends had a boy/girlfriend (i.e., female version, "Imagine a girl your age, Sara, has a boyfriend Brad and a best friend Pam. Pam does not have a boyfriend. When Sara talks to Pam about a problem in her relationship with Brad they'll ... "). Items referred to excessively discussing problems, focusing on the negative feelings associated with the problems, and discussing problems instead of engaging in other activities (e.g., "talk about every part of the problem over and over."). Reliability was high ($\alpha = .92$).

Encouragement. Based on research on adults' perceptions of their friends' approval of romantic relationships (Sprecher & Felmlee, 2000), a 12-item measure was created to capture cognitions of encouragement (i.e., female version, "A girl your age has a best friend named Cindy and a boyfriend named Ted. Cindy does not have a boyfriend. Please answer the following questions about how you think Ted would act."). A sample item from the female version is, "How likely is Ted to say he's glad his girlfriend has a best friend she can share her problems with." Seven negatively worded items were reverse scored. Cronbach's alpha was .86.

Conflict Resolution Strategies. Three hypothetical situations were created in which one member of a friendship choose to spend time with a romantic partner instead of his/her best friend (see Table 1). The use of hypothetical situations to examine conflict resolution is common (Rose & Asher, 1999), and responses corresponded with one's actual behavior in conflict situations (Chung & Asher, 1996). Situations were created based on research that indicated adolescents often feel excluded by friends who are romantically involved, and they exclude their

TABLE 1. Example of Hypothetical Conflict and Conflict Resolution Strategies, Female Version

Example Hypothetical Situation	Strategy Type	Example Responses
At the beginning of the week Sue and her best friend, Mary, decide that on Friday night they will go to the movies together. But on Thursday Sue's boyfriend, Ed, asks her to go to a different movie with him on Friday night. Sue decides to break her plans with Mary and go to a movie with Ed instead.	Compromise	"After Sue decides to go to the movie with Ed, how likely is she to suggest that she and Mary see the other movie together the next day?"
	Voicing Concern	"How likely is Mary to suggest to Sue that in the future they should talk before Sue breaks their plans to spend time with Ed?"
	Withdrawal from Friendship	"How likely is Mary to decide to ask Sue to go to the movies with her less often?"
	Threat of Friendship Termination	"How likely is Mary to say she won't be friends with Sue if Sue continues to choose Ed over her?"

Note. Responses are measured on a 5-point Likert scale (1 = *not at all likely* and 5 = *very likely*). Boys and girls were given gender-specific versions of the questionnaire such that the sex of the friends in each vignette matched the sex of the participant.

friends when they have a romantic partner (Roth & Parker, 2001). After each situation, adolescents rated how likely the friend with the romantic partner was to engage in compromise and the other friend was to engage in voicing concern, withdrawal from friendship, and threat of friendship termination (see Table 1). Six items comprised compromise and voice (two items from each vignette) and three items comprised withdrawal and threat (one item from each vignette). A principal axis factor analysis with oblimin rotation revealed a four factor solution that replicated the conceptual structure of the measure and explained 60.29% of the variance. Reliability of scales was: compromise $\alpha = .89$, voice $\alpha = .87$, withdrawal $\alpha = .84$, threat $\alpha = .88$.

Cognitive Representations of Friendship Quality. Students answered questions about a hypothetical best friendship in which one of the friends had a romantic partner (female version, "Think about two girls your own age, Mandy and Kim, who are best friends. Mandy has a boyfriend but Kim does not."). Parallel items were included for cognitive representations of a friendship in which neither friend had a romantic relationship, but are not reported here. The intimacy, support, companionship, conflict, and rivalry subscales of Berndt and Keefe's (1995) friendship measure were used. Subscales consisted of six items. Positive friendship quality was created by averaging the positive items and a negative quality score was created by averaging the conflict and rivalry items. Measures had high internal consistency (α for positive = .92; α for negative = .91).

Actual Friendship Quality. Nearly all students (99%) reported having a best friend, defined as someone of the same sex with whom the student felt very close to and with whom the student spent much of his/her free time. Questions were similar to cognitive representations of friendship items. For example, "How often does Ann tell Judy about something that is bothering her?" was changed to, "How often does your best friend tell you about something that is bothering her?" Derivation of the final measures was comparable to that for cognitive representations of friendship. Internal consistency was high (positive quality α = .92; negative quality α = .93).

Romantic Involvement. Forty-two percent of students (n = 144) reported having a romantic relationship, defined as a relationship with someone of the other sex to whom the student felt close and considered more than a "friend." Romantic relationships ranged from 1 to 35 months (M = 8.7 months, SD = 8.1 months) in duration. In addition, 44% of students (n = 150) reported that their best friend had a boyfriend or girlfriend.

Results

Preliminary Analyses

Associations between potential confounding variables and the processes variables were examined before conducting the primary analyses. For example, participants in a romantic relationship may have cognitive representations of relationship processes that are more positive than those who are not dating. However, beliefs about processes did not significantly vary according to one's romantic relationship status or to friend's romantic status. In addition, for those in a romantic relationship, the duration of the romantic relationship was unrelated to interactional processes.

Descriptive Information for Interactional Processes

The first goal was to identify processes through which adolescents believe romantic relationships may influence friendship. The first hypothesis was that compromise and voice would be more strongly endorsed than threat and withdrawal. T-tests revealed that adolescents believe intimate exchange, co-rumination, encouragement, and conflict resolution about a friend's romantic partner are processes used within friendships when one friend has a boyfriend or girlfriend (see Table 2). Intimate exchange was more strongly endorsed than co-rumination,

TABLE 2. Descriptive Information for Interactional Process Variables

	Males		Females		All	
Interactional Processes	n	M (SD)	n	M (SD)	n	M (SD)
Intimate Exchange	131	2.76 (0.63)	204	3.54 (0.69)	335	3.23 (0.77)
Co-rumination	131	2.14 (0.76)	204	2.71 (0.90)	335	2.48 (0.89)
Encouragement	131	3.06 (0.62)	204	3.50 (0.73)	335	3.33 (0.72)
Conflict Resolution Strategies						
Compromise	128	3.01 (0.83)	194	3.76 (0.88)	322	3.47 (0.94)
Voice	128	3.06 (0.88)	194	3.45 (0.86)	322	3.30 (0.89)
Withdrawal	128	2.50 (0.92)	194	2.47 (1.01)	332	2.49 (0.97)
Threat	128	2.11 (0.97)	194	2.15 (1.06)	332	2.15 (1.03)

Note. All values are mean scores measured on a 5-point Likert scale (for co-rumination 1 = *not at all true* and 5 = *really true*; all other scales 1 = *not at all likely* and 5 = *very likely*).

$t(335) = 17.54$, $p < .001$, $d = .89$. And encouragement was viewed as more frequent than co-rumination, $t(334) = 12.91$, $p < .001$, $d = 1.04$. Frequency of intimacy and encouragement were similar. In support of the first hypothesis, compromise was more strongly endorsed than any other conflict strategy: $t(321) = 3.05$, $p = .002$, $d = .18$ for voice; $t(321) = 12.54$, $p < .001$, $d = 1.03$ for withdraw; $t(321) = 16.98$, $p < .001$, $d = 1.35$ for threat. Voice was more frequent than withdrawal, $t(321) = 12.21$, $p < .001$, $d = .87$ and threat, $t(321) = 18.36$, $p < .001$, $d = 1.21$. Withdrawal was more strongly endorsed than threat $t(334) = 6.67$, $p < .001$, $d = .34$.

Sex Differences in Cognitive Representations of Interactional Processes

To address the second aim of the study, two 2 × 2 (Sex [male, female] × Grade [ninth, eleventh]) multivariate analyses of variance (MANOVAs) were conducted. The interactional processes variables served as the dependent variables.

Intimate Exchange, Co-rumination, and Encouragement. The first MANOVA revealed significant multivariate effects of sex, Wilks' $\Delta = .67$, $F(3, 329) = 54.46$, $p < .001$, $\eta_p^2 = .33$ and grade, Wilks' $\Delta = .97$, $F(3, 329) = 3.21$, $p = .023$, $\eta_p^2 = .03$. Univariate effects of sex were significant for intimacy, co-rumination, and encouragement ($p < .001$). Consistent with the gender hypothesis, girls were more likely to conceive of friends as utilizing a romantic partner as a source of intimacy and co-rumination and to view a romantic partner as encouraging of a friendship than were boys (η_p^2's = .235, .096, and .099 respectively; see Table 2). Although there was a multivariate effect of grade, follow-up univariate tests were not significant.

Conflict Resolution Strategies. The second MANOVA examined sex and age differences in adolescents' beliefs about conflict resolution. Multivariate effects were significant for sex, Wilks' $\Delta = .85$, $F(4, 315) = 14.40$, $p < .001$, $\eta_p^2 = .16$. Univariate effects were significant ($p < .001$) for compromise and voice. Consistent with the hypothesis, girls were more likely than boys to endorse compromise and voice (η_p^2's $= .152$ and $.040$; see Table 2).

Relationships Between Interactional Processes and Friendship Quality

The final purpose of the study was to determine whether the interactional process variables were associated with adolescents' beliefs about the quality of friendships when one friend is dating. As a first step, correlations were run among the process variables and both cognitive representations of and actual positive and negative friendship quality.

Modest correlations were revealed among the interactional processes variables (see Table 3). In addition, consistent with the assumption based on social information processing theory (Crick & Dodge, 1994) and theories of social cognition (Fiske & Taylor, 2007) that beliefs about relationship should resemble adolescents' actual relationships, cognitive representations of positive and negative friendship quality closely resembled adolescents' perceptions of their own friendships. Furthermore, cognitive representations of friendship and actual friendship quality were meaningfully related to interactional processes. Cognitive representations of and actual positive friendship quality were significantly correlated with all the process variables except for threat. Fewer of the process variables were correlated with negative quality.

Predicting Cognitive Representations of Friendship Quality From Interactional Processes

Hierarchical regression analyses were conducted to further address the final aim of the study and to examine the hypothesis that friendships would be viewed as higher in positive and lower in negative quality when adolescents more strongly endorsed intimacy, co-rumination, encouragement, and constructive conflict resolution strategies as processes that occur within friendships when a friend is dating. The criterion variables included cognitions of positive and negative friendship quality. For each regression analysis, sex, grade, romantic relationship status (current romantic relationship: yes or no), and the matching actual friendship quality score (positive or negative quality) were entered on the first step. The seven interactional process variables were entered on the second step. Results are presented in Tables 4 and 5.

Sex and perceptions of actual positive friendship quality were significant predictors of cognitive representations of positive friendship quality (see Table 4). Girls and students with higher quality best friendships believed friendships would be characterized by more positive features when a friend has a girlfriend or boyfriend than did boys and students with lower quality best friendships. When

TABLE 3. Correlations Between Interactional Processes, Cognitive Representations of Friendship Quality, and Actual Friendship Quality

Measures	1	2	3	4	5	6	7	8	9	10
Interactional Processes										
1. Intimacy	—									
2. Co-rumination	0.57***	—								
3. Encouragement	0.02	−0.08	—							
Conflict Resolution Strategies										
4. Compromise	0.40***	0.33***	0.33***	—						
5. Voice	0.35***	0.23***	0.05	0.40***	—					
6. Withdraw	0.05	0.18*	−0.33***	−0.08	0.18**	—				
7. Threat	0.11*	0.19**	−0.29***	−0.02	0.31***	0.57***	—			
Cognitive Representations of Friendship Quality										
8. Positive Quality	0.49***	0.24****	0.34***	0.50***	0.34***	−0.11*	−0.03	—		
9. Negative Quality	0.05	0.21***	−0.28***	−0.07	0.12*	0.25***	0.25***	−0.34***	—	
Actual Friendship Quality										
10. Positive Quality	0.52***	0.32**	0.31***	0.45***	0.31***	−0.12*	−0.08	0.70***	−0.13*	—
11. Negative Quality	−0.04	0.07	−0.17**	−0.11	−0.01	0.15**	0.16**	−0.26**	0.61***	−0.25***

Note. N's 316–340; *p < .05; **p < .01; ***p < .001; ****p < .0001.

TABLE 4. Regression Predicting Cognitive Representations of Positive Friendship Quality from Interactional Processes

	B	SE(B)	β	ΔR²	R²	F	df
Step 1				0.513***	0.513***		
Sex	0.284	0.065	0.208***				
Grade	−0.004	0.065	−0.003				
Romantic Relationship Status	0.017	0.056	0.013				
Actual Positive Friendship Quality	0.527	0.044	0.579***				
Step 2				0.058***	0.571***		
Sex	0.186	0.067	0.136**				
Grade	0.001	0.054	0.001				
Romantic Relationship Status	0.001	0.055	0.001				
Actual Positive Friendship Quality	0.415	0.047	0.456***				
Intimate Exchange	0.130	0.047	0.152**				
Co-rumination	−0.077	0.036	−0.104*				
Encouragement	0.095	0.043	0.103*				
Compromise	0.103	0.034	0.144**				
Voice	0.060	0.034	0.079				
Withdrawal from Friendship	−0.027	0.033	−0.039				
Threat of Friendship Termination	0.019	0.032	0.029				
Final Model						36.41***	11, 312

Note. $^*p < .05$; $^{**}p < .01$; $^{***}p < .001$.

TABLE 5. Regression Predicting Cognitive Representations of Negative Friendship Quality from Interactional Processes

	B	SE(B)	β	ΔR²	R²	F	df
Step 1				0.384***	0.384***		
Sex	−0.022	0.064	−0.016				
Grade	0.044	0.065	0.032				
Romantic Relationship Status	0.042	0.064	0.031				
Actual Negative Friendship Quality	0.599	0.044	0.622***				
Step 2				0.077***	0.461***		
Sex	−0.063	0.073	−0.045				
Grade	0.060	0.063	0.044				
Romantic Relationship Status	0.001	0.063	0.001				
Actual Negative Friendship Quality	0.545	0.043	0.566***				
Intimate Exchange	0.004	0.051	0.005				
Co-rumination	0.101	0.041	0.135*				
Encouragement	−0.116	0.048	−0.124*				
Compromise	−0.010	0.039	−0.013				
Voice	0.064	0.038	0.082				
Withdrawal from Friendship	0.050	0.038	0.071				
Threat of Friendship Termination	0.035	0.036	0.053				
Final Model						23.34***	11, 311

Note. $^*p < .05$; $^{**}p < .01$; $^{***}p < .001$.

the seven interactional process variables were entered on the second step, the betas for sex and actual positive friendship quality decreased but remained significant. Consistent with the hypothesis, cognitive representations of friendships as being characterized by more intimate exchange, encouragement, and compromise predicted beliefs about friendships as being characterized by more positive features when one friend has a romantic relationship. Inconsistent with the hypothesis, less co-rumination also predicted beliefs about friendships as characterized by more positive features.

Students' reports of the negative quality of their actual best friendship were a significant predictor of their beliefs about the amount of conflict and rivalry within a friendship in which one friend has a romantic partner (see Table 5). Students who reported more conflict and rivalry within their best friendship believed a friendship would be characterized by more negative features when one friend is dating than did students who reported less conflict and rivalry within their best friendship. When the seven interactional process variables were entered on the second step, the beta for actual negative quality decreased but remained significant. Consistent with the hypothesis, students who thought a romantic partner would be less encouraging of a friendship believed a friendship would be characterized by more negative features when one friend is dating. Inconsistent with the hypothesis, those who believed a friend's romantic partner would serve as a more frequent topic of co-rumination also believed friendships would be characterized by more conflict and rivalry when one friend has a romantic partner.

Discussion

Although many studies have investigated the influence of friends on adolescents' romantic relationships (e.g., Wood et al., 2002), this exploratory study represents a first step in probing the unexamined question of how adolescents' romantic relationships influence their friendships. Findings reveal that intimate exchange, co-rumination, encouragement, and conflict resolution about a friend's romantic partner represent processes that adolescents believe occur regularly within friendships when a friend has a boyfriend or girlfriend. In addition, gender differences suggest that romantic relationships may have stronger influence over the friendships of girls than boys. Furthermore, regression analyses revealed that intimate exchange, co-rumination, encouragement, and conflict resolution may represent important processes through which adolescents' romantic relationships influence the positive quality of friendships. In addition, romantic relationships may contribute to the deterioration of friendships if friends co-ruminate about a romantic partner and if a romantic partner discourages a friendship. Results illustrate that a more comprehensive understanding of adolescent friendship will occur when these social ties are examined within a network that includes romantic partners. From an applied standpoint, findings highlight the need for those who work with youth to help them develop skills necessary to simultaneously maintain friendships and romantic relationships. For instance, the interactional processes identified all require the ability to take another's perspective. The development and practice of these skills may allow youth to develop more satisfying friendships and romantic relationships.

Interactional Processes

As expected, findings suggest that just as adolescents' friendships influence their romantic relationships, the interactional processes identified may shape adolescents' friendships once friends gain a boyfriend or girlfriend. Behaviors such as intimacy and encouragement may allow friends to remain close or even strengthen a friendship once friends begin dating. In addition, the fact that self-disclosures about a romantic relationship were unrelated to whether adolescents believed a romantic partner encourages a friendship, suggests that when examining how romantic relationships influence friendships, both direct (e.g., encouragement) and indirect behaviors (e.g., self-disclosure) should be examined.

Gender Differences. Gender differences emerged for cognitive representations of interactional processes that were consistent with predictions based on theories of social-cognitive relationship style or relational orientation (Rose & Rudolph, 2006). However, there are several alternative explanations and important implications of these findings. For instance, the hypothesis that romantic relationships become important topics of conversation between friends and may draw friends closer during adolescence (Connolly & Goldberg, 1999) may be more applicable to girls' than boys' friendships. Alternatively, because boys disclose personal information to friends less frequently than girls do, when boys talk about a romantic partner with a friend this may be especially important for the closeness and quality of boys' friendships. Future research could clarify gender differences by having friends talk with one another about their romantic relationships and measure changes in friendship quality before and after these conversations.

Gender differences also signify that the interactional processes identified may be more relevant to girls' than boys' friendships. For example, while girls create intimacy and closeness with friends through self-disclosure, boys are more likely to establish intimacy and closeness through shared activities with friends (McNelles & Connolly, 1999). The extent to which romantic relationships hinder or promote shared activities with friends may be a mechanism through which romantic relationships are particularly influential for boys' friendships.

Findings also reveal that romantic relationships may have a greater impact on girls' than boys' friendships. Past research lends credence to this claim. Specifically, girls are more invested in their relationships than are boys (Rose & Rudolph, 2006) and they report romantic relationships characterized by more positive features than do boys (Connolly, Furman, & Konarski, 2000), suggesting a desire by girls to develop close, intimate connections with a romantic partner sooner than boys do. Girls' greater desire for a close romantic relationship may lead them to be more susceptible to the influence of a romantic partner on their other peer relationships. Additional evidence that a romantic partner's influence may vary according gender comes from recent investigations into peer networks. Studies have revealed that the sex of one's friends is important for understanding peer influence (Arndorfer & Stormshak, 2008; Haynie, Steffensmeier, & Bell, 2007). Indeed, for the development of certain risky behaviors, friendships with girls serve as protective factors for boys while friendships with boys serve as risk factors for girls (Haynie et al.). Taken together, findings suggest that a better understanding of adolescent friendship and the processes of peer influence will be achieved if researchers investigate peer relationships within a context that includes both gender and romantic ties.

Interactional Processes and Friendship Quality

Consistent with interdependence theory and the principle of transitivity derived from balance theory (Heider, 1946) stronger endorsement of intimate exchange, encouragement, and compromise and less co-rumination were related to beliefs about friendships as being higher in positive quality when friends are dating. In addition, more co-rumination about a romantic partner and less encouragement of a friendship were related to beliefs about friendship as characterized by more conflict and rivalry. Because co-rumination and encouragement were the only variables associated with both positive and negative friendship quality, these processes may be especially important for understanding how romantic relationships influence friendships.

Discussing problems about a romantic partner was not associated with beliefs that friendships would be higher in quality. Although co-rumination may appear to be a behavior that elicits social support from friends, it may instead result in perceiving a friendship to be less supportive and intimate and to be characterized by more conflict and rivalry. This is in contrast to research that has shown co-rumination in general to be associated with increases in adolescents' perceptions of the positive quality of their friendships (Rose et al., 2007). Findings suggest that the content of the problem being discussed may be critical for friendship quality. Specifically, co-rumination about a romantic partner may increase tension and negative interactions between friends, as these discussions may lead friends to be unsupportive of the romantic relationship. In fact, avoiding conflict and fear that a friendship will be damaged are reasons given for avoiding discussing topics such as romantic relationships with friends (Afifi & Guerroro, 1998). And, individuals are motivated to have others view their romantic relationships positively, thus they often withhold negative information about romantic partners from friends (Loving & Agnew, 2001). Co-rumination may represent an important process through which romantic relationships contribute to the deterioration of friendships.

Few conflict resolution variables were predictive of friendship quality. Compromise was the only strategy associated with positive quality and none of the conflict variables were associated with of negative quality. Because past investigations showed that compromise is the strategy of choice among adolescents when resolving conflicts with friends (Laursen et al., 2001), findings may indicate that the other strategies investigated are relied upon rarely. Alternatively, although the strategies examined were based on theory and past research (e.g., Rusbult et al., 1991), strategies not included in this study, specifically behaviors meant to damage friendship (e.g., revenge, aggression), may be more important for understanding friendship quality when a friend is dating. Although threat and friendship withdrawal seem like behaviors intended to harm a friendship, they are accommodative processes and do not reveal a motivation to hurt a friendship (Rusbult et al.).

Associations between the interactional process variables and friendship quality have important applied consequences. For instance, youth need to be made aware of the possible negative consequences that talking about problems concerning their romantic relationships may have for their friendships. In addition, individuals who work with teens should redirect teens who continually co-ruminate about romantic relationships to activities that are more likely to result in the resolution of these issues. Results for conflict resolution and friendship quality suggest that adolescents who have difficulty simultaneously maintaining friendships and romantic relationships may benefit from activities that allow them to learn and practice compromise skills.

Limitations and Conclusions

Several methodological limitations should be considered when interpreting the findings of this study. First, adolescents' beliefs about interactional processes and relationships are thought to resemble their actual behaviors (Crick & Dodge, 1994) and although cognitive representations were strongly related to adolescents' reports of their actual friendships, adolescents should be surveyed about their actual relationships. Second, adolescents' cognitive representations were assessed from the point of view of the peer without a romantic partner (with the exception of compromise) because this situation should be perceived as most troublesome for a friendship (Rusbult & Arriaga, 1997). Research is necessary to determine whether interactional processes and their relationship with friendship quality varies according to whether adolescents are queried from the point of view of the friend who has the romantic relationship and for situations in which both friends are dating. Third, data were cross-sectional. Although various conceptual frameworks lead to the hypothesis that interactional processes are predictive of friendship quality, longitudinal data are necessary to determine the directional nature of these relationships or whether another, unidentified variable is responsible for the relationships between these variables. Last, the sample was restricted to rural, Midwestern, European-Americans and their beliefs about heterosexual romantic relationships. Connections between friendship and romantic relationships may vary for adolescents according to race/ethnicity, whether they live in rural, suburban, or urban areas, and according to their sexual orientation. Future research would benefit from examining the experiences of adolescents from more diverse backgrounds.

These limitations aside, this is the first study to identify and explore potential processes through which romantic relationships may influence adolescents' friendships. Adolescents believe that intimate exchange, co-rumination, encouragement, and conflict resolution represent behaviors that frequently occur within friendships when friends are dating. Gender differences suggest that girls' friendships may be more susceptible to the influence of a friend's romantic partner than are boys' friendships. Regression analyses revealed that the processes identified were meaningfully related to beliefs about the quality of friendships when a friend is dating. Behaviors such as intimate self-disclosure and compromise may enable adolescents to remain close to a friend even when the friend is dating whereas co-rumination and discouragement may be especially detrimental to friendships. From a theoretical standpoint, findings suggest that a more comprehensive understanding of adolescent friendship, the processes of peer influence, and gender differences in peer experiences may come from examining friendship from a social network perspective that includes romantic ties.

From a practical standpoint, findings have implications for helping youth develop, manage, and maintain more satisfying relationships. Successfully maintaining multiple social relationships entails skills individuals will need to draw upon throughout their lifetime. However, results suggest that romantic relationships may pose a problem for the maintenance of friendships, thus adolescents should be taught skills necessary for close relationships. Because intimacy, encouragement, and constructive conflict resolution strategies were related to higher quality friendships, adolescents should be taught behaviors necessary for these strategies such as perspective taking and being a good listener. Links between co-rumination and negative friendship quality imply that youth should be encouraged to find ways to manage negative feelings about a romantic partner aside from co-ruminating with friends. Parents, teachers, and professionals who work with adolescents should help them to recognize how focusing on problems is damaging to friendships. In addition, adults should also be aware that romantic relationships may have greater consequences for the peer experiences of girls than boys. Compared to boys, girls' more communal relationship orientation may make them more sensitive to stresses associated with simultaneously maintaining a friendship and a romantic relationship.

AUTHOR NOTES

Jennifer J. Thomas is an Associate Professor of Psychology at Wilkes University. Her research interests include adolescent friendships and romantic relationships, their associations with positive development, and the processes of peer influence.

REFERENCES

Afifi, W. A., & Guerroro, L. K. (1998). Some things are better left unsaid II: Topic avoidance in friendship communication. *Communication Quarterly, 45*, 231– 249.

Arndorfer, C. L., & Stormshak, E. A. (2008). Same-sex versus other-sex best friendship in early adolescence: Longitudinal predictors of antisocial behavior throughout adolescence. *Journal of Youth and Adolescence, 37*, 1059–1070.

Berndt, T. J., & Keefe, K. (1995). Friends' influence on students' adjustment to school. *Child Development, 66*, 1312–1329.

Brown, B. B. (1999). "You're going out with who?": Peer group influences on adolescent romantic relationships. In W. Furman, B. Brown, & C. Feiring (Eds.), *The development of romantic relationships in adolescence* (pp. 291–329). New York, NY: Cambridge University Press.

Brown, B. B., Feiring, C., & Furman, W. (1999). Missing the love boat: Why researchers have shied away from adolescent romance. In W. Furman, B. Brown, & C. Feiring (Eds.), *The development of romantic relationships in adolescence* (pp. 1–16). New York, NY: Cambridge University Press.

Burhrmester, D., & Prager, K. (1995). Patterns and functions of self-disclosure during childhood and adolescence. In K. J. Rotenberg (Ed.,), *Disclosure processes in children and adolescents* (pp. 10–56). New York, NY: Cambridge University Press.

Cavanagh, S. E. (2007). The social construction of romantic relationships in adolescence: Examining the role of peer networks, gender, and race. *Sociological Inquiry, 77*, 572–600.

Chung, T., & Asher, S. R. (1996). Children's goals and strategies in peer conflict situations. *Merrill-Palmer Quarterly, 42*, 125–147.

Collins, W. A. (2003). More than myth: The developmental importance of romantic relationships during adolescence. *Journal of Research on Adolescence, 13*, 1–25.

Connolly, J., Furman, W., & Konarski, R. (2000). The role of peers in the emergence of heterosexual romantic relationships in adolescence. *Child Development, 71*, 1395–1408.

Connolly, J., & Goldberg, A. (1999). Romantic relationships in adolescence: The role of friends and peers in their emergence. In W. Furman, B. Brown, & C. Feiring (Eds.), *The development of romantic relationships in adolescence* (pp. 266–290). NY: Cambridge University Press.

Crick, N. R., & Dodge, K. A. (1994). A review of social-information processing mechanisms in children's social adjustment. *Psychological Bulletin, 115*, 74–101.

Etcheverry, P. E, & Agnew, C. R. (2004). Subjective norms and the prediction of romantic relationship state and fate. *Personal Relationships, 11*, 409–428.

Felmlee, S. (2001). No couple is an island: A social network perspective on dyadic stability. *Social Forces, 79*, 1259–1287.

Fiske, S. T., & Taylor, S. E. (1991). *Social cognition* (2nd ed.). New York: McGraw-Hill.

Furman, W. (1996). The measurement of friendship perceptions: Conceptual and methodological issues. In W. M. Bukowski, A. F. Newcomb, & W. W. Hartup (Eds.), *The company they keep: Friendship in childhood and adolescence* (pp. 41–65). New York, NY: Cambridge University Press.

Furman, W., & Buhrmester, D. (1992). Age and sex differences in perceptions of networks of personal relationships. *Child Development, 63*, 103–115.

Furman, W. & Simon, V. A. (2006). Actor and partner effects of adolescents' working models and styles on interactions with romantic partners. *Child Development, 77*, 241–255.

Haynie, D. L., Steffensmeier, D., & Bell, K. E. (2007). Gender and serious violence: Untangling the role of friendship sex composition and peer violence. *Youth Violence and Juvenile Justice, 5*, 235–253.

Heider, F. (1946). Attitudes and cognitive organization. *Psychology, 21*, 107–122.

Laursen, B. (1996). Closeness and conflict in adolescent peer relationships: Interdependence with friends and romantic partners. In W. M. Bukowski, A. F. Newcomb, & W. W. Hartup (Eds.), *The company they keep: Friendship in childhood and adolescence* (pp. 186–210). New York, NY: Cambridge University Press.

Laursen, B., & Collins, A. W. (1994). Interpersonal conflict during adolescence. *Psychological Bulletin, 115*, 197–209.

Laursen, B., Finkelstein, B. D., & Betts, N. T. (2001). A developmental meta-analysis of peer conflict. *Developmental Review, 21*, 423–449.

Loving, T. J., & Agnew, C. R. (2001). Socially desirable responding in close relationships: A dual-component approach and measure. *Journal of Social and Personal Relationships, 18*, 551–573.

McNelles, L. R., & Connolly, J. A. (1999). Intimacy between adolescent friends: Age and gender differences in intimate affect and intimate behaviors. *Journal of Research on Adolescence, 9*, 143–159.

Reis, H. T., & Patrick, B. C. (1996). Attachment and intimacy: Component processes. In E. T. Higgins & A. W. Kruglanski (Eds.), *Social Psychology: Handbook of basic principles* (pp. 523–563). New York, NY: Guilford.

Reis, H. T., & Shaver, P. (1988). Intimacy as an interpersonal process. In S. Duck (Ed.), *Handbook of personal relationships* (pp. 367–389). Chichester, England: Wiley.

Rodkin, P. C., & Hanish, L. D. (Eds.) (2007). *Social network analysis and children's peer relationships.* In L. A. Jensen and R. W. Larson (Series Ed.), New Directions for Child and Adolescent Development (No. 118). New York, NY: Wiley.

Rose, A. J. (2002). Co-rumination in the friendships of girls and boys. *Child Development, 73*, 1830–1843.

Rose, A. J., & Asher, S. R. (1999). Children's goals and strategies in response to conflicts within a friendship. *Developmental Psychology, 35*, 69–79.

Rose, A. J., Carlson, W., & Waller, E. M. (2007). Prospective associations of co-rumination with friendship and emotional adjustment: Considering the socioemotional trade-offs of co-rumination. *Developmental Psychology, 43*, 1019–1031.

Rose, A. J., & Rudolph, K. D. (2006). A review of sex differences in peer relationship processes: Potential trade-offs for the emotional and behavioral development of girls and boys. *Psychological Bulletin, 132*, 98–131.

Roth, M. A., & Parker, J. G. (2001). Affective and behavioral responses to friends who neglect their friends for dating partners: Influence of gender, jealousy, and perspective. *Journal of Adolescence, 24*, 281–296.

Rubin, K. H., Bukowski, W., & Parker, J. G. (2006). Peer interactions, relationships, and groups. In W. Damon (Series Ed.), & N. Eisenberg (Vol. Ed.), *Handbook of child psychology: Vol. 3. Social, emotional, and personality development* (7th ed., pp. 571–645). New York, NY: Wiley.

Rusbult, C. E., & Arriaga, X. B. (1997). Interdependence theory. In S. Duck (Ed.), *Handbook of personal relationships* (2nd ed., pp. 221–250). New York, NY: Wiley.

Rusbult, C. E., Verette, J., Whitney, G. A., Slovik, L. F., & Lipkus, I. (1991). Accomodating processes in close relationships: Theory and preliminary empirical evidence. *Journal of Personality and Social Psychology, 60*, 53–78.

Shulman, S. (1993). Close friendships in early and middle adolescence: Typology and friendship reasoning. In B. Laursen (Ed.), *Close friendships in adolescence*, (No. 60, pp. 55–71). San Francisco, CA: Jossey-Bass.

Simon, R., Eder, D., & Evans, C. (1992). The development of feeling norms underlying romantic love among adolescent females. *Social Psychology Quarterly, 55*, 29–46.

Sprecher, S., & Felmlee, D. (2000). Romantic partners' perceptions of social network attributes with the passage of time and relationship transitions. *Personal Relationships, 7*, 325–349.

Sullivan, H. S. (1953). *The interpersonal theory of psychiatry*. New York: Norton.

Thompson, S. (1994). Changing lives, changing genres: Teenage girls' narratives about sex and romance, 1978–1986. In A. S. Rossi (Ed.), *Sexuality across the life course* (pp. 209–232). Chicago, IL: University of Chicago Press.

Wood, E., Senn, C. Y., Desmarais, S., Park, L., & Vernberg, N. (2002). Sources of information about dating and their perceived influence on adolescents. *Journal of Adolescent Research, 17*, 401–417.

Zimmer-Gembeck, M. J., & Kindermann, T. (2010). Capturing the peer context: Developmental issues, statistical methods, and new directions. *Journal of Adolescence, 33*, 783–786.

How Do Romantic Relationship Satisfaction, Gender Stereotypes, and Gender Relate to Future Time Orientation in Romantic Relationships?

NURAY SAKALLI-UGURLU

ABSTRACT. The present study is an investigation into how romantic relationship satisfaction and attitudes toward gender stereotypes about romantic relationship and gender are related to future time orientation in romantic relationships (FTORR). Four hundred and thirteen (208 men and 205 women) university students taking elective psychology courses at Middle East Technical University were given a scale including items about FTORR, romantic relationship satisfaction, and attitudes toward gender stereotypes about romantic relationships. All the participants were then involved in a heterosexual romantic relationship. Multiple regression results showed that for the women, attitudes toward men's assertiveness and men's dominance in relationships were more important predictors of FTORR than relationship satisfaction. For the men, attitudes toward men's assertiveness and romantic relationship satisfaction were important predictors of FTORR, but attitude toward men's dominance was not a predictor of FTORR. Women were more future oriented in their ongoing romantic relationships than were men. Finally, participants who were highly satisfied with their relationships scored higher on FTORR than those who were less satisfied.

IN THE PRESENT STUDY I explored how romantic relationship satisfaction, attitudes toward gender stereotypes about romantic relationship, and gender are related to future time orientation in romantic relationships in a sample of university students who were currently in heterosexual dating relationships. A great deal of research has been focused on satisfaction in dating and in marital relationships. *Satisfaction* can be defined as an intrapersonal evaluation of the positivity of feelings for one's partner and attraction to the relationship (Rusbult, 1983). Romantic relationship satisfaction has been shown to be associated with various factors such as commitment (Rusbult, 1980), rewards, costs (Sabatelli, 1988), relationship stability (White, 1990), perceived relationship alternatives (Attridge, Berscheid, & Simpson, 1995), time spent together (Vangelisti & Banski, 1993), power (Gray-Kittle & Burke, 1983), and future time orientation (Öner, 2000a).

Future orientation is defined as a collection of schemata or attitudes based on previous experiences that interact with incoming information from the individual's environment to form expectations for the future (Nurmi, 1991; Trommsdorff, 1983). Gjesme (1983) defined the concept as "the ability to forsee and anticipate, to make plans and organize future possibilities" (p. 347). Recently, Öner (2000a) argued that the concept of future time orientation can be context related, and future time orientation for romantic relationship (FTORR) might be different from general future time orientation.

Öner (2000a) developed a scale to measure FTORR, including one's need for future commitment and the degree of future investment put into relationships with the opposite sex. In a subsequent study (Öner, 2000b), she found that participants who were more future time oriented were less satisfied with their relationships with the opposite sex than were participants who were more satisfied with their relationships with the opposite sex. However, some respondents in Öner's (2000b) study may not have been involved in ongoing romantic relationships at the time of the study. To better understand the relationship between FTORR and romantic relationship satisfaction, in this study I examined the relationship between FTORR and satisfaction in a sample consisting of participants all of whom were involved in ongoing romantic relationships. One purpose of the present study was to examine the association between satisfaction and FTORR with dating heterosexual individuals.

Furthermore, relationship satisfaction might not be the only predictor of FTORR. Social or cultural factors should also be considered. In the present study I also expanded on the studies of Öner (2000a, 2000b, 2001) by exploring the association between FTORR and other important social factors such as attitudes toward gender stereotypes about romantic relationships and gender differences. Together, these factors might better predict FTORR because stereotypes about romantic relationships in different cultures and the degree of their acceptance might affect individuals' future expectations, commitment, and investment in their relationships.

Gender stereotypes refer to the structural set of beliefs about the personal attributes of men and women. Thus, the definition of gender stereotypes is similar to future time orientation in terms of being collections of schemata. Having a set of beliefs about how men and women should behave in a romantic relationship might exert a strong influence on future plans and expectations that are formed through interacting with incoming information from the individuals' social environment (e.g., norms, culture). As the research literature shows, gender stereotypes give clear messages about how women and men are supposed to behave in a dating script.

According to traditional stereotypes, men are supposed to be leaders who are assertive, dominant decision makers in romantic relationships, whereas women are supposed to be submissive, passive conformists (Peplau & Gordon, 1985). For example, at the beginning of the relationship, initiation is assumed to be the man's role. Women, however, are expected to refuse or accept the man's offer and are expected to resist men's sexual advances (Basow, 1992; Peaplau, Rubin, & Hill, 1977). Results of a study conducted by Sakallı and Curun (2001) on students' attitudes toward stereotypes about romantic relationships showed that Turkish women agreed with stereotypes that men ought to be assertive in romantic relationships, whereas Turkish men were more likely to accept stereotypes about both the men's dominance and the compliance of women in romantic relationships. Thus, these attitudes toward the stereotypes about romantic relationships might exert an influence on FTORR, including future commitment and the degree of future investment in the relationship.

Gender differences might also affect FTORR and satisfaction. As earlier studies (Gjesme, 1979) showed, gender may influence individuals' future time orientation. Specifically, women are more future time oriented than men. Nurmi (1991) found that women have more detailed future plans about relationships and families. In addition, results of earlier studies on romantic relationship satisfaction showed that women tend to report greater relationship satisfaction than their male partners (Attridge et al., 1995). Women also work harder to maintain their romantic relationships than men and have significantly higher commitment scores than men (Sacher & Fine, 1996). Thus, gender differences should be considered one of the important predictors of FTORR.

The purpose of the present research was to examine the relationship between romantic relationship satisfaction, FTORR, attitudes toward gender stereotypes about romantic relationships, and gender among currently dating university students. I expected that satisfaction, attitudes toward gender stereotypes about romantic relationship, and gender would predict FTORR. In addition, I predicted that the variables of relationship satisfaction and attitudes toward gender stereotypes about romantic relationship would affect FTORR of women and men differently.

Method

Participants and Procedure

Participants were 413 (208 men and 205 women) heterosexual university students taking elective psychology courses at Middle East Technical University. I distributed questionnaires, informed the students about the topic of the study, and promised anonymity. All participants were currently involved in a romantic relationship. I asked any student who did not have a boyfriend or girlfriend at the time of data collection to pass the questionnaire on to a student who was involved in a romantic relationship. The questionnaire took approximately 15 min to complete, after which I thanked the students. They received a course credit for their participation in the study.

The mean age of the participants was 21.65 ($SD = 2.27$). The mean length of time of the current romantic relationship was 15.69 months ($SD = 14.88$), ranging from 1 month to 96 months. The participants were generally of a high socioeconomic status.

Measures

The Future Time Orientation in Romantic Relationship Scale (FTORR) was developed by Öner (2000a). A few examples from the scale are "I do not search for temporary romantic relationships," "As far as romantic relationships are concerned, I am very much involved with thinking about the future of my relationships," and "I can readily make sacrifices today in order to organize the future of my relationships with the opposite sex." Participants indicate their degree of agreement on a 7-point scale ranging from *strongly disagree* (1) to *strongly agree* (7). High scores indicate high FTORR.

I performed a factor analysis, the results of which were inconsistent with the results of Öner's study (2000a) in that only one factor explained 50.34% of the total variance with an eigenvalue of 3.52. Cronbach's alpha for the whole scale was .83. Consequently, I combined the seven items of the Öner's scale and generated a FTORR variable.

After I had examined the literature on romantic relationship satisfaction, I developed the following semantic differential scale in Turkish to measure romantic relationship satisfaction. At the top of the scale was the statement "In general, I have a ____ relationship with my partner." The participants read the following 9 adjective pairs and indicated which adjective defined their romantic relationship on a 7-point scale: good–bad, happy–unhappy, satisfactory–unsatisfactory, content–not content, rewarding–punishing, passionate–not passionate, full of love–full of hate, enjoyable–irritable, and exciting–unexciting. The participants also stated their degree of agreement with the following statement: "Overall, I am satisfied with my relationship with my partner." I averaged the scores so that high scores indicated more satisfaction.

The factor analysis showed that one factor—Romantic Relationship Satisfaction—explained 54.38% of the total variance. The Cronbach alpha for the scale was .90. I used the median value (6.20) to divide the participants into two groups, one low on satisfaction (below the median) and the other high on satisfaction (above the median).

I used the Attitudes Toward Gender Stereotypes About Romantic Relationships (AGSRR) scale, developed by Sakallı and Curun (2001), to measure Turkish individuals' attitudes toward gender stereotypes about romantic relationships. The scale consists of 11 items concerning stereotypic behaviors in romantic relationships, such as male assertiveness and female passivity. The participants were asked to indicate their degree of agreement with each item on a 7-point scale ranging from *strongly disagree* (1)) to *strongly agree* (7). High scores indicate agreement with traditional gender related stereotypes in romantic relationships.

I performed a factor analysis, demonstrating that there were two factors for the scale that explained 59.33% of the total variance. The first factor was Attitudes Toward Men's Assertiveness in Romantic Relationships (AMARR), which explained 31.20% of the variance, with an eigenvalue of 4.29. The items on the scale representing the first factor were "I think that the first step for romantic relationships should come from men," "Men should be the ones to propose marriage in romantic relationships," "I think men should call their partners more often than should women in romantic relationships," "Women can ask men whom they admire for a date (reverse item)," and "It is more acceptable for women to refuse men's sexual advances in romantic relationships." Cronbach's alpha for the factor was .84.

The second factor was Attitudes Toward Women's Compliance in Romantic Relationships (AWCRR), which explained 28.12% of the variance, with an eigenvalue of 1.64. The items on the scale representing the second factor were "Men can tell their girlfriends what to wear," "Women publicly should not behave in a way that is inconsistent with their boyfriends," "Women should be virgins at the beginning of a romantic relationship," "Women can go anywhere without their boyfriends during the night (reverse item)," and "Men should be always one step ahead of their girlfriends (in terms of status, money, etc.) in romantic relationships." Cronbach's alpha was .80 for the second factor.

Design

I calculated correlations among the variables and the means of each variable for the whole data set. I also examined correlations and means separately for men and women. I used multiple regression analysis to discover whether satisfaction, the two factors of AGSRR (AMARR and AWCRR), and gender predicted FTORR in the present sample. I also performed separate multiple regression analyses for women and for men to examine the predictive values of satisfaction and attitudes toward gender stereotypes about romantic relationships on FTORR. Finally, I subjected FTORR to a 2 (Satisfaction: low vs. high) × 2 (Gender: female or male) analysis of covariance (ANCOVA), with AMARR and AWCRR as covariates to examine the consistency between the results of the present study and Öner's study (2000a).

Results

I calculated correlations between variables and means of each variable for the whole data set and separately for men and women (see Table 1). Analyses of variance indicated that there were significant differences between women and men on AMARR, $F(1, 408) = 11.36$, $p < .01$, on AWCRR, $F(1, 407) = 56.57$, $p < .01$, and on satisfaction, $F(1, 407) = 4.13$, $p = .04$. Women scored higher on attitudes toward men's assertiveness and on satisfaction than did men, whereas men scored higher on attitudes toward women's compliance in romantic relationships (Table 1).

A multiple regression analysis with the whole data set demonstrated that satisfaction ($\beta = .15$, $t = 3.31$, $p < .01$), AMARR ($\beta = .28$, $t = 4.92$, $p < .01$), and AWCRR ($\beta = .21$, $t = 3.61$, $p < .01$), and gender ($\beta = .17$, $t = 3.20$, $p < .01$) were significant predictors for FTORR, $R^2 = .22$, $F(4, 391) = 27.13$, $p < .01$. A multiple regression analysis for only female participants showed that satisfaction ($\beta = .11$, $t = 1.70$, $p = .09$), AMARR ($\beta = .25$, $t = 3.17$, $p < .01$), and AWCRR ($\beta = .30$, $t = 3.87$, $p < .01$) were significant predictors for FTORR, $R^2 = .25$, $F(3, 192) = 21.50$, $p < .01$. A multiple regression analysis for only male participants revealed

TABLE 1. Means and Standard Deviations for Each Variable and Correlations Between Them

Variable	M	SD	1	2	3	4
For whole data						
1. FTORR	4.49	1.32	—	.40**	.27**	.15**
2. AMARR	3.25	1.55		—	.48**	−.002
3. AWCRR	3.45	1.53			—	−.07
4. Satisfaction	6.04	0.86				—
For female participants						
1. FTORR	4.69	1.27	—	.43**	.45**	.09
2. AMARR	3.50	1.65		—	.61**	−.007
3. AWCRR	2.88	1.38			—	−.04
4. Satisfaction	6.14	0.86				—
For male participants						
1. FTORR	4.29	1.33	—	.35**	.27**	.18**
2. AMARR	3.01	1.40		—	.57**	−.03
3. AWCRR	4.00	1.46			—	−.04
4. Satisfaction	5.95	0.85				—

Note. FTORR = Future Time Orientation in Romantic Relationships. AMARR = Attitudes Toward Men's Assertiveness in Romantic Relationships. AWCRR = Attitudes Toward Women's Compliance in Romantic Relationships.
*$p < .05$. **$p < .01$.

that satisfaction ($\beta = .19$, $t = 2.99$, $p < .01$) and AMARR ($\beta = .29$, $t = 3.64$, $p < .01$) were significant predictors for FTORR, $R^2 = .17$, $F(3, 196) = 13.25$, $p < .01$, but not for AWCRR ($\beta = .11$, $t = 1.45$, $p = .14$).

As indicated earlier, I subjected FTORR to a 2 (Satisfaction: low vs. high) × 2 (Gender Difference: female or male) ANCOVA, with attitudes toward men's dominance and men's assertiveness as covariates, to explore the consistency between the results of the present study and those of Öner (2000a). There was not a statistically significant interaction between sex and satisfaction. The results of this analysis revealed a significant main effect for satisfaction, $F(1, 390) = 17.65$, $p < .01$, $\eta^2 = .032$, suggesting that participants who were high on satisfaction ($M = 4.71$, $SD = 1.31$) scored higher on FTORR than did participants who were low on satisfaction ($M = 4.27$, $SD = 1.29$). Results also demonstrated a significant main effect for gender, $F(1, 390) = 10.00$, $p < .01$, $\eta^2 = .025$, suggesting that the women ($M = 4.69$; $SD = 1.27$) were more future time oriented than were the men ($M = 4.29$; $SD = 1.33$).

Discussion

In the present study I investigated how romantic relationship satisfaction, AGSRR, and gender difference are relevant to FTORR in currently dating heterosexual university students. Multiple regression analysis on the whole data set showed that satisfaction, AMARR and AWCRR, and gender differences were significant predictors of FTORR. Because gender was a significant predictor of FTORR, I performed separate multiple regression analyses for men and women. Regression analysis for the female participants revealed that AMARR and AWCRR were more important factors in explaining FTORR than was relationship satisfaction.

That the two factors of AGSRR were positively and significantly related to FTORR suggests that women are more affected by gender stereotypes when they are in romantic relationships. It can be argued that men's dominance, decisiveness, and authority over women, and women's acceptance, dependence, and compliance still remain strong in Turkey. It is not surprising that gender stereotypes are more relevant to female participants' FTORR in Turkey, which is a country in transition from traditional to egalitarian views about gender roles (Kagıtçıbası, 1983; Tekeli, 1995). The present finding may differ in less conservative and less sexist cultures.

Multiple regression results for male participants indicated that satisfaction and AMARR were important predictors of FTORR but that AWCRR was not a predictor of FTORR for men. Thus, the male participants not only accepted men as being initiators, being more active, and being the decision maker in their relationships but were also concerned with happiness, rewards, enjoyment, and excitement, that is, satisfaction, in their romantic relationships. This finding might be consistent with ambivalent sexist ideology (Glick & Fiske, 1996), suggesting that men want to keep their superior position in society but also want to show that they do not want to control but to protect and cherish women in their relationships. Male participants might expect that their girlfriends' tasks should be to create an atmosphere in which their male partners can be leaders and initiators. The male participants also desired to have happy, content, loving, and understanding relationships. In such a situation, they may be more concerned with the future of their relationships.

In addition, the results of 2×2 ANCOVA demonstrated that there were significant main effects of gender differences and satisfaction on FTORR. Women were more future time oriented in ongoing romantic relationships than were men. The result is consistent with earlier research on future time orientation (Gjesme, 1979; Nurmi, 1991; Öner, 2001), in which men were found to be less future oriented than women. This finding suggests that women care about the future of their romantic relationships and family more than do men. These concerns may be associated with gender stereotypes. Turkish culture still keeps its traditionality and gives less freedom to women in terms of sexuality, dating, and marriage (Imamoglu, 1991; Tekeli, 1995). Consequently, women may be more concerned with their relationships with the opposite sex and with the future of their romantic relationships than are men.

Furthermore, the present data are inconsistent with results of Öner's studies (2000a, 2000b) in that participants who were highly satisfied with their current romantic relationship scored higher on FTORR than those who were less satisfied with their current romantic relationship. Thus, participants who defined their romantic relationships as good, contenting, happy, enjoyable, rewarding, passionate, and full of love—in short, satisfactory—considered and thought about the future of their relationship. This is consistent with the investment model of Rusbult (1983), suggesting that commitment is enhanced when individuals experience relationship satisfaction.

At this point, the question that comes to mind is why are the results of present study, in term of the relationship between FTORR and satisfaction, inconsistent with the results of Öner's (2000a) study? The answer may be that the present study used university students who were currently in romantic relationships. The satisfaction items in the scale were also directly relevant to students' ongoing romantic relationships. Öner (2000a), however, did not specifically use dating students even though she asked her participants to state the degree of satisfaction in their relationships with the opposite sex. Thus, Öner's single-item satisfaction question may not directly measure attitudes about ongoing romantic relationships but instead may measure relationships with the opposite sex in general. Participants in Öner's (2000a) study might have interpreted the satisfaction item as measuring satisfaction in their general friendships with the opposite sex.

One may also argue that the participants of the present study were not seeking a relationship but were already involved in a romantic relationship and had therefore already passed through an initial thinking process about whom to select as a partner and how much investment they could make to start a relationship. Because they had already made important choices about their romantic relationship partners, they might assume that their current romantic relationship was linked to future goals such as marriage, which is highly endorsed in Turkish society. As Öner (2001) suggested, individuals with extended future time orientation seek to maintain their ongoing relationships. Thus, before having a romantic relationship, future time orientation might increase anxiety (Öner, 2000a), but after establishing a romantic relationship, future time orientation might have different effects on satisfaction. As Öner (2001) argued, "When individuals felt satisfied with what they had, their concern for the future of their romantic relationships increased" (p. 437). Thus, satisfied individuals may make commitments to their future, as similarly suggested by the investment model of Rusbult (1983).

The present finding on the association between romantic relationship satisfaction and FTORR is consistent with some researchers' suggestion that the value of future time orientation might depend on cultural and situational social factors (Trommsdorff, 1983). Turkish society has been documented to be both a collectivist (Hofstede, 1980) and sexist culture (Tekeli, 1995). Because Turkish culture requires its members to have traditional heterosexual relationships, participants who are already in a romantic relationship might be more concerned about the future of their relationship (e.g., marriage), especially when they have a satisfactory relationship. Also, results of other studies (Agnew & Loving, 1998) have suggested that "individuals who are more concerned with future events and circumstances are more likely to behave presently in a manner which works to facilitate the attainment of desired future outcomes (p. 757)." Thus, individuals who have satisfactory relationships might behave in a way that provides the desired outcomes, which in Turkish culture would tend to be commitment and marriage.

The present study showed that not only personality characteristics but also cultural and social factors influence individuals' perceptions of the future of their romantic relationships. Gender differences and attitudes toward stereotypes about romantic relationships may affect how individuals feel about their relationships and how they plan their future. Future researchers ought to explore what other social and cultural variables might affect romantic relationship satisfaction and FTORR, such as attitudes toward family, how romantic relationships are perceived by the wider society, and social norms about romantic relationships and sexuality, especially in collectivist and Moslem cultures.

REFERENCES

Agnew, C. R., & Loving, T. J. (1998). Future time orientation and condom use attitudes, intentions, and behavior. *Journal of Social Behavior & Personality, 13,* 755-765.
Attridge, M., Berscheid, E., & Simpson, J. A. (1995). Predicting relationship stability from both partners versus one. *Journal of Personality and Social Psychology, 69,* 445-454.
Basow, S. A. (1992). *Gender and stereotypes and roles.* Pacific Grove, CA: Brooks/Cole.
Gjesme, T. (1979). Future time orientation as a function of achievement motives, ability,

delay of gratification, and sex. *The Journal of Psychology, 101,* 173-188.

Gjesme, T. (1983). Introduction: An inquiry into the concept of future orientation. *International Journal of Psychology, 18,* 347-350.

Glick, P., & Fiske, T. S. (1996). The ambivalent sexism inventory: Differentiating hostile and benevolent sexism. *Journal of Personality and Social Psychology, 70,* 491-512.

Gray-Kittle, B., & Burke, N. (1983). Power and satisfaction in marriage: A review and critique. *Psychological Bulletin, 93,* 513-538.

Hofstede, G. (1980). *Culture's consequences: Individual differences in work-related values.* Beverly Hills, CA: Sage.

Imamoglu, O. (1991). Evaluating his/her success/failure at breadwinning/homemaking: A case of double standards. *Journal of Human Sciences, 2,* 50-70.

Kagıtçıbası, Ç. (1983). Women and development in Turkey. *International Journal of Turkish Studies, 2,* 59-70.

Nurmi, J. E. (1991). How do adolescents see their future? A review of the development of future orientation and planning. *Developmental Review, 11,* 1-59.

Öner, B. (2000a). Future time orientation and relationships with the opposite sex. *The Journal of Psychology, 134,* 306-314.

Öner, B. (2000b). Relationship satisfaction and dating experience: Factors affecting future time orientation in relationships with the opposite sex. *The Journal of Psychology, 134,* 527-536.

Öner, B. (2001). Factors predicting future time orientation for romantic relationships with the opposite sex. *The Journal of Psychology, 135,* 430-438.

Peplau, A. L., & Gordon, S. L. (1985). Women and men in love: Gender differences in close relationships. In V. E. Oleary, K. R. Unger, & S. B. Watson (Eds.), *Women, gender and social psychology* (pp. 257-291). Hillsdale, NJ: Erlbaum.

Peplau, A. L., Rubin, Z., & Hill, C. T. (1977). Sexual intimacy in dating relationships. *Journal of Social Issues, 33,* 86-109.

Rusbult, C. E. (1980). Commitment and satisfaction in romantic associations: A test of the investment model. *Journal of Experimental Social Psychology, 16,* 172-186.

Rusbult, C. E. (1983). A longitudinal test of investment model: The development (and deterioration) of satisfaction and commitment in heterosexual investment. *Journal of Personality and Social Psychology, 45,* 101-117.

Sabatelli, R. M. (1988). Exploring relationship satisfaction: A social exchange perspective on the interdependence between theory, research, and practice. *Family Relations, 37,* 217-222.

Sacher, J. A., & Fine, M. A. (1996). Predicting relationship status and satisfaction after six months among dating couples. *Journal of Marriage and the Family, 58,* 21-32.

Sakallı, N., & Curun, F. (2001). Romantik iliskilerle ilgili kalıpyargılara karsı tutumlar [Attitudes toward stereotypes about romantic relationships]. *Tecrübi Psikoloji Dergisi, 22,* 31-45.

Tekeli, S. (1995). *Women in modern Turkish society.* London: Zed Books.

Trommsdorff, G. (1983). Future orientation and socialization. *International Journal of Psychology, 18,* 381-406.

Vangelisti, A. L., & Banski, M. A. (1993). Couples' debriefing conversations: The impact of gender, occupational, and demographic characteristics. *Family Relations, 42,* 149-157.

White, L. K. (1990). Determinants of divorce: A review of research in the eighties. *Journal of Marriage and the Family, 52,* 904-912.

Empathy and Social Support Provision in Couples: Social Support and the Need to Study the Underlying Processes

INGE DEVOLDRE
Ghent University

MARK H. DAVIS
Eckerd College

LESLEY L. VERHOFSTADT
Université Catholique de Louvain

ANN BUYSSE
Ghent University

ABSTRACT. Social support researchers and clinicians have repeatedly expressed the need to identify the antecedents of social support provision within close relationships. The aim of the present study is to investigate the extent to which individual differences in cognitive empathy (perspective taking) and affective empathy (empathic concern and personal distress) are predictive of social support provision in couples. Study 1 involved 83 female participants in a relatively young relationship; Study 2 involved 128 married couples. The authors used self-report measures in both studies to assess individual differences in empathy and participants' support provision behaviors. The main findings suggest a significant contribution of the different components of empathy with rather different pictures for each of these components. The authors discuss the present findings in light of existing theory and research on social support in relationships.

SOCIAL SUPPORT REFERS GENERALLY to the way people help each other cope with personal difficulties and how they provide everyday support to one another (Pasch & Bradbury, 1998). Such support can be offered to anyone but may be an especially important component of marital relationships (Cutrona,

1996a). Considerable research has demonstrated that receiving beneficial support is associated with better mental and physical health of individuals confronted with a stressor (for a review, see Cohen, Gottlieb, & Underwood, 2000). In addition, social support is considered a key element of relationship maintenance and marital well-being (Bradbury, Fincham, & Beach, 2000; Bradbury & Karney, 2004). There is consistent evidence regarding the favorable effect of support interactions on relationships themselves (Cutrona, 1996b). For example, greater support from the partner is associated with greater marital satisfaction (Cramer, 2004; Pasch & Bradbury; Pasch, Bradbury, & Sullivan, 1997).

Despite this recent interest in the role of social support in marital functioning and despite important advances in our knowledge in this area, many fundamental issues regarding social support in marriage remain unresolved. To date, little is known about the processes underlying marital support provision. However, the identification of the factors that contribute to social support is considered an important research objective by many researchers and clinicians for at least several reasons (e.g., Lakey & Cohen, 2000; Lindorff, 2005; Verhofstadt, Buysse, Devoldre, & De Corte, 2007). First, because of its central role within relationships (Bradbury & Karney, 2004). Second, the provision of support is not as easy as intuition would presume. It is a complex process, and it proved to be difficult to provide effective support (Rafaeli & Gleason, 2009). Further insight in how effective support comes about may inform us about the nature of this process. Last, from a clinical point of view, understanding the determinants of spousal support is important, given the value of designing effective support interventions (Lakey & Cohen; Rafaeli & Gleason).

A variety of factors no doubt contribute to the provision of effective marital support. One such factor is the set of personal characteristics possessed by support providers (e.g., Pierce, Lakey, Sarason, Sarason, & Joseph, 1997; Verhofstadt et al., 2007). A particular characteristic put forward as a likely contributor to social support is *empathy* (see Reis & Collins, 2000). Therefore, the focus of this investigation is on the dispositional empathy of the support provider and on the ways in which it influences the actual level of support provision in romantic relationships.[1]

Empathy and Social Support

Empathy has a long history marked by recurring debates regarding its definition. One major approach has been to view empathy as a cognitive phenomenon in which one person attempts to understand the internal state of another person (e.g., Hogan, 1969). The term perspective taking (or role taking) is often used to describe this process. The other major approach has been to define the term empathy as an affective reaction in the observer that results from observing the target. However, no clear consensus exists regarding the precise nature of this emotional response. Some have argued that empathy consists of the observer and target experiencing the same or similar emotions (e.g., Eisenberg & Strayer, 1987). For example, observers may feel personal distress or feelings of discomfort when witnessing a target's negative experiences (Davis, 1994). Others have argued that empathy occurs when the observer comes to have feelings of sympathy, concern, and compassion for the target (e.g., Batson, 1991), so-called feelings of empathic concern. Other affective states have been offered as well, such as empathic anger or empathic joy. However, in recent years there has been growing acceptance of the view that empathy can best be considered a multidimensional phenomenon that encompasses both cognitive and affective elements (e.g., Davis).

What effect might empathy have on social support? Evidence from the past 2 decades suggests that both its cognitive and affective facets are associated with important social behaviors (for a detailed review, see Davis, 2004). For example, perspective taking has been linked with acting in less aggressive ways (e.g., Richardson, Hammock, Smith, Gardner, & Signo, 1994), experiencing less interpersonal conflict (Davis & Kraus, 1991), and being more helpful to those in need (Underwood & Moore, 1982). Empathic concern has been similarly linked to being more helpful to those in need (Batson, 1991), supportive responses to peers (Trobst, Collins, & Embree, 1994), and engaging in greater self-disclosure (Davis, Franzoi, & Wellinger, 1985). In contrast with the socially beneficial effects of perspective taking and empathic concern, personal distress has demonstrated positive associations with shyness and social anxiety (Davis, 1983) and negative associations with reported number of friends (Davis & Kraus, 1991).

More specifically, some evidence suggests that individual differences in empathy are related to the social support occurring within romantic relationships. In a pair of studies, Davis and Oathout (1987, 1992) examined dispositional empathy and relationship behaviors in young adult romantic relationships, and some of those behaviors can be considered forms of social support for the partner. They found that for both men and women, dispositional empathic concern was positively associated with a cluster of behaviors that included being supportive, generous, and loving toward one's partner. Dispositional perspective taking, for both men and women, was inversely related to what can be considered negative social support: a cluster of behaviors including being critical, nagging, rude, and dominating. Personal distress was not related to either of these behavior clusters; it is interesting that, however, it was associated with higher self-reported levels of possessiveness in the relationship.

The Present Research

To summarize, considerable research has demonstrated links between dispositional empathy and social behavior (Batson, Chang, Orr, & Rowland, 2002; Davis, 1983, 1994; Reis & Collins, 2000). However, this link has been investigated largely outside the context of intimate relationships and virtually never among married couples. Because the specific qualities of marital relationships can compromise the generalizability of results from samples of nonintimates (Pasch et al., 1997; Verhofstadt et al., 2007), the present study aimed to investigate whether individual differences in cognitive and affective components of empathy are linked to several types of support provision within marriage.

Although *social support* can be broadly defined as the way people help each other with personal difficulties, it is also possible to distinguish among different types of spousal support. In particular, researchers have identified both positive and negative forms of support provision (Pasch, Harris, Sullivan, & Bradbury, 2004). Two different positive forms can be distinguished, namely *emotional* and *instrumental* support provision. Reassuring the spouse and providing genuine encouragement are examples of emotional support provision, which is aimed at the management of emotions. The provision of instrumental support is characterized by the support provider making specific suggestions, giving helpful advice, or providing access to information regarding the problem. This kind of support attempts to deal directly with the problem. In contrast, examples of negative support provision would include criticizing or blaming the spouse, expressing negative affect at the spouse, and minimizing or maximizing the problem (Bradbury & Pasch, 1994; S. Cohen et al., 2000). Previous research has often failed to distinguish (a) between positive and negative types of support and (b) between instrumental and emotional types of support provision. Therefore, we included all three categories of support in this study.

Although the focus of this study is on individual differences in empathy, the association between *relational characteristics* (i.e., relationship length and depth of the relationship) and social support will also be examined in the present investigation, as recommended by previous theory and research. The reason for this is that relationship characteristics are found to be important predictors of social support interactions in couples (Dunkel-Schetter & Skokan, 1990; Iida, Seidman, Shrout, Fujita, & Bolger, 2008; Verhofstadt et al., 2007). We did so in two ways. First, we tested empathy's association with social support in two kinds of relationships. Study 1 used female members of relatively young romantic relationship; Study 2 focused on both members of longer-term marriages. Second, within each study, we directly examined the effect of relationship length (Davis & Oathout, 1987) and relationship quality (Lawrence et al., 2008).

More specifically, we tested a hypothesis drawn from Davis and Oathout's (1987) study. That investigation found that the association between dispositional empathy and relationship behavior depended in part on the length of the romantic relationship. Empathy was associated with more kinds of behavior, and these associations were stronger for the longer relationships in their dating sample, dispositional perspective taking in particular demonstrated this pattern. Thus, we expected to find in these studies somewhat stronger and more consistent associations between dispositional empathy and social support in longer relationships. We are confident to make this prediction because Davis and Oathout found that chronic dispositional tendencies may be less influential at the early stages of the relationship because of the greater salience of constraints with regard to roles, concerns about self-presentation and other situational forces. In time, as situational factors become less important, stable personality traits may gain in strength.

We also expected each of the empathy subscales to be related to support behaviors in specific ways. On the basis of the research already cited, we developed hypotheses concerning the different components of empathy (i.e., perspective taking, empathic concern, and personal distress) and spousal support provision (i.e., emotional, instrumental, and negative support).

> Hypothesis 1: Attempts to imagine the partner's point of view (i.e., perspective taking) are expected to aid in the provision of instrumental support. The more successful that support providers are in adopting their partner's perspective, the better able they should be to offer appropriate information and assistance.

> Hypothesis 2: Second, we assume that a tendency to feel sympathy for others will lead to the provision of more emotional support. Thus, the higher that support providers are in dispositional empathic concern, the more likely they should be to provide comfort and reassurance to their partner.

> Hypothesis 3: It seems reasonable to assume that a tendency to feel distressed and anxious when faced with partners' distress (i.e., personal distress) will lead to the provision of more negative support. The more likely that support providers are to experience such self-oriented feelings, the more likely they should be to respond to their partners in unhelpful ways.

STUDY 1

Method

Participants

We used a convenience sample of 83 female college students. All participants were in a committed heterosexual relationship of at least 3 months' duration but no longer than 15 months. The mean age of the participants was 20.33 years ($SD = 2.31$ years, range $= 17$–27 years). The average length of their relationship was 6.55 months ($SD = 2.95$ months, range $= 3$–15 months). All participants were students; 88% of them were students in the Department of Psychology at Ghent University.

Procedure

An invitation for participation was sent by e-mail to all psychology students at Ghent University. Students who met the criteria and wanted to participate were redirected to an online questionnaire. Before completing the questionnaire, a description of the project (i.e., aims and procedure) was given and the criteria for participation were repeated. Students participating in this study did so voluntarily and gave their informed consent. The participants were debriefed after the completion of the questionnaires.

Measures

Empathy

We assessed individual differences in empathy using the Interpersonal Reactivity Index (IRI, Davis, 1994; Dutch version by De Corte et al., 2008). This self-report measure consists of 28 items and yields four subscales, only three of which were used in this study. The perspective-taking subscale measures the cognitive tendency to adopt another's psychological perspective and consists of seven items (e.g., "I try to look at everybody's side of a disagreement before I make a decision"). The empathic-concern subscale assesses the tendency to experience feelings of warmth, sympathy, and concern toward others and consists of seven items (e.g., "When I see someone taken advantage of, I feel kind of protective towards them"). Last, the personal-distress subscale measures feelings of discomfort and distress when witnessing other's negative experiences and consists of seven items (e.g., "I sometimes feel helpless when I am in the middle of a very emotional situation"). We did not use the fantasy subscale because it focuses on identifying with fictional characters, which seems less relevant in daily social interactions between partners. Each item was rated on a five-point Likert-type scale ranging from 0 (*does not describe me well*) to 4 (*describes me very well*). We computed subscale scores by summing scores for all items included in a specific subscale. The possible range of scores for each subscale is 0 to 28. Previous studies have provided evidence for the reliability and validity of the IRI (Davis, 1983, 1994; De Corte et al.) and have supported the psychometric adequacy of the scores of the Dutch version, in terms of factor structure (De Corte et al.). In the present study, the internal consistencies (Cronbach's alphas) for the IRI subscales were as follows: .70 for perspective taking, .73 for empathic concern, and .81 for personal distress.

Support Behavior

To assess the provision of social support, a self-report measure was designed that was based on the Social Support Interaction Coding System (SSICS; Bradbury & Pasch, 1994). Participants were asked (a) to reflect on discussions with their partner about personal problems and (b) to rate the likelihood of several types of support solicitation and provision behavior that might occur during these discussions. The questionnaire assessed the respondents' own support behaviors and the partners' support behaviors, in both the helpee and the helper role. This questionnaire included 54 items and each item was rated on a nine-point Likert-type scale ranging from 1 (*very unlikely*) to 9 (*very likely*). In the present study, we used three subscales indicating the likelihood of the following: (a) emotional support provision (8 items; e.g., reassures, expresses care for help seeker, understanding, provides genuine encouragement; sample item: "When my partner asks for support, then I give my partner the feeling to be loved and esteemed"); (b) instrumental support provision (8 items; e.g., offers a specific plan or assistance, gives helpful advice, asks specific questions aimed at defining the problem; sample item: "When my partner asks for support, then I make specific suggestions, give helpful advice or information to handle the problem"); and (c) negative support provision (16 items; e.g., criticizes, minimizes problem, is inattentive or disengaged, offers unhelpful advice; sample item: "When my partner asks for support, then I am inattentive, draw back, or do nothing"). Because of the rationale of the present study, we did not include the support-seeking subscales (i.e., positive support seeking and negative support seeking). We calculated subscales scores by computing the mean response across all items in the respective subscales. Confirmatory factor analysis confirmed the postulated three-factor structure of support provision behavior within the support provision questionnaire used.[2] In previous studies, researchers have found evidence for the validity and reliability of the SSICS, on which the questionnaire used in this study was based (Pasch et al., 2004). Cronbach's alpha values ranged between .66 and .76, indicating an acceptable internal consistency for all three subscales.

Relationship Length

We determined length of the relationship by participant reports of the number of months they had been together with their partner.

Relationship Quality

To measure relationship quality, we used the depth subscale of the Quality of Relationships Inventory (QRI; Pierce, Sarason, & Sarason, 1991; Dutch version by Verhofstadt, Buysse, Rosseel, & Peene, 2006). The QRI depth subscale consists of six items (e.g., "How much do you depend on this person?"; "How positive a role does this person play in your life?") that assess the perceived importance of the relationship. In the present study, we asked participants to reflect on the relationship with their spouse and to answer each QRI item using a 4-point Likert-type scale ranging from 1 (*not at all*) to 4 (*very much*). We obtained the total scale scores of the participants by computing the mean of their responses across all items in the scale. Verhofstadt et al. found evidence for the factorial validity of the three-factor structure of the QRI. The alpha reliability for the depth subscale used in this study was .78.

Results

Test of the Hypotheses

In Table 1, we report the means, standard deviations, and ranges for our primary variables of relationship characteristics, support provision, and empathy.

We used hierarchical multiple regression analysis to test whether participants' self-reported tendency to provide support could be predicted from individual differences in empathy. We carried out separate regressions for each of the support

TABLE 1. Descriptive Statistics for Relationship Characteristics, Spousal Support Provision, and Individual Differences in Empathy (Study 1; $N = 83$)

Variable	M	SD	Minimum	Maximum
Length of relationship (months)	6.55	2.95	3.00	15.00
Depth of relationship	3.33	0.45	2.00	4.00
Emotional support provision	8.15	0.76	4.75	9.00
Instrumental support provision	7.62	0.92	4.50	9.00
Negative support provision	2.38	0.99	1.00	5.00
Perspective taking	18.61	4.02	10.00	26.00
Empathic concern	19.83	3.94	10.00	27.00
Personal distress	13.90	5.15	3.00	26.00

provision behaviors: emotional, instrumental, and negative. To control for possible effects of the participants' relational characteristics (i.e., length of the relationship and relationship depth), we entered these variables on the first step. In the second step, participants' empathy scores (i.e., perspective taking, empathic concern and personal distress) were entered. Last, on the third step, three terms were entered to examine possible interactions between length of relationship and dispositional empathy.[3] Scores on each IRI scale were standardized, as was relationship length; length was then separately multiplied by each of the empathy scores. Before each regression analysis, we performed collinearity diagnostics using the variance inflation factors (VIF) as criteria. No multicollinearity was evident, because the VIF for the predictors ranged between 1.01 and 1.40 (<10; Cohen, Cohen, West, & Aiken, 2003).

When predicting participants' emotional support provision, the relational characteristics (i.e., length of the relationship and relationship depth) accounted for 25% of the variance, $F(2, 80) = 13.53, p < .01$ (see Table 2). This was due entirely to the depth variable; higher levels of depth were associated with higher levels of emotional support provision, $t(77) = 4.54, p < .01, \beta = .50$. The variables entered on the second step of the model (i.e., participants' empathy scores) accounted for an additional 15% of the variance, $F(3, 77) = 6.65, p < .01$. The addition of the interaction terms on the third step did not add significantly to R^2. Overall, we found the model to be significant, $F(8, 74) = 7.12, p < .01$, and accounted for 44% of the variance in emotional support provision. Only perspective taking contributed significantly to the model, with higher levels of perspective taking corresponding with higher levels of emotional support provision, $t(77) = 3.47, p < .01, \beta = .34$. Neither empathic concern, $t(77) = 1.06$, ns, nor personal distress, $t(77) = -.76$, ns, contributed significantly to the model.

TABLE 2. Summary of Hierarchical Multiple Regression Analyses to Predict Emotional, Instrumental, and Negative Support Provision From Marital Characteristics and Individual Empathy Scores ($N = 83$)

Variable	β	ΔR^2	F for ΔR^2
Predicting emotional support provision			
Step 1: Marital characteristics		.25	13.53**
Length	−.08		
Depth	.50**		
Step 2: Empathy scores		.15	6.65**
Empathic concern	.11		
Perspective taking	.34**		
Personal distress	−.07		
Step 3: Interactions		.03	1.25
Length × Empathic concern	.11		
Length × Perspective taking	.08		
Length × Personal distress	−.10		
Predicting instrumental support provision			
Step 1: Marital characteristics		.06	2.36
Length	−.17*		
Depth	.17		
Step 2: Empathy scores		.12	3.70*
Empathic concern	−.02		
Perspective taking	.05		
Personal distress	−.33**		
Step 3: Interactions		.01	0.14
Length × Empathic concern	−.07		
Length × Perspective taking	.02		
Length × Personal distress	−.02		
Predicting negative support provision			
Step 1: Marital characteristics		.03	0.97
Length	.04		
Depth	−.15		
Step 2: Empathy scores		.16	5.16**
Empathic concern	−.10		
Perspective taking	−.24*		
Personal distress	.28*		
Step 3: Interaction terms		.05	1.48
Length × Empathic concern	.03		
Length × Perspective taking	−.17		
Length × Personal distress	−.18		

For predicting emotional support provision, R^2 total = .44, $F(8, 74) = 7.12$**; for predicting instrumental support provision, R^2 total = .18, $F(8, 74) = 2.02°$; for predicting negative support provision, R^2 total = .23, $F(8, 74) = 2.81$**.
$°p < .10$. *$p < .05$. **$p < .01$.

When predicting participants' *instrumental support provision*, relational characteristics only accounted for 6% of the variance, and did not make a significant contribution to the regression model. (see Table 2). Adding participants' empathy scores on the second step of the model accounted for an additional 12% of the variance, $F(3, 77) = 3.70, p < .05$. Adding the interaction terms on the third step accounted for no additional variance. Overall, the model was found to be marginally significant, $F(8, 74) = 2.02, p < .06$, and accounted for 18% of the variance in instrumental support provision. empathic concern and perspective taking did not contribute significantly to the model (for empathic concern $t(77) = -.02$, *ns;* for perspective taking $t(77) = .05$, *ns*). In contrast, personal distress did significantly contribute to the model, with lower levels of personal distress in the provider corresponding with higher levels of instrumental support provision, $t(77) = -3.02, p < .01, \beta = -.33$.

When predicting participants' negative support provision, relational characteristics accounted for only 3% of the variance, and did not make a significant contribution in the regression model (see Table 2). Entering participants' empathy scores on the second step of the model accounted for an additional 16% of the variance, $F(3, 77) = 5.16, p < .01$. Adding the interaction terms on the third step accounted for no additional variance. Overall, the model was found to be significant, $F(8, 74) = 2.81, p < .01$, and accounted for 23% of the variance in negative support provision. empathic concern did not contribute significantly to the model, $t(77) = -.10$, *ns*. However, both personal distress and perspective taking did so, with higher levels of personal distress associated with higher levels of negative support provision, $t(77) = 2.59, p < .05, \beta = .28$, and higher levels of perspective taking associated with lower levels of negative support provision, $t(77) = -2.09, p < .05, \beta = -.24$.

Discussion

Consistent with our expectations, the results of Study 1 revealed a significant contribution of individual differences in empathy to the provision of support. For each type of support, the addition of IRI scores on the second step of the model produced a significant increase in R^2, indicating an influence of dispositional empathy above and beyond the effect of relationship length and depth. Also as expected, higher levels of personal distress were associated with providing higher levels of unhelpful support to the spouse. Interestingly, it was also negatively related to instrumental support.

However, perspective taking and empathic concern did not display the expected relations with social support provision. perspective taking failed to exhibit a significant relationship with instrumental support, although it was significantly and positively related to affective support, and negatively related to negative support. Unexpectedly and contrary to previous research (Trobst et al., 1994), empathic concern was not associated with any form of social support. Thus dispositional empathy proved to be a substantial predictor of social support provision, but not in the expected ways. In addition, there was no evidence that dispositional empathy interacted with relationship length to influence the provision of social support.

Subsequently, Study 2 was designed to replicate and extend the findings of Study 1. First, we wanted to determine whether the Study 1 findings were robust. In particular, we wanted to see if these findings could be replicated in the context of marital relationships. Virtually all the evidence bearing on the empathy-support link has been carried out using relationships other than marriages. Study 2 sought to rectify this shortcoming.

Second, on the basis of the findings of Davis and Oathout's (1987) investigation of dispositional empathy and relationship behaviors, we again examined the possibility that stronger associations between dispositional empathy and self-reported support behavior may be found in longer relationships. The married sample in Study 2 contains greater variation in relationship length and thus may provide a better test of this possibility.

STUDY 2

Method

Participants

The sample consisted of the 256 members of 128 heterosexual married couples. In this study, we used a snowball sampling method to select the participants. A team of research assistants recruited an initial set of 50 couples in shopping areas. These couples were then asked to participate in the study and to screen their circle of acquaintances for potential participants. Additional couples were further obtained from the second sample and so on.

Research assistants contacted participants by telephone and gave a short, standardized description of the research (e.g., inclusion criteria, aims, and procedure). Inclusion criteria included being involved in a heterosexual relationship for at least 1 year and being married for at least 6 months. All couples who participated did so voluntarily. For the eligible couples who expressed interest in the study, a home visit was scheduled to complete a packet of questionnaires.

The mean ages for husbands and wives were 44.65 years ($SD = 12.31$ years, range $= 20$–82 years), and 42.89 years ($SD = 12.47$ years, range $= 19$–87 years), respectively. The couples had an average of 1.65 children ($SD = 1.15$ children, range $= 0$–4 children). The average length of their relationships was 19.67 years ($SD = 12.36$ years, range $= 0.5$–60 years). Among the men, 69% were white-collar workers, 28% were blue-collar workers, and 3% had other professional activities. Among the women, 76% were white-collar workers, 11% were blue-collar workers, and 13% had other professional activities.

Procedure

We collected data using home surveys. As agreed in the first telephone contact, couples were visited at home by one of the research assistants. Both partners then completed a variety of measures. At the end of the session, couples were debriefed more fully about the global aim of the study and thanked for their participation. We assured couples that their data would be analyzed anonymously and confidentially, and we asked them to grant written permission to use the collected data for scientific goals.

Measures

Empathy

See Study 1 for a description of the empathy measure. The alpha coefficients ranged between .61 and .70 for the husbands and between .60 and .70 for the wives.

Spousal Support Behavior

See Study 1 for a description of the spousal support behavior measure. Subscale scores were created separately for husbands and wives by computing the mean of their responses across all items in the scale. Cronbach's alphas ranged between .71 and .82 for husbands and between .79 and .84 for wives, indicating a good internal consistency for all three subscales.

Relationship Quality

See Study 1 for a description of the relationship quality measure. Cronbach's alpha was .78 for the husbands and .79 for the wives.

Relationship Length

Length of the relationship was determined by participant reports of the number of months they had been together.

Results

Test of the Hypotheses

In Table 3, we report the means, standard deviations, and ranges for our primary variables of relationship characteristics, support provision, and empathy.

Hierarchical multiple regression analysis was used to test whether provision of social support could be predicted by considering the providers' dispositional empathy. Separate regressions were carried out for each support provision behavior: emotional, instrumental and negative support. In each regression model, one of the reported support behaviors of one of the spouses served as a dependent variable.

TABLE 3. Descriptive Statistics for Relationship Characteristics, Spousal Support Provision, and Individual Differences in Empathy (Study 2)

Variable	Husbands ($N = 128$)				Wives ($N = 128$)			
	M	SD	Minimum	Maximum	M	SD	Minimum	Maximum
Length of relationship (years)	19.67	12.35	0.50	60.83	19.67	12.35	0.50	60.83
Depth of relationship	3.44	0.47	1.83	4.00	3.36	0.51	1.50	4.00
Emotional support provision	6.64	1.25	2.88	8.75	6.84	1.16	3.46	8.75
Instrumental support provision	6.63	1.20	3.25	8.88	6.64	1.10	3.50	8.75
Negative support provision	3.35	1.11	1.44	6.88	3.20	1.09	1.13	6.94
Perspective taking	15.74	4.29	4.00	26.00	16.42	4.10	4.00	27.00
Empathic concern	16.90	4.17	4.00	27.00	20.20	3.97	11.00	28.00
Personal distress	11.31	4.45	0.00	20.00	14.84	4.83	3.00	27.00

To control for possible effects of marital characteristics (i.e., length of the relationship and relationship depth scores of both spouses), these variables were entered on the first step. At the second step, both spouses' empathy scores (i.e., perspective taking, empathic concern and personal distress) were entered. On the third step, six terms were entered to examine possible interactions between length of relationship and dispositional empathy. Husbands' and wives' scores on each IRI scale were standardized, as was relationship length; length was then separately multiplied by each of the six empathy scores. Before each regression analysis, we performed collinearity diagnostics using the VIF as criteria. No multicollinearity was evident because the VIF for the predictors ranged between 1.03 and 1.35 (<10; J. Cohen et al., 2003).

Husbands' Support

When predicting husbands' emotional support provision, marital characteristics (i.e., length of the relationship and relationship depth scores of both spouses) accounted for 17% of the variance and made a significant contribution to the regression model, $F(3, 124) = 8.26, p < .01$ (see Table 4). Both relationship length and wives' depth contributed significantly to the model, with longer relationships corresponding to lower levels of emotional support provision, $t(118) = -1.75, p < .10, \beta = -.15$, and wives' depth corresponding to higher levels of emotional support provision, $t(118) = 3.23, p < .01, \beta = .30$. Entering both spouses' empathy scores on the second step of the model accounted for an additional 6% of the variance, $F(6, 118) = 1.46, ns$, but it did not make a significant contribution to the regression model. Similarly, adding the six interaction terms on the third step of the model did not significantly increase the R^2. Overall, we found the model to be significant, $F(15, 112) = 2.79, p < .001$, and it accounted for 27% of the variance in husbands' emotional support provision.

Although the addition of the interaction terms on Step 3 did not account for a significant amount of additional variance, there were two significant interactions involving relationship length: Length × Husband's empathic concern and Length × Wife's perspective taking. To determine the nature of these interactions, we computed the correlation between husbands' emotional support provision and the appropriate empathy variable, separately for shorter (fewer than 18.9 years) and longer (more than 18.9 years) marriages. The correlations were somewhat stronger for the longer relationships (husband's empathic concern, $r = .29, p < .02$; wife's perspective taking, $r \doteq .21, p < .11$) than shorter ones (husband's empathic concern, $r = .06, ns$; wife's perspective taking, $r = .02, ns$).

When predicting husbands' instrumental support provision, marital characteristics accounted for 13% of the variance, and it made a significant contribution to the regression model, $F(3, 124) = 6.21, p < .01$ (see Table 5). Wives' depth contributed significantly to the model; higher levels of depth were associated with higher levels of instrumental support provision, $t(118) = 3.17, p < .01, \beta = .30$. Entering both spouses' empathy scores on the second step of the model accounted for an additional 17% of the variance, $F(6, 118) = 4.62, p < .01$. Both husbands' empathic concern and perspective taking significantly contributed to the model. Higher levels of empathic concern were associated with lower levels of instrumental support provision, $t(118) = -2.09, p < .05, \beta = -.19$, and higher levels of perspective taking were associated with offering greater instrumental support, $t(118) = 4.00, p < .01, \beta = .36$. In addition, wives' empathic concern significantly contributed to the model, with higher levels of empathic concern associated with higher levels of instrumental support provision behavior, $t(118) = 2.44, p < .05, \beta = .22$. Entering the interaction terms on the third step of the model did not significantly increase the R^2. Overall, we found the model to be significant, $F(15, 112) = 4.17, p < .001$, and accounted for 36% of the variance in instrumental support provision.

Although the addition of the interaction terms on Step 3 did not account for a significant amount of additional variance, there was a significant interaction between relationship length and wives' personal distress. To determine the nature of the interaction, we computed the correlation between wives' personal distress

TABLE 4. Summary of Hierarchical Multiple Regression Analyses to Predict Husbands' Emotional Support Provision from Marital Characteristics and Individual Empathy Scores

Variable	β	ΔR^2	F for ΔR^2
Predicting husbands' emotional support provision			
Step 1: Marital characteristics		.17	8.26**
Length	−.15°		
Depth (husband)	.11		
Depth (wife)	.30**		
Step 2: Empathy scores		.06	1.46
Empathic concern (husband)	.10		
Perspective taking (husband)	.12		
Personal distress (husband)	.01		
Empathic concern (wife)	.14		
Perspective taking (wife)	−.05		
Personal distress (wife)	−.11		
Step 3: Interaction terms		.05	1.23
Length × Empathic concern (husband)	.19*		
Length × Perspective taking (husband)	−.10		
Length × Personal distress (husband)	−.01		
Length × Empathic concern (wife)	−.11		
Length × Perspective taking (wife)	.20*		
Length × Personal distress (wife)	.04		

For predicting husbands' emotional support provision, R^2 total $= .27, F(15, 112) = 2.79^{**}$.
°$p < .10$. *$p < .05$. **$p < .01$.

TABLE 5. Summary of Hierarchical Multiple Regression Analyses to Predict Husbands' Instrumental Support Provision from Marital Characteristics and Individual Empathy Scores ($N = 128$ Husbands and 128 Wives)

Variable	β	ΔR^2	F for ΔR^2
Predicting husbands' instrumental support provision			
Step 1: Marital characteristics		.13	6.21**
Length			
Depth (husband)	.07		
Depth (wife)	.30**		
Step 2: Empathy scores		.17	4.62**
Empathic concern (husband)	−.19*		
Perspective taking (husband)	.36**		
Personal distress (husband)	.00		
Empathic concern (wife)	.22*		
Perspective taking (wife)	.02		
Personal distress (wife)	−.15		
Step 3: Interaction terms		.06	1.81
Length × Empathic concern (husband)	.13		
Length × Perspective taking (husband)	−.11		
Length × Personal distress (husband)	.04		
Length × Empathic concern (wife)	−.11		
Length × Perspective taking (wife)	.15		
Length × Personal distress (wife)	.22**		

For predicting husbands' instrumental support provision, R^2 total $= .36$, $F(15, 112) = 4.17**$.
*$p < .05$. **$p < .01$.

and husbands' instrumental support provision for shorter and longer marriages. It was unexpected that there was no relationship among marriages of either kind. Thus, we next examined the correlation for two more extreme groups: marriages more than one standard deviation shorter than the mean (i.e., fewer than 7.3 years) and those more than one standard deviation longer than the mean (i.e., more than 32 years). With this more extreme comparison, there was a significant negative correlation between wives' personal distress and husbands' instrumental support provision for the shorter relationships ($r = -.40$, $p < .05$) but no correlation for the longer ones ($r = .16$, ns).

When predicting husbands' negative support provision, marital characteristics accounted for 11% of the variance and made a significant contribution in the regression model, $F(3, 124) = 5.05$, $p < .01$ (see Table 6). Entering both spouses' empathy scores on the second step of the model accounted for an additional 10% of the variance, $F(6, 118) = 2.63$, $p < .05$. Husbands' perspective taking was significantly associated with negative support; higher levels of perspective taking corresponded to lower levels of such support, $t(118) = -2.47$, $p < .05$,

TABLE 6. Summary of Hierarchical Multiple Regression Analyses to Predict Husbands' Negative Support Provision from Marital Characteristics and Individual Empathy Scores ($N = 128$ Husbands and 128 Wives)

Variable	β	ΔR^2	F for ΔR^2
Predicting husbands' negative support provision			
Step 1: Marital characteristics		.11	5.05**
Length	.09		
Depth (husband)	−.19		
Depth (wife)	−.18		
Step 2: Empathy scores		.10	2.63*
Empathic concern (husband)	−.04		
Perspective taking (husband)	−.23*		
Personal distress (husband)	.05		
Empathic concern (wife)	−.12		
Perspective taking (wife)	.06		
Personal distress (wife)	.19*		
Step 3: Interaction terms		.02	0.36
Length × Empathic concern (husband)	−.08		
Length × Perspective taking (husband)	.09		
Length × Personal distress (husband)	.10		
Length × Empathic concern (wife)	.09		
Length × Perspective taking (wife)	−.08		
Length × Personal distress (wife)	−.03		

For predicting husbands' negative support provision, R^2 total $= .23$, $F(15, 112) = 2.22*$.
*$p < .05$. **$p < .01$.

$\beta = -.23$. In addition, wives' personal distress significantly contributed to the model, with higher levels of personal distress related to higher levels of negative support provision, $t(118) = 2.28$, $p < .05$, $\beta = .19$. The addition of the six interaction terms on Step 3 did not significantly increase the model's R^2. Overall, we found the model to be significant, $F(15, 112) = 2.22$, $p < .01$, and it accounted for 23% of the variance in negative support provision.

Wives' Support

When predicting wives' emotional support provision, marital characteristics accounted for 29% of the variance, and it made a significant contribution to the regression model, $F(3, 124) = 16.46$, $p < .01$ (see Table 7). Both wives' and husbands' depth contributed significantly to the model, with higher depth scores associated with higher levels of emotional support provision, $t(118) = 4.34$, $p < .001$, $\beta = .37$ (wives' depth) and $t(118) = 2.91$, $p < .05$, $\beta = .24$ (husbands' depth). Entering both spouses' empathy scores on the second step of the model accounted for an additional 12% of the variance, $F(6, 118) = 4.01$, $p < .01$. Both

TABLE 7. Summary of Hierarchical Multiple Regression Analyses to Predict Wives' Emotional Support Provision from Marital Characteristics and Individual Empathy Scores ($N = 128$ Husbands and 128 Wives)

Variable	β	ΔR^2	F for ΔR^2
Predicting wives' emotional support provision			
Step 1: Marital characteristics		.29	16.46**
Length	−.05		
Depth (husband)	.24**		
Depth (wife)	.37**		
Step 2: Empathy scores		.12	4.01**
Empathic concern (husband)	−.10		
Perspective taking (husband)	.15		
Personal distress (husband)	−.01		
Empathic concern (wife)	.20*		
Perspective taking (wife)	.15		
Personal distress (wife)	−.16*		
Step 3: Interaction terms		.05	1.58
Length × Empathic concern (husband)	.10		
Length × Perspective taking (husband)	−.14		
Length × Personal distress (husband)	−.11		
Length × Empathic concern (wife)	−.08		
Length × Perspective taking (wife)	.23**		
Length × Personal distress (wife)	−.03		

For predicting wives' emotional support provision, R^2 total $= .45$, $F(15, 112) = 6.16$**.
*$p < .05$. **$p < .01$.

wives' empathic concern and personal distress contributed significantly to the model. Higher levels of empathic concern were associated with greater emotional support provision, $t(118) = 2.39$, $p < .05$, $\beta = .20$, and higher levels of personal distress were associated with lower levels of such support, $t(118) = -2.22$, $p < .05$, $\beta = -.16$. Entering the interaction terms on the third step of the model did not significantly increase the R^2. Overall, we found the model to be significant, $F(15, 112) = 6.16$, $p < .001$, and it accounted for 45% of the variance in wives' emotional support provision.

Although the addition of the interaction terms on Step 3 did not account for a significant amount of additional variance, there was a significant interaction between relationship length and wives' perspective taking. The interaction resulted because wives' perspective taking was related less strongly to their offering of emotional support in shorter marriages ($r = .23$, ns), but it was more strongly associated in the longer ones ($r = .45$, $p < .001$).

When predicting wives' instrumental support provision, marital characteristics accounted for 22% of the variance, and it made a significant contribution to

TABLE 8. Summary of Hierarchical Multiple Regression Analyses to Predict Wives' Instrumental Support Provision from Marital Characteristics and Individual Empathy Scores ($N = 128$ Husbands and 128 Wives)

Variable	β	ΔR^2	F for ΔR^2
Predicting wives' instrumental support provision			
Step 1: Marital characteristics		.22	11.89**
Length	−.05		
Depth (husband)	.34**		
Depth (wife)	.20*		
Step 2: Empathy scores		.12	3.54**
Empathic concern (husband)	−.09		
Perspective taking (husband)	.11		
Personal distress (husband)	−.07		
Empathic concern (wife)	.05		
Perspective taking (wife)	.26**		
Personal distress (wife)	−.14		
Step 3: Interaction terms		.04	1.31
Length × Empathic concern (husband)	.04		
Length × Perspective taking (husband)	−.11		
Length × Personal distress (husband)	−.01		
Length × Empathic concern (wife)	−.05		
Length × Perspective taking (wife)	.21*		
Length × Personal distress (wife)	−.10		

For predicting wives' instrumental support provision, R^2 total $= .39$, $F(15, 112) = 4.67**$.
*$p < .05$. **$p < .01$.

the regression model, $F(3, 124) = 11.89, p < .01$ (see Table 8). Both wives' and husbands' depth contributed significantly to the model, with higher depth scores corresponding to higher levels of instrumental support provision, $t(118) = 2.20$, $p < .05$, $\beta = .20$ (wives' depth) and $t(118) = 3.92, p < .01, \beta = .34$ (husbands' depth). Entering both spouses' empathy scores on the second step of the model accounted for an additional 12% of the variance, $F(6, 118) = 3.54, p < .01$. Wives' perspective taking contributed significantly to the model, with higher levels of perspective taking associated with higher levels of instrumental support provision, $t(118) = 3.06, p < .01, \beta = .26$. Adding the six interaction terms to the model on the third step did not significantly increase the R^2. Overall, the model was found to be significant, $F(15, 112) = 4.67, p < .001$, and it accounted for 39% of the variance in wives' instrumental support provision.

Although the addition of the interaction terms on Step 3 did not account for a significant amount of additional variance, there was a significant interaction between relationship length and wives' perspective taking. Wives' perspective

TABLE 9. Summary of Hierarchical Multiple Regression Analyses to Predict Wives' Negative Support Provision from Marital Characteristics and Individual Empathy Scores ($N = 128$ Husbands and 128 Wives)

Variable	β	ΔR^2	F for ΔR^2
Predicting wives' negative support provision			
Step 1: Marital characteristics		.15	7.27**
Length	−.04		
Depth (husband)	−.28**		
Depth (wife)	−.18		
Step 2: Empathy scores		.08	1.96
Empathic concern (husband)	.01		
Perspective taking (husband)	−.18		
Personal distress (husband)	.12		
Empathic concern (wife)	−.07		
Perspective taking (wife)	−.01		
Personal distress (wife)	.17*		
Step 3: Interaction terms		.03	.72
Length × Empathic concern (husband)	−.12		
Length × Perspective taking (husband)	.17		
Length × Personal distress (husband)	.09		
Length × Empathic concern (wife)	.07		
Length × Perspective taking (wife)	−.02		
Length × Personal distress (wife)	−.07		

For predicting wives' negative support provision, R^2 total $= .26$, $F(15, 112) = 2.56$**.
*$p < .05$. **$p < .01$.

taking was unrelated to offering instrumental support in shorter marriages ($r = .21$, ns) but was significantly related in the longer ones ($r = .49, p < .001$).

When predicting wives' negative support provision, marital characteristics accounted for 15% of the variance, and it made a significant contribution to the regression model, $F(3, 124) = 7.27, p < .01$ (see Table 9). Husbands' depth contributed significantly to the model; higher depth scores were related to higher levels of negative support provision, $t(118) = -3.04, p < .01, \beta = -.28$. Entering both spouses' empathy scores on the second step of the model accounted for an additional 8% of the variance, but it did not make a significant contribution in the regression model, $F(6, 118) = 1.96$, ns. Wives' personal distress contributed significantly to the model, with higher scores on personal distress associated with higher levels of negative support provision, $t(118) = 1.97, p < .05, \beta = .17$. Adding the six interaction terms to the model on the third step did not significantly increase the R^2. Overall, we found the model to be significant, $F(15, 112) = 2.56, p < .01$, and it accounted for 26% of the variance in wives' negative support provision.

Discussion

We found considerable but not complete support in Study 2 for the hypothesized links between empathy and social support. The results for support provision by wives were as expected, with each type of dispositional empathy displaying the predicted relationship with a particular type of support. In addition, instrumental support by husbands was predictably associated with husbands' dispositional perspective taking. Thus, four of the six predicted findings clearly emerged from this study. Further, husbands' empathic concern interacted with relationship length to influence husbands' provision of emotional support. In the longer marriages, husbands higher in empathic concern offered more of this form of support, thus providing partial support for this hypothesis as well. Only husbands' personal distress was completely unrelated to the predicted type of support.

The finding that dispositional empathy was a more reliable predictor of social support for wives is similar to the pattern reported by Davis and Oathout's (1987) study. Those investigators found stronger and more consistent links between dispositional empathy and relationship behaviors for the female members of their dating couples. Davis and Oathout offered an explanation for their findings on the basis of the traditional social roles assigned to women and men. According to this argument, the expressive role in romantic relationships—which includes the responsibility to monitor and maintain a pleasant emotional tone—typically falls to women. Dispositional empathy, especially empathic concern and perspective taking, can therefore be seen as role relevant for women because such skills aid in fulfilling this role. Empathy seems less relevant to the instrumental role typically assigned to men. Thus, empathy may more reliably affect social support among women because such support is a larger part of their social role (Trobst et al., 1994).

Study 2 also provided partial support for the prediction that dispositional empathy would be a stronger predictor of support provision in longer relationships. Although it was never the case that entering the interaction terms on the third step of the model produced a significant increase in R^2, there were five significant interactions between relationship length and dispositional empathy. In four of those interactions, we found the expected pattern: stronger associations between empathy and support in longer relationships. It is also noteworthy that two of these interactions were consistent with a specific pattern found in Davis and Oathout's (1987) study: dispositional perspective taking is a stronger predictor of supportive behavior in longer relationships.

Also of particular interest in Study 2 was the finding that the support offered by husbands was influenced by the dispositional empathy of their partners. More specifically, wives' affective empathy was associated with the support they received from their husbands. Wives with higher scores on other-oriented affective empathy (empathic concern) received more instrumental support from their husbands; wives with higher scores on the self-oriented component of affective empathy (personal distress) received higher levels of negative support. To a lesser degree, husband perspective taking also influenced the support offered by wives, but these associations were only of borderline significance.

This finding is broadly congruent with the notion of mutual influence in dyadic relationships proposed by Campbell and Kashy (2002). According to this view, interdependence in dyads results in features of one dyad member influencing the outcomes of the other dyad member. Thus, it is not difficult to imagine that relationship partners may "invite" certain kinds of support by virtue of their personality or behavior. Warm and sympathetic wives may receive more (instrumental) support from their husbands because such aid is more visibly appreciated. Wives who are prone to distress and anxiety may receive more negative support from husbands because other forms of support (e.g., soothing, problem solving) have failed. Such interpretations are only speculative, however, and must await more systematic investigation.

GENERAL DISCUSSION

This research investigated how individual differences in cognitive and affective components of empathy can be linked to the provision of social support between marital partners, and the results presented here both broaden and add specificity to our knowledge in this area. Both studies found that support provision was significantly affected by the emotional depth of the relationship, although this pattern was noticeably stronger in Study 2. More important, the results revealed that individual differences in empathy still made a significant and substantial contribution to the prediction of romantic relationship support provision beyond such relational variables. In seven of the nine regression analyses, the addition of dispositional empathy significantly improved the amount of variance accounted for. In addition, it is worth noting that all three types of social support were associated with at least one kind of empathy, and all three kinds of empathy were associated with at least one kind of support. These findings complement Verhofstadt, Buysse, Ickes, Davis, and Devoldre's (2008) work, which showed that cognitive (i.e., empathic accuracy) and affective (i.e., emotional matching) dimensions of empathy are both of importance in the prediction of support provision.

However, rather different pictures emerge for each of the three facets of dispositional empathy. Somewhat surprising is that empathic concern had the weakest influence on spousal support provision. Only twice was it significantly related to such support: a positive association with wives' emotional support provision in Study 2 but a negative relationship with husbands' instrumental support provision in that study.

In contrast, both perspective taking and personal distress displayed four significant associations with social support, and all of them were either predicted or reasonable given the nature of the constructs. Higher perspective taking was associated with greater instrumental support provision for both husbands and wives in Study 2 and was associated (for husbands) with offering less negative support. In addition, perspective taking was positively associated with providing emotional support in Study 1. Thus, perspective taking displayed a consistently constructive pattern of associations for both men and women.

In contrast, personal distress exhibited a completely opposite pattern of associations with support. Higher personal distress was associated with offering more negative spousal support in Study 1, and this pattern emerged for wives in Study 2. However, the harmful effect of dispositional personal distress was not limited to negative support; dispositional distress was also associated with offering lower levels of emotional and instrumental aid. Thus, in one form or another, the dispositional tendency to react to others' distress with personal unease had a harmful effect on all three types of support. This finding is in line with Batson et al. (2002) who argue that experiencing personal distress provokes largely egoistic motivations.

Future Research

Although we have described our findings as providing evidence that dispositional empathy has an effect on spousal support provision, there are several limitations that may limit their generalizability. It should be taken into account that our studies relied exclusively on self-report, and that we can not determine the accuracy of such reports. Future research should use additional techniques, including observational measures of the variables under study. Considering the robust effects of cognitive empathy on spousal support provision, the empathic accuracy paradigm (Ickes, 1997)—which provides situational measures of successful perspective taking—might be adopted as an observational measure of cognitive empathy. In addition, all of the data reported here are correlational in nature and were measured at a single time point. Thus, the associations we report between empathy and support cannot be taken as definitive evidence of causality. The present study is also limited by our sample, which included only White, middle-class, nonclinical individuals and couples. Future research should investigate the generalizability of the present findings to couples drawn from more diverse samples (e.g., couples who are seeking marital counseling, homosexual couples).

Despite these limitations, our confidence in these results is enhanced by a number of strengths in our methodology and design. Foremost among these strengths was that we examined empathy's role in social support using two different samples—women in relatively young relationships and couples in well-established marriages. That dispositional empathy was significantly related to support provision in each study reinforces our faith in the theoretical rationale guiding this work. In addition, we adopted a multidimensional approach for the measurement of both empathy and spousal support. Doing so allowed a more detailed examination of the links between these two variables. Our findings emphasize the importance of a multicomponent approach, showing that the different components of empathy are distinctly related to different types of social support.

Conclusion

In sum, perhaps the most important lesson to be learned from the present study is that different facets of dispositional empathy do seem to play distinctive, meaningful roles in shaping support provision in marriage. It happens not only in the most obvious ways through the positive routes of providing one's partner with instrumental help and emotional reassurance, but also through the less-obvious route of refraining from criticizing and blaming the partner—even if, as must be true in some circumstances, such reactions may be justified.

NOTES

1. One caution should be voiced concerning such causal inferences. Most probably, the influence is bidirectional. However, on the basis of the theoretical model outlined, it seems logical to predict social support behavior is based on individual differences in empathy.

2. Further information concerning the data analyses can be obtained from the first author.

3. In the tables, only the beta coefficients are represented for the predictors added in the respective step.

AUTHOR NOTES

Inge Devoldre is a PhD student at Ghent University. Her current research interests are empathy and social support. **Mark H. Davis** is a professor at Eckerd College in St. Petersburg, Florida. His current research interests are empathy, helping behavior, and interpersonal conflict. **Lesley L. Verhofstadt** is an assistant professor at the Université Catholique de Louvain in Louvain-la-Neuve, Belgium. Her current research interests are social support and relationship functioning. **Ann Buysse** is a professor at Ghent University. Her current research interests are empathy, divorce and sexual health.

REFERENCES

Batson, C. D. (1991). *The altruism question: Toward a social-psychological answer.* Hillsdale, NJ: Erlbaum.

Batson, C. D., Chang, J., Orr, R., & Rowland, J. (2002). Empathy, attitudes, and action: Can feeling for a stigmatized group motivate one to help the group? *Personality and Social Psychology Bulletin, 28,* 1656–1666.

Bradbury, T. N., Fincham, F. D., & Beach, S. R. H. (2000). Research on the nature and determinants of marital satisfaction: A decade in review. *Journal of Marriage and the Family, 62,* 964–980.

Bradbury, T. N., & Karney, B. R. (2004). Understanding and altering the longitudinal course of marriage. *Journal of Marriage and the Family, 66,* 862–881.

Bradbury, T. N., & Pasch, L. A. (1994). *The Social Support Interaction Coding System (SSICS).* Unpublished coding manual. Los Angeles: University of California.

Campbell, L., & Kashy, D. A. (2002). Estimating actor, partner, and interaction effects for dyadic data using PROC MIXED and HLM: A user-friendly guide. *Personal Relationships, 9,* 327–342.

Cohen, J., Cohen, P., West, S. G., & Aiken, L. S. (2003). Applied multiple regression/correlation analysis for the behavioural sciences. Mahwah, NJ: Erlbaum.

Cohen, S., Gottlieb, B. H., & Underwood, L. G. (2000). Social relationships and health. In S. Cohen, B. H. Gottlieb, & L. G. Underwood (Eds.), *Social support measurement and intervention: A guide for health and social scientists* (pp. 3–28). New York: Oxford University Press.

Cramer, D. (2004). Emotional support, conflict, depression, and relationship satisfaction in a romantic partner. *The Journal of Psychology, 138*, 532–542.

Cutrona, C. E. (1996a). *Social support in couples*. Thousand Oaks, CA: Sage.

Cutrona, C. E. (1996b). Social support as a determinant of marital quality: The interplay of negative and supportive behaviors. In G. R. Pierce, B. R. Sarason, & I. G. Sarason (Eds.), *Handbook of social support and the family* (pp. 173–194). New York: Plenum.

Davis, M. H. (1983). Measuring individual differences in empathy: Evidence for a multidimensional approach. *Journal of Personality and Social Psychology, 44*(1), 113–126.

Davis, M. H. (1994). *Empathy: A social psychological approach*. Madison: Westview Press.

Davis, M. H. (2004). Empathy: Negotiating the border between self and other. In L. Z. Tiedens & C. W. Leach (Eds.), *The social life of emotions* (pp. 19–42). Cambridge: Cambridge University Press.

Davis, M. H., Franzoi, S. L., & Wellinger, P. (1985, August). *Personality, social behavior, and loneliness*. Paper presented at the 93rd Annual Convention of the American Psychological Association, Los Angeles, CA.

Davis, M. H., & Kraus, L. A. (1991). Dispositional empathy and social relationships. In W. H. Jones & D. Perlman (Eds.), *Advances in personal relationships* (Vol. 3, pp. 75–115).

Davis, M. H., & Oathout, H. A. (1987). Maintenance of satisfaction in romantic relationships: Empathy and relational competence. *Journal of Personality and Social Psychology, 53*, 397–410.

Davis, M. H., & Oathout, H. A. (1992). The effect of dispositional empathy on romantic relationship behaviors: Heterosocial anxiety as a moderating influence. *Personality and Social Psychology Bulletin, 18*, 76–83.

De Corte, K., Buysse, A., Verhofstadt, L. L., Roeyers, H., Ponnet, K., & Davis, M. H. (2008). Measuring empathic tendencies: Reliability and validity of the Dutch version of the Interpersonal Reactivity Index. *Psychologica Belgica, 47*, 235–260.

Dunkel-Schetter, C., & Skokan, L. A. (1990). Determinants of social support provision in personal relationships. *Journal of Social and Personal Relationships, 7*, 437–450.

Eisenberg, N., & Strayer, J. (1987). Critical issues in the study of empathy. In N. Eisenberg & J. Strayer (Eds.), *Empathy and its development* (pp. 3–13). Cambridge: Cambridge University Press.

Hogan, R. (1969). Development of an empathy scale. *Journal of Consulting and Clinical Psychology, 33*, 307–316.

Ickes, W. (1997). *Empathic accuracy*. New York: Guilford.

Iida, M., Seidman, G., Shrout, P. E., Fujita, K., & Bolger, N. (2008). Modeling support provision in intimate relationships. *Journal of Personality and Social Psychology, 94*, 460–478.

Lakey, B., & Cohen, S. (2000). Social support theory and measurement. In S. Cohen, L. G. Underwood, & B. H. Gottlieb (Eds.), *Social support measurement and intervention: A guide for health and social scientists* (pp. 29–52). London: Oxford University Press.

Lawrence, E., Bunde, M., Barry, R. A., Brock, R., Sullivan, K. T., Pasch, L., et al. (2008). Spousal support and marital satisfaction among newlyweds: Support amount, adequacy, provision, and solicitation. *Personal Relationships, 15*, 445–463.

Lindorff, M. (2005). Determinants of received social support: Who gives what to managers? *Journal of Social and Personal Relationships, 22*, 323–337.

Pasch, L. A., & Bradbury, T. N. (1998). Social support, conflict, and the development of marital dysfunction. *Journal of Consulting and Clinical Psychology, 66*, 219–230.

Pasch, L. A., Bradbury, T. N., & Sullivan, K. T. (1997). Social support in marriage: An analysis of intraindividual and interpersonal components. In G. R. Pierce, B. Lakey, I. G. Sarason, & B. R. Sarason (Eds.), *Sourcebook of social support and personality* (pp. 229–256). New York: Plenum.

Pasch, L. A., Harris, K. W., Sullivan, K. T., & Bradbury, T. N. (2004). The social support interaction coding system. In P. Kerig & D. Baucom (Eds.), *Couple observational coding systems* (pp. 319–334). New York: Guilford.

Pierce, G. R., Lakey, B., Sarason, I. G., Sarason, B. R., & Joseph, H. (1997). Personality and social support processes: A conceptual overview. In G. R. Pierce, B. Lakey, I. G. Sarason, & B. R. Sarason (Eds.), *Sourcebook of social support and personality* (pp. 3–18). New York: Plenum.

Pierce, G. R., Sarason, I. G., & Sarason, B. R. (1991). General and relationship-based perceptions of social support: Are two construct better than one? *Journal of Personality and Social Psychology, 61*(6), 1028–1039.

Rafaeli, E., & Gleason, M. E. J. (2009). Skilled support within intimate relationships. *Journal of Family Theory and Review, 1*, 20–37.

Reis, H. T., & Collins, N. (2000). Measuring relationship properties and interactions relevant to social support. In S. Cohen, L. G. Underwood, & B. H. Gottlieb (Eds.), *Social support measurement and intervention: A guide for health and social scientists* (pp. 136–194). New York: Oxford University Press.

Richardson, D. R., Hammock, G. S., Smith, S. M., Gardner, W., & Signo, M. (1994). Empathy as a cognitive inhibitor of interpersonal aggression. *Aggressive Behavior, 20*, 275–289.

Trobst, K. K., Collins, R. L., & Embree, J. M. (1994). The role of emotion in social support provision: Gender, empathy, and expressions of distress. *Journal of Social and Personal Relationships, 11*(1), 45–62.

Underwood, B., & Moore, B. (1982). Perspective-taking and altruism. *Psychological Psychological, 91*, 143–173.

Verhofstadt, L. L., Buysse, A., Rosseel, Y., & Peene, O. J. (2006). Confirming the three-factor structure of the Quality of Relationships Inventory within couples. *Psychological Assessment, 18*, 15–21.

Verhofstadt, L. L., Buysse, A., Devoldre, I., & De Corte, K. (2007). The influence of personal characteristics and relationship properties on social support in marriage. *Psychologica Belgica, 43*, 195–217.

Verhofstadt, L. L., Buysse, A., Ickes, W., Davis, M., & Devoldre, I. (2008). Support provision in marriage: The role of emotional matching and empathic accuracy. *Emotion 8*, 792–802.

Relationship Satisfaction and Conflict Over Minor and Major Issues in Romantic Relationships

DUNCAN CRAMER

ABSTRACT. In this study the question of whether conflicts over minor issues and over major issues were equally strongly related to satisfaction in romantic relationships was examined. Sixty-four women and 29 men completed the Hendrick (1988) Relationship Assessment Scale for their current main romantic relationship and a 12-item conflict scale (Cramer, 2000b) for minor and major issues. All the relationships were heterosexual. Satisfaction was significantly and equally negatively correlated with conflict over minor and major issues, suggesting that whether an issue is of major or minor importance does not affect satisfaction or dissatisfaction in a romantic relationship. Thus, assessing conflict over major issues may be unnecessary in predicting relationship satisfaction. Conflict over minor and major issues was significantly and positively correlated even when satisfaction was controlled, indicating consistency in conflict resolution.

RESOLVING CONFLICT may play an important role in promoting compatibility in romantic relationships in that both self-report and observation measures of conflict resolution have been found to predict satisfaction (Heavey, Layne, & Christensen, 1993; but see Cramer, 2000a) and stability (Filsinger & Thoma, 1988; McGonagle, Kessler, & Gotlib, 1993) in such relationships. Most studies have been based on observation measures, and couples have generally been asked to discuss a serious problem in their relationship (Cramer, 1998).

Studies using the observation technique are important for determining the behavior shown when conflicts are enacted. However, four potential problems with observation methods may limit their usefulness. First, it may be more difficult to record couples' attempts to avoid discussing conflicts. Second, asking participants to record problem-solving behavior or to resolve problems may cause them to engage in atypical behavior. Third, the time period during which a conflict may be resolved may not be restricted to a relatively brief observation period but may extend beyond that. And fourth, affect as well as outcome may be harder to assess because the manner in which these two variables are experienced may not be readily discernible.

Surprisingly, few studies compare the extent to which participants and observers agree on what has occurred or the relative strengths of either observation or self-report in predicting relationship compatibility. Those that have been published show that self-report is strongly associated with observer ratings (Heavey, Larson, Zumtobel, & Christensen, 1996) and that both self-report and observer ratings are related to concurrent marital satisfaction (Heavey et al., 1993). If this is the case, self-report is a quicker and more efficient way to investigate the association between conflict resolution and relationship satisfaction.

Self-reported negative conflict resolution has been found to predict relationship satisfaction (Heavey et al., 1993; Kurdek, 1995) and stability (McGonagle et al., 1993). Conflict questionnaires typically ask participants how they deal with problems, arguments, or disagreements in general (Christensen & Sullaway, 1984; Kurdek, 1994) rather than specify the severity of these conflicts. Partners dissatisfied with their relationship have been shown to rate these conflicts as being more serious than partners who are satisfied with their relationships (Cramer, 2001; Storaasli & Markman, 1990). Thus, the association between negative conflict resolution and relationship satisfaction may be that dissatisfied couples have more serious problems rather than that they simply show a negative conflict resolution style. In other words, the severity of a problem may be more strongly associated with relationship satisfaction than negative conflict behavior.

Although of less importance, negative conflict resolution over minor issues was found to be associated with relationship satisfaction even when the extent of disagreement was controlled (Cramer, 2001), implying that this association is not solely due to the level of disagreement. Furthermore, the magnitude of the simple correlation between relationship satisfaction and negative conflict resolution style was greater than that, for example, of those reported by Kurdek (1994, 1995) for all four conflict styles of his Conflict Resolution Style Inventory. These four conflict styles were called *conflict engagement* (e.g., launching personal attacks), *positive problem solving* (e.g., negotiating and compromising), *withdrawal* (e.g., remaining silent), and *compliance* (e.g., giving in). Because this inventory does not specify the importance of the issues raised, the difference in the size of the correlation may have resulted from dissatisfied partners' referring to major issues and satisfied partners' referring to minor issues.

In the present study I had three aims. My first aim was to ascertain whether the association between negative conflict resolution and relationship satisfaction was similar for minor and for major issues. Observation studies of conflict resolution have shown that a greater increase in distress occurs when major rather than minor problems are discussed (Simpson, Rholes, & Phillips, 1996). In the Simpson et al. study, distress was measured with three questions on how stressful participants found the discussion, how upset they felt, and how major the problem was. Gottman et al. (1976) found that high-conflict tasks did not yield more negative impacts on the other person than low-conflict tasks. Low-conflict tasks involved personal preferences and high-conflict tasks involved relationship differences. As distress over a discussion may not necessarily be synonymous with feeling negative toward another person, I anticipated that the size of these correlations would be similar. If the correlations are shown to differ, self-report measures of conflict resolution may need to specify the importance of the issues to ensure that partners are referring to issues of similar importance. The advantage of specifying minor or major issues is that more people are likely to have and to admit to having disagreements over minor issues. Thus, the questionnaire would be applicable to more people. Moreover, disagreements over minor issues are less likely to refer to a disagreement over whether the relationship should continue, which would be expected to be strongly associated with relationship satisfaction.

The second aim was to determine whether negative conflict resolution in romantic relationships over minor issues was related to that over major issues. Although Gottman et al. (1976) had the same couples try to resolve low- and high-conflict tasks, the consistency in behavior across these two types of task was not reported. If relationship satisfaction is correlated with conflict over both major and minor issues equally, conflict over the two kinds of issues might be related. Consequently, the association between major and minor issues needs to be examined with relationship satisfaction partialled out.

My third aim was to determine whether participants who reported never having different opinions over minor or major issues responded to the remaining questions on how these differences were handled and, if they answered these questions, how this affected the reliability of the two conflict measures and their association with each other and relationship satisfaction. Self-report conflict questionnaires do not ask whether respondents never have problems, arguments, or disagreements. If respondents do not experience these conflicts, assessing their style of resolving them would not be possible. Studies using these measures have not included any discussion of this issue. I anticipated that more people would report having different opinions over minor than major issues because minor issues, by their very nature, may be more common, and differences over major issues may lead to relationship dissolution.

Method

Participants

Participants were a convenience sample of British undergraduates. Of the 199 participants, 108 responded in terms of a current romantic relationship, varying in seriousness. The duration of the relationship varied from about 1 to 30 months ($M = 4.81$, $SD = 7.27$).

Measures

I measured re;ationship satisfaction with the Hendrick (1988) Relationship Assessment Scale, which Hendrick found was correlated (.80) with the Spanier (1976) Dyadic Adjustment Scale. Hendrick's scale consists of 7 items (e.g., "In general, how satisfied are you with your relationship?") to be answered on a 5-point Likert-type scale. In this study the last item ("How many problems are there in your relationship?") was excluded from the analyses because it overlapped conceptually with the content of the questions on differences of opinion. High scores indicate greater relationship satisfaction.

Handling differences of opinion was measured with 11 items (Cramer, 2000b) to which each participant responded separately for differences of opinion over minor and major issues. Responses were given on a 7-point Likert-type scale ranging from *never* (1) to *always* (7). The first item concerned the frequency of different opinions, the next five were about the frequency of various negative experiences during such differences (such as avoiding discussing them and feeling irritated), and the last five concerned the frequency with which the differences were satisfactorily resolved (i.e., whether differences remained unresolved or whether they had a satisfactory outcome). The score on each scale was the average of the sum of the items so that the scores corresponded to the scale used.

Participants answered the questions in terms of their current main romantic relationship if they had one, a past romantic relationship if they did not have a current romantic relationship, or their current closest friend if they had never had a romantic partner. The latter relationships were included so that all the participants approached could respond to the questionnaire, thereby avoiding having to ask the potentially embarrassing question of whether they were currently in a romantic relationship and excluding them if they were not. The gender and age of the participant and of the person in the relationship were also obtained, together with the duration of the relationship in years and months.

Results

Of the 108 participants answering the questionnaire in terms of a current romantic relationship, 3 and 12 people said that they never had different opinions over minor (3) or major (12) issues. These participants completed the remaining items, varying their responses nevertheless. The means, standard deviations, reliabilities and correlations for the complete sample and the sample excluding participants not having differences of opinions on both minor and major issues did not differ substantially.

The analyses were conducted on 64 women (mean age = 23.31, SD = 8.75) and 29 men (mean age = 24.00, SD = 8.77) who completed data on the main variables of interest. One individual who did not have different opinions on major issues was excluded because of missing data. Because the results were similar for women and men, they are not presented separately. All relationships were heterosexual.

The alpha reliability of the 6-item Relationship Assessment Scale ($M = 4.17$, $SD = 0.68$) was .86, which is the same as that of .86 reported by Hendrick (1988) for the 7-item scale. The alpha reliability of the minor issues conflict scale ($M = 2.93$, $SD = 0.84$) was .90 and of the major issues conflict scale ($M = 2.63$, $SD = 0.80$) was .89. Minor issues conflict was greater than major issues conflict. Participants were generally satisfied with their relationships and did not often experience negative conflict over minor and major issues.

Relationship satisfaction was significantly and negatively correlated with both minor issues conflict ($r = -.51$, $p < .001$) and major issues conflict ($r = -.48$, $p < .001$). These two correlations did not differ significantly. Minor and major issues conflict were significantly and positively correlated ($r = .82$, $p < .001$) even when relationship satisfaction was partialled out ($r = .76$, $p < .001$). Longer relationship duration was significantly correlated with both major ($r = .24$, $p < .05$) and minor ($r = .21$, $p < .05$) issues conflict but not with relationship satisfaction ($r = .03$, ns).

Discussion

The number of people reporting not having different opinions over minor (3) or major (12) issues was relatively small. Most people's differences of opinion were more frequent for minor than major issues. Those not having differences over minor issues also did not have differences over major issues. Participants not having differences nonetheless answered the questions on how these differences were experienced. Their responses varied, implying that they responded to these questions as though they had different opinions. The correlations between the three variables of relationship satisfaction and conflict over minor and major issues did not differ substantially when those not having differences over either minor and major issues were included or excluded from the analysis. These results suggest that taking into account whether participants have different opinions does not affect the relationship between these three variables.

Conflict over minor and major issues was significantly and positively correlated even when relationship satisfaction was partialled out. In other words, there was consistency in the frequency of the way conflict is handled over minor and major issues. The extent to which this consistency is not a self-report artefact but is reflected in observed behavior needs to be established.

Although relationship satisfaction was more strongly correlated with conflict over minor than over major issues, the size of the two correlations did not differ significantly. This finding implies that specifying the importance of the issues does not influence the correlation among these variables. Thus, the difference in the size of the correlations of conflict and relationship satisfaction for this study and those of Kurdek (1994, 1995) is unlikely to be attributable to the varied importance of the issues. Because both the level of consensus and conflict over minor issues have been found to contribute independently to relationship satisfaction (Cramer, 2001), relationship satisfaction appears to be associated with the way conflict is handled. If this is the case, it may be just as beneficial to have couples in marital therapy work on minor problems (Jacobson & Margolin, 1979, pp. 252-253) as major ones. The similarity in the correlation of relationship satisfaction and conflict over major and minor issues suggests that conflict over minor issues may predict relationship satisfaction as well as conflict over major issues.

The results of this study on self-reported conflict resolution concur with those of Gottman et al. (1976) on observed conflict resolution. Results in both studies showed that low-conflict tasks and high-conflict tasks equally discriminated satisfied from dissatisfied couples. However, Gottman et al. (1976) included discussing a salient marital problem as one of four high-conflict tasks in the first of their two studies. Thus, the extent to which major and minor relationship problems affect relationship satisfaction equally needs to be determined in further research. Because the discussion of major relationship problems has sometimes been found to be more distressing than that of minor ones (Simpson et al., 1996), the answer to this question is particularly important for minimizing the potential distress experienced by individuals involved in a romantic relationshp.

REFERENCES

Christensen, A., & Sullaway, M. (1984). *Communication Patterns Questionnaire*. Unpublished manuscript, University of California, Los Angeles.

Cramer, D. (1998). *Close relationships: The study of love and friendship.* New York: Oxford University Press.

Cramer, D. (2000a). *A cautionary tale of two statistics: Partial correlation and standardised partial regression.* Manuscript submitted for publication.

Cramer, D. (2000b). Relationship satisfaction and conflict style in romantic relationships. *The Journal of Psychology, 134,* 337-341.

Cramer, D. (2001). Consensus change, conflict and relationship satisfaction in romantic relationships. *The Journal of Psychology, 135,* 313-320.

Filsinger, E. E., & Thoma, S. J. (1988). Behavioral antecedents of relationship stability and adjustment: A five-year longitudinal study. *Journal of Marriage and the Family, 50,* 785-795.

Gottman, J., Notarius, C., Markman, H., Bank, A., Yoppi, B., & Rubin, M. E. (1976). Behavior exchange theory and marital decision making. *Journal of Personality and Social Psychology, 34,* 14-23.

Heavey, C. L., Larson, B. M., Zumtobel, D. C., & Christensen, A. (1996). The Communication Patterns Questionnaire: The reliability and validity of a constructive communication subscale. *Journal of Marriage and the Family, 58,* 796-800.

Heavey, C. L., Layne, C., & Christensen, A. (1993). Gender and conflict structure in marital interaction: A replication and extension. *Journal of Consulting and Clinical Psychology, 61,* 16-27.

Hendrick, S. S. (1988). A generic measure of relationship satisfaction. *Journal of Marriage and the Family, 50,* 93–98.

Jacobson, N. S., & Margolin, G. (1979). *Marital therapy: Strategies based on social learning and behavior exchange principles.* New York: Brunner/Mazel.

Kurdek, L. A. (1994). Conflict resolution styles in gay, lesbian, heterosexual nonparent, and heterosexual parent couples. *Journal of Marriage and the Family, 56,* 705–722.

Kurdek, L. A. (1995). Predicting change in marital satisfaction from husbands' and wives' conflict resolution styles. *Journal of Marriage and the Family, 57,* 153–164.

McGonagle, K. A., Kessler, R. C., & Gotlib, I. H. (1993). The effects of marital disagreement style, frequency, and outcome on marital disruption. *Journal of Social and Personal Relationships, 10,* 385–404.

Simpson, J. A., Rholes, W. S., & Phillips, D. (1996). Conflict in close relationships: An attachment perspective. *Journal of Personality and Social Psychology, 71,* 899–914.

Spanier, G. B. (1976). Measuring dyadic adjustment: New scales for assessing the quality of marriage and similar dyads. *Journal of Marriage and the Family, 38,* 15–28.

Storaasli, R. D., & Markman, H. J. (1990). Relationship problems in the early stages of marriage: A longitudinal investigation. *Journal of Family Psychology, 4,* 80–98.

Socially Desirable Responding and Impression Management in the Endorsement of Love Styles

MARTIN F. DAVIES

ABSTRACT. In 2 experiments, the researcher investigated the social desirability of different love styles (Eros, Ludus, Storge, Pragma, Mania, and Agape). In Experiment 1, the Marlowe-Crowne measure of social desirability (D. P. Crowne & D. Marlowe, 1960) was correlated negatively with possessive, dependent (Mania) love styles in both men and women. In men, social desirability was correlated positively with romantic, passionate love (Eros) and game-playing love (Ludus), but negatively with all-giving, selfless love (Agape). In women, social desirability was correlated positively with Agape, but negatively with Ludus. In Experiment 2, the researcher replicated these findings using an impression management manipulation (good, bad, and honest responding). The gender differences in social desirability of different love styles are explained in terms of traditional and nontraditional gender role socialization.

A NUMBER OF THEORIES have proposed that love is a multidimensional concept. Walster and Walster (1978) suggested that there are two kinds of love: passionate love, involving a short and intense relationship; and companionate love, involving a close and enduring relationship. Clark and Mills (1979) differentiated between exchange relationships (based on interpersonal economics) and communal relationships (based on altruistic motives), suggesting that a benefit given in response to a benefit received would be appropriate in an exchange but not in a communal relationship, in which a benefit is given specifically to satisfy the other's need. Sternberg (1986) conceived of love as having three components: an emotional component, intimacy; a motivational component, passion; and a cognitive component, decision/commitment. Hazan and Shaver (1987) suggested that adult love can be traced to prototypical infant–mother attachment styles of security, anxiety/ambivalence, and avoidance.

An increasing amount of research on love has been devoted to investigating different styles of loving following Lee's (1973) typology of love styles. Lee's love styles consist of three primary and three secondary types. Primary types are Eros, romantic, passionate love; Ludus, game-playing love; and Storge, friendship love. Secondary types are Mania, possessive, dependent love; Pragma, logical, "shopping list" love; and Agape, all-giving, selfless love. Lee's typology of love styles refers to types of relationships rather than to types of people, and he considered it possible to be simultaneously one type in one relationship (e.g., Eros) and a different type in another relationship (e.g., Ludus).

Hendrick and Hendrick (1986) considered Lee's (1973) typology "exceedingly rich theoretically" (p. 393) because of its multidimensionality and because it can encompass other, less extensive, theories of love. For example, Clark and Mills's (1979) communal love is exemplified by Agape, whereas Walster and Walster's (1978) passionate love and companionate love represent Eros and Storge, respectively. Lee's original research was based on qualitative analyses of interview data, which Hendrick and Hendrick (1986) used to devise a Likert-type questionnaire to produce a quantitative assessment of love styles. They found that responses to the questionnaire produced a six-factor solution corresponding to the six love styles defined by Lee.

Much research has now examined the psychometric properties of love styles, including studies of reliability and consistency (e.g., Hendrick & Hendrick, 1986), factor-analytic studies (e.g., Critelli, Myers, & Loos, 1986; Hendrick & Hendrick, 1986), and studies of convergent and discriminant validity (e.g., Hendrick & Hendrick, 1987; Woll, 1989). One issue that has not been adequately addressed so far is the role of response bias in questionnaire measures of love. Given the importance and value accorded to love in Western societies ("all the world loves a lover"), in this study I expected participants to be motivated to respond to all questions about love in ways that are socially desirable and that present the respondent in a favorable light.

However, some love styles seem to be more socially desirable than others. For example, the Mania love style (possessive, dependent) is characterized by loneliness, discontent, and desperation, so people would be expected to perceive it as socially undesirable. Conversely, the Eros love style (romantic, passionate) is commonly regarded as an idealized type of love, as portrayed in poetry, songs, plays, novels, films, and television (Sprecher & Metts, 1989), and so it should be judged as socially desirable—particularly by young people. For older people, however, the Storge love style (friendship, companionship) is often portrayed as the norm and, therefore, desirable (Hieger & Troll, 1973). Given that student samples were used in the present research, I expected that Eros would be associated with social desirability, whereas Storge would not.

I also expected gender differences in the social desirability of love styles. According to Hendrick, Hendrick, Slapion-Foote, and Foote (1985), men are more permissive and instrumental in their sexual attitudes than women, who are traditionally more conservative, because they are socialized to view sex as a precious commodity to be guarded and to marry a partner who will be a good provider. If gender differences in love attitudes parallel those of sexual attitudes, then men should favor the game-playing style of love, and women should favor the pragmatic style. Hendrick and Hendrick (1986) provided evidence that this is indeed the case for the endorsement of love styles. Consequently, I expected that Ludus would be positively associated with social desirability in men, and Pragma would be positively associated with social desirability in women.

EXPERIMENT 1: Social Desirability Correlates of Love Styles

Method

The Marlowe-Crowne (MC; Crowne & Marlowe, 1960) questionnaire of social desirability and Hendrick and Hendrick's (1986, 1990) Love Attitudes Scale (LAS; which measures Lee's love styles) were administered to 122 college students (51 men and 71 women) aged 18 to 38 years. The MC questionnaire consists of 33 items describing either desirable but uncommon behaviors (e.g., admitting mistakes) or undesirable but common behaviors (e.g., gossiping). Participants respond "true" or "false" to 18 items keyed in the true direction and 15 in the false direction. Higher scores represent greater socially desirable responding. The LAS consists of 42 items, 7 items for each of the six love styles: Eros, romantic, passionate (e.g., "My lover and I were attracted to each other immediately after we first met"); Ludus, game-playing (e.g., "I try to keep my lover a little uncertain about my commitment to him or her"); Storge, friendship (e.g., "It is hard to say exactly where friendship ends and love begins"); Pragma, logical (e.g., "I consider what a person is going to become in life before I commit myself to him/her"); Mania, possessive, dependent (e.g., "When my love affairs break up, I get so depressed that I have even thought of suicide"); and Agape, selfless (e.g., "I try always to help my lover through difficult times"). Participants respond on 5-point Likert scales (1 = *strongly disagree*, 5 = *strongly agree*), answering the questionnaire items with their current partner in mind.

Results

The means, standard deviations, and correlations of the MC scores and love styles are shown in Table 1. There were significant differences in endorsement of the different love styles, multivariate $F(5, 116) = 42.47$, $p < .001$. Overall, participants in the present sample showed most endorsement of the Storge ($M = 23.13$), Eros ($M = 22.67$), and Agape ($M = 20.20$) love styles and least endorse-

TABLE 1
Experiment 1: Means, Standard Deviations, and Correlations of Social Desirability (Marlowe-Crowne) With Love Styles

Participants	Love style						M	SD
	Eros	Ludus	Storge	Pragma	Mania	Agape		
Men								
Social desirability	.34*	.36**	−.02	−.13	−.54***	−.33*	12.63	6.31
M	23.84	18.29	22.47	15.92	17.22	18.96		
SD	4.71	4.96	5.04	4.51	5.03	5.67		
Women								
Social desirability	.03	−.28*	.01	.01	−.37**	.32**	13.44	5.68
M	21.83	16.44	23.61	16.32	19.31	21.08		
SD	4.23	5.60	6.49	4.83	6.64	4.19		
Overall								
Social desirability	.16	−.03	.01	−.05	−.41***	−.01	13.10	5.94
M	22.67	17.21	23.13	16.16	18.43	20.20		
SD	4.53	5.40	5.93	4.68	6.08	4.96		

*$p < .05$. **$p < .01$. ***$p < .001$ two-tailed tests.

ment of the Mania ($M = 18.43$), Ludus ($M = 17.21$), and Pragma ($M = 16.16$) love styles. There were also significant differences in endorsement of love styles as a function of gender, multivariate $F(5, 116) = 3.07$, $p < .02$. Men chose Eros ($M = 23.84$) more often than women did ($M = 21.83$), $F(1, 120) = 6.11$, $p < .02$. Men also chose Ludus ($M = 18.29$) more than women did ($M = 16.44$), $F(1, 120) = 3.59$, $p < .06$. Women selected Mania ($M = 19.31$) more frequently than men did ($M = 17.22$), $F(1, 120) = 3.59$, $p < .06$, and Agape ($M = 21.08$) more than men did ($M = 18.96$), $F(1, 120) = 5.66$, $p < .02$.

Of particular relevance to this study were the correlations between social desirability and love styles. Correlations between MC and LAS scores showed a significant overall relation only for Mania, with higher scores associated with lower social desirability in both men and women. However, there were gender differences in the correlations. Social desirability was correlated positively with Eros in men but not in women ($z_{diff} = 1.72$, $p < .06$), and it was correlated positively with Ludus in men but negatively in women ($z_{diff} = 3.53$, $p < .001$). Conversely, social desirability was correlated negatively with Agape in men but positively in women ($z_{diff} = 3.58$, $p < .001$).

Although age has been suggested as an important factor in research on love, in the present study this was not found, either in terms of endorsement of love styles or as a moderator of the relationship between social desirability and love styles. This was probably because the sample participants were college students who showed little variation in age ($SD = 3.80$ years). Similar conditions were present in studies by Hendrick and Hendrick (1986) and Woll (1989), who also reported null findings with respect to age.

Discussion

In this study, gender differences in endorsement of love styles varied from those found in previous studies performed in the United States. For example, Hendrick and Hendrick (1986) found that men scored higher on Ludus, but not on Eros and women scored higher, not only on Mania, but also on Storge and Pragma. Dion and Dion (1973) found that men were more idealistic and also more cynical about love, whereas women were more pragmatic. The present results confirm these findings for men, who scored higher on Eros (idealistic) and Ludus (cynical), but not for women who did not score higher on Pragma. This discrepancy between the present findings and previous findings on gender differences may be attributable to cross-cultural (US–UK) differences in love styles. However, differences in findings have also been reported across various college samples within the United States (Woll, 1989).

Mania (possessive, dependent love) was found to be associated with lower social desirability in both men and women, a finding that is not surprising because it involves feelings of loneliness, discontent, and desperation. Given that the present sample consisted of young adults, it is also not surprising that Eros (romantic, passionate love) was associated with greater social desirability. Yet, this was found to be true only for men. Perhaps the two most interesting findings were that Ludus (game-playing love) was associated with greater social desirability in men but lower social desirability in women, and that Agape (selfless love) was associated with lower social desirability in men but greater social desirability in women. Before speculating further about the meaning of these gender differences, I tested the present findings using a different methodology.

EXPERIMENT 2: Impression Management in Reporting Love Styles

The effects of impression management on responding to self-report questionnaires have often been studied by inducing different impression sets in participants (for reviews, see Nederhof, 1985; Paulhus, 1991). In addition to the standard honesty instructions, respondents have been instructed to create a good impression ("faking good") or to create a bad impression ("faking bad"). Susceptibility to impression management is shown if scores increase with the good impression set and decrease with the bad impression set. In the following experiment, therefore, I investigated the influence of impression-management set on the endorsement of different love styles.

Method

The LAS was administered to 89 college students (39 men and 50 women) aged 18 to 44 years. Participants were randomly assigned to one of three instructional conditions. In the honest impression condition, participants were advised to respond as honestly as possible in order to give a true and accurate impression of themselves. In the good impression condition, participants were advised to respond so as to create a good impression by presenting themselves in the best light possible. In the bad impression condition, participants were advised to respond so as to create a bad impression by presenting themselves in the worst light possible.

Results and Discussion

The mean LAS scores are shown in Table 2 as a function of impression-management set and gender of respondent. There were significant differences in endorsement of the different love styles, multivariate $F(5, 79) = 29.79$, $p < .001$. As in Experiment 1, respondents showed most endorsement of the Storge ($M = 23.48$), Eros ($M = 22.74$), and Agape ($M = 20.54$) love styles and least endorsement of Mania ($M = 19.02$), Ludus ($M = 17.20$), and Pragma ($M = 16.30$) love styles. The gender differences in endorsement of love styles found in Experiment 1 were also replicated, multivariate $F(5, 79) = 3.47$, $p < .01$. Men chose Eros ($M = 23.77$) more than women did ($M = 21.94$), $F(1, 83) = 6.50$, $p < .02$. They

TABLE 2
Experiment 2: Mean Love Style Scores for Different Impression Management Sets

Participants/ Impression set	Love style					
	Eros	Ludus	Storge	Pragma	Mania	Agape
Men						
Bad	22.23$_a$	17.54$_a$	20.92	15.69	20.54$_a$	20.77
Honest	22.31$_a$	16.25$_a$	24.31	16.69	19.00$_a$	20.69
Good	28.10$_b$	22.60$_b$	22.90	15.40	13.40$_b$	16.00
Women						
Bad	21.27	19.55$_a$	24.91	16.45	21.27	17.91$_a$
Honest	22.95	16.60$_{ab}$	23.50	16.95	20.85	22.30$_b$
Good	21.26	14.21$_b$	24.00	16.11	17.74	22.32$_b$
Overall						
Bad	21.79	18.46	22.75	16.04	20.88$_a$	19.46
Honest	22.67	16.44	23.86	16.83	20.03$_a$	21.58
Good	23.62	17.10	23.62	15.86	16.24$_b$	20.14

Note. Within rows and columns, means with different subscripts are significantly different from each other at the .05 level by Student-Newman-Keuls.

also chose Ludus ($M = 18.31$) more than women did ($M = 16.34$), $F(1, 83) = 3.47$, $p < .07$. Women endorsed Mania ($M = 19.76$) more than men did ($M = 18.08$), $F(1, 83) = 3.50$, $p < .07$, and they chose Agape ($M = 21.34$) more than men did ($M = 19.51$), $F(1, 83) = 2.32$, $p < .15$.

Impression-management set had a significant overall effect on the endorsement of love styles, multivariate $F(12, 158) = 2.43$, $p < .01$. However, on only one love style, Mania, was the difference significant, $F(2, 83) = 6.70$, $p < .01$, such that lower scores were associated with greater favorability of impression. Interestingly, the effect of a bad impression set (relative to the honest set) was much less, multivariate $F(6, 51) = 1.13$, ns, than the effect of a good impression set, multivariate $F(6, 56) = 3.63$, $p < .01$.

Gender differences in impression management were found as a function of love style, multivariate $F(12, 158) = 3.18$, $p < .001$. As can be seen from Table 2, scores on Eros increased with favorability of impression for men, $F(2, 36) = 6.79$, $p < .01$, but not for women, $F < 1$. Scores on Ludus increased with favorability of impression for men, $F(2, 36) = 6.13$, $p < .01$, but decreased for women, $F(2, 47) = 3.78$, $p < .05$. For Agape, scores decreased slightly for men, $F(2, 36) = 2.23$, $p < .12$, but increased for women, $F(2, 47) = 4.99$, $p < .01$. These findings confirmed those of Experiment 1.

GENERAL DISCUSSION

The results of both experiments are consistent in showing that the social desirability of different love styles is strongly affected by the gender of the respondent. Only Mania was associated (negatively) with social desirability for both men and women. This does not come as a great surprise, because Mania is associated with a number of negative emotional states (loneliness, discontent, and desperation). From a methodological point of view, researchers might be advised to take special care when interpreting the level of endorsement of the manic love style, because the strong social undesirability of this style may result in an underestimation of its incidence.

The gender differences in social desirability of the different love styles found in these studies can be summarized as follows:

1. Eros (romantic, passionate love) is associated with social desirability in men but not in women.
2. Ludus (game-playing love) is associated with social desirability in men, but with social undesirability in women.
3. Agape (selfless love) is associated with social desirability in women but with social undesirability in men.

Some of these observed gender differences can be explained in terms of differences in attitudes to sex. Men tend to be permissive and instrumental in their attitudes, whereas women tend to be more conservative (e.g., Hendrick et al.,

1985). This explanation may account for why Ludus (game-playing love) is socially desirable for men but socially undesirable for women. However, it would also suggest that Pragma (logical love) should be socially desirable for women but socially undesirable for men—neither of which was found in the present studies.

Gender role socialization theory provides an influential explanation of gender differences in love. Dion and Dion (1985, 1991) argued that those who contribute less to economic subsistence have the most to gain by love being linked to marriage. They theorized that because women customarily have contributed less to the economic subsistence of the nuclear family, they should be more prone to value love in pragmatic terms—as a basis for marriage—rather than for idealistic reasons. Women following such traditional gender role patterns determine their standard of living by their choice of a husband. In contrast, because men have traditionally been socialized to be economically self-sufficient, their choice of a wife is not as strongly affected by factors that determine their standard of living. Thus, theorists conclude that women tend to be more pragmatically concerned about love and also less idealistic than men. Similarly, women are viewed as being less cynical about the importance of love to marriage, because it functions as an inducement for marriage. In contrast, men are seen as being less concerned about practical aspects of relationships and as being more influenced by both idealistic and cynical factors.

This gender role socialization explanation may account for why Eros and Ludus are associated with social desirability in men (and not in women). However, as with the explanation in terms of sexual attitudes, it does not account for the lack of an association in this study between Pragma and social desirability in women. Possibly, Pragma was not found to be associated with social desirability because it is rather a neutral kind of love, in the sense of being logical and sensible. Generally, being logical and sensible may not be perceived as particularly desirable traits by young people. Alternatively, pragmatic love may be less important to women nowadays because of changes in traditional gender role socialization. Women have become more economically self-sufficient and independent, so that the link between love and marriage has weakened. This would seem to be especially the case in college women (as in the present sample). Nontraditional attitudes toward love would mean that women should be more idealistic in their love styles. But rather than manifesting itself in erotic love styles (as in men), this idealism may be manifested in the all-giving, selfless love style. Further research is needed to test this gender role socialization account by, for example, comparing the love styles of traditional and nontraditional men and women and their perceptions of the desirability of different love styles.

REFERENCES

Clark, M. S., & Mills, J. S. (1979). Interpersonal attraction in exchange and communal relationships. *Journal of Personality & Social Psychology, 37*, 12–24.

Critelli, J. W., Myers, E., & Loos, V. E. (1986). The components of love: Romantic attraction and sex role orientation. *Journal of Personality, 54,* 354–370.

Crowne, D. P., & Marlowe, D. (1960). A new scale of social desirability independent of psychopathology. *Journal of Consulting Psychology, 24,* 349–354.

Dion, K. K., & Dion, K. L. (1985). Personality, gender, and the phenomenology of romantic love. In P. Shaver (Ed.), *Self, situations, and social behavior: Review of personality and social psychology* (Vol. 6, pp. 209–239). Beverly Hills, CA: Sage

Dion, K. K., & Dion, K. L. (1991). Psychological individualism and romantic love. *Journal of Social Behavior and Personality, 6,* 17–33.

Dion, K. L., & Dion, K. K. (1973). Correlates of romantic love. *Journal of Consulting and Clinical Psychology, 41,* 51–56.

Hazan, C., & Shaver, P. (1987). Romantic love conceptualized as an attachment process. *Journal of Personality and Social Psychology, 52,* 511–524.

Hendrick, C., & Hendrick, S. S. (1986). A theory and method of love. *Journal of Personality & Social Psychology, 50,* 392–402.

Hendrick, C., & Hendrick, S. S. (1990). A relationship specific version of the Love Attitude Scale. *Journal of Social Behavior and Personality, 5,* 239–254.

Hendrick, C., Hendrick, S. S., Slapion-Foote, M. J., & Foote, F. H. (1985). Gender differences in sexual attitudes. *Journal of Personality & Social Psychology, 48,* 1630–1642.

Hendrick, S. S., & Hendrick, C. (1987). Love and sex attitudes and religious beliefs. *Journal of Social and Clinical Psychology, 5,* 391–398.

Hieger, L. J., & Troll, L. A. (1973). A three-generation study of attitudes concerning the importance of romantic love in mate selection. *Gerontologist, 13,* 86–88.

Lee, J. A. (1973). *The colors of love.* Don Mills, Ontario, Canada: New Press.

Nederhof, A. J. (1985). Methods of coping with social desirability bias: A review. *European Journal of Social Psychology, 15,* 263–280.

Paulhus, D. L. (1991). Measurement and control of response bias. In J. P. Robinson, P. R. Shaver & L. S. Wrightsman (Eds.), *Measures of personality and social psychological attitudes* (Vol. 1, pp. 17–59). London: Academic Press.

Sprecher, S., & Metts, S. (1989). Development of the "Romantic Beliefs Scale" and examination of the effects of gender and gender-role orientation. *Journal of Social and Personal Relationships, 6,* 387–411.

Sternberg, R. J. (1986). A triangular theory of love. *Psychological Review, 93,* 119–135.

Walster, E., & Walster, G. W. (1978). *A new look at love.* Reading, MA: Addison-Wesley.

Woll, S. B. (1989). Personality and relationship correlates of loving styles. *Journal of Research in Personality, 37,* 480–505.

Humor Use in Romantic Relationships: The Effects of Relationship Satisfaction and Pleasant Versus Conflict Situations

BETHANY BUTZER
NICHOLAS A. KUIPER
University of Western Ontario

ABSTRACT. In this study, the authors explored the use of positive, negative, and avoiding humor in 2 types of situations by individuals in romantic relationships. Participants ($N = 154$) rated their frequency of humor use in either a typical conflict scenario with their partner or a typical pleasant event. Participants also indicated their overall degree of romantic relationship satisfaction. Hierarchical regression analyses revealed that individuals who were more satisfied with their relationship reported higher levels of positive humor use and lower levels of negative and avoiding humor use. Furthermore, lower levels of negative and avoiding humor use were reported for the conflict situation. Last, a significant 2-way interaction revealed that individuals who were high in relationship satisfaction reported significantly lower levels of negative humor use in a conflict situation as compared with a pleasant encounter. In contrast, individuals who were low in relationship satisfaction reported the same high levels of negative humor use regardless of whether they were in a conflict situation or a pleasant encounter. The authors discuss these findings in terms of the need for further research to clearly delineate the factors that may influence the complex use of humor in romantic relationships.

HUMOR IS AN IMPORTANT ASPECT of many romantic relationships (Goodwin & Tang, 1991). As one example, Lauer, Lauer, and Kerr (1990) found that wives and husbands considered humor to be among the more important ingredients for a successful marriage. Similarly, researchers have found that individuals place a great deal of importance on humor when selecting a mate (Buss, 1988; Goodwin, 1990; Murstein & Brust, 1985). In addition, greater humor appreciation has been linked to positive relational processes, such as increased intimacy and interpersonal attraction (Cann, Calhoun, & Banks, 1997; Hampes, 1992).

The authors gratefully acknowledge the support of an SSHRC-CGS award to the first author to assist in the preparation of this article.

Research on the use of humor in close relationships has suggested that individuals in romantic relationships generally use humor in three main ways with their partners (Alberts, 1990; De Koning & Weiss, 2002; Jacobs, 1985). *Positive humor* is used to feel closer to one's partner and to ease tension, whereas *negative humor* is used to express hostility toward one's partner (De Koning & Weiss; Jacobs; Ziv, 1988). Last, *avoiding humor* is used to either minimize or avoid conflict entirely, often by changing the focus of conversation (Alberts; De Koning & Weiss).

In the present study, we explored how positive, negative, and avoiding humor use might relate to two other important relational constructs: (a) the degree of relationship satisfaction and (b) the type of situation involved (conflict situation vs. a pleasant encounter). We first describe how individuals in close relationships report using humor and then delineate how both relationship satisfaction and the type of situation might pertain to humor use in romantic relationships, including the proposal that these two constructs might interact to predict humor use.

Humor Use in Romantic Relationships

With regard to positive humor, several researchers have shown that individuals in romantic relationships may use humor to feel closer to one another and to help them cope with various aspects of their lives (Alberts, 1990; Bippus, 2000; Lefcourt & Martin, 1986; Ziv, 1988). For example, after interviewing 61 couples about humor use in their relationships, Ziv found that the most frequently reported role of humor in marriage was to enhance closeness and bonding. In a similar fashion, Bippus interviewed young couples about their conceptualizations of humor and found that bonding, a relationship-specific category of humor, emerged as an important positive use of humor. Bonding serves as a form of communication within the relationship, to both increase warmth and strengthen closeness between couples. Last, De Koning and Weiss (2002) asked married couples to report on their own and their partner's uses of humor by answering a self-report questionnaire that assessed the functions of humor in marriage. They found that participants endorsed items indicating that humor can play a positive role in relationships when couples appreciate each other's humor and when humor is used to bring couples closer to each other.

Individuals in romantic relationships also sometimes use negative humor with each other. For example, in an examination of adjusted and maladjusted married couples during conflict interactions, Alberts (1990) found that humor can be used between partners to provoke conflict by allowing them to conceal hostility or to allow for hostility without the negative consequences of overt behavior. In support of this notion, De Koning and Weiss (2002) found that their sample of married couples indicated on a self-report questionnaire that they sometimes used humor as a form of aggression or manipulation against their partner. Similarly, by asking married women to self-report on their humor use with their partner, Jacobs (1985) also identified a negative aspect of humor in the context of marital relationships, namely, the expression of hostility and creation of distance.

Last, researchers have found that individuals in romantic relationships may also use avoiding humor with each other to minimize conflict or avoid it entirely. As one illustration, De Koning and Weiss (2002) found that some couples self-reported using humor as a way to diffuse negative feelings during tense interactions. Similarly, Jacobs (1985) found that humor could be used in the context of marital relationships to manage conflict by reducing tension and Alberts (1990) found that romantic couples sometimes used humor as an avoidance tactic to move the conversation away from the matter at hand.

In summary, our review suggests that humor is used in three main ways in romantic relationships: in positive, negative, and avoiding manners. Accordingly, our goal in the present study was to determine (a) the extent to which individuals in romantic relationships report using humor in each described manner with their partners, and (b) how this use may relate to both the type of situation involved (pleasant event vs. conflict) and the degree of relationship satisfaction.

Humor Use and Relationship Satisfaction

Relationship satisfaction can have important implications for individuals in romantic relationships. Considerable research has shown that couples who report lower levels of satisfaction generally behave less positively toward each other, exhibiting higher levels of negative affect and lower levels of relationship stability (Gottman, 1994; Schaap & Jansen-Nawas, 1987). Consequently, an examination of the association between relationship satisfaction and humor use in romantic relationships was one of the goals of the present study. Prior research with married couples offers some initial insights concerning potential links between relationship satisfaction and the differential use of humor.

Ziv and Gadish (1989) administered a self-report questionnaire assessing humor creation and appreciation to 50 married couples and found that higher levels of these positive uses of humor were related to greater marital satisfaction for husbands. In addition, in her examination of married couples during conflict interactions, Alberts (1990) found that couples who were more satisfied with their marriage were more likely to use benign forms of humor (e.g., jokes about the self, relationship, or partner made in a gentle manner), whereas unsatisfied couples were more likely to use hostile humor (e.g., humor that joked about the partner in a negative way, such as sarcasm). Furthermore, satisfied couples report using friendly teasing with their partners, whereas unsatisfied couples do not (Ting-Toomey, 1983). Finally, both greater self-reported positive humor use and increased perceptions of the use of positive humor by one's partner have been linked to higher marital satisfaction (De Koning & Weiss, 2002; Jacobs, 1985). In contrast, fewer researchers have focused on romantic relationship satisfaction and negative uses of humor. However, the researchers who have examined these relationships have found that lower marital satisfaction is related to greater self-reported negative humor use and greater perceptions of one's partner's use of negative humor (De Koning & Weiss; Jacobs).

In summary, prior research with married couples has suggested that individuals who are more satisfied with their relationship may use more positive humor, whereas individuals who are less satisfied may use more negative humor. Despite these intriguing findings, two limitations of this research are that these studies (a) have not directly compared how different situations, such as a conflict situation versus a pleasant encounter, may have a different impact on humor use and (b) have not examined how relationship satisfaction may be associated with differences in humor use for each of these two situations. Type of situation is an important relational construct to consider because the ways in which married couples interact with each other during conflict situations is a strong predictor of marital quality and longevity (Gottman, 1994). Thus, in the present study, we examined (a) how the humor used in a typical conflict situation may differ from the humor used in a pleasant encounter and (b) how the degree of romantic relationship satisfaction may be differentially associated with humor use in each of these two types of situations.

Humor Use in Conflict Versus Pleasant Situations

Previous researchers have found that the escalation of conflict situations is generally associated with lower levels of relationship satisfaction, whereas greater conflict resolution is associated with higher levels of satisfaction (Billings, 1979; Gottman, 1979; Pike & Sillars, 1985). In addition, researchers have found that humor is used in conflict situations by individuals in romantic relationships for a variety of positive or negative reasons (Krokoff, 1991), such as to de-escalate the conflict (Alberts, 1990), or to express hostility or create distance (Jacobs, 1985). Thus, it appears that both the type of situation, particularly the presence or absence of conflict, and the degree of relationship satisfaction can have significant implications for how humor is used in romantic relationships.

An important limitation regarding previous research is that researchers have focused either on how humor is related to relationship satisfaction or on how humor is used in conflict situations but not on both. Thus, prior researchers have not examined, in one study, how both situational context and romantic relationship satisfaction may contribute to humor use. To illustrate, Alberts (1990) found that couples engaging in a conflict discussion tended to use more hostile humor when they were not satisfied with their relationships. However, Alberts did not compare these couples with couples in other pertinent situations, such as engaging in a pleasant event.

Thus, in the present study we examined how both the type of situation and individuals' relationship satisfaction may be related to positive, negative, and avoiding humor use by individuals in romantic relationships. In particular, we examined both the individual effects of the type of situation and relationship satisfaction when predicting humor and how these two constructs might interact to predict humor use. The fact that other research on romantic relationships has demonstrated major implications of both the type of situation and relationship satisfaction reinforces the importance of simultaneously investigating these two relational constructs in one humor study.

Overview and Hypotheses

In the present study, we asked university students who were involved in a romantic relationship for 3 months or longer to report on their relationship satisfaction and their use of positive, negative, and avoiding humor with their romantic partner, for either a typical conflict situation or a pleasant encounter. We assessed positive humor using self-report items (described in more detail in the Method section) that involved the use of humor to increase closeness and relieve tension. We assessed negative humor with items reflecting the use of humor to express hostility toward one's partner. Last, the items for avoiding humor reflected the use of humor to avoid discussing a topic.

Based on well-established and validated procedures used in both survey research (Alexander & Becker, 1978) and the literature on romantic relationships (e.g., Jackson & Ebnet, 2006), we used brief descriptive vignettes to tap both a conflict situation (dealing with jealousy issues) and a pleasant encounter (having an enjoyable lunch with one's partner). We then used hierarchical regression analyses to examine how both (a) the degree of relationship satisfaction and (b) the type of situation (conflict vs. pleasant encounter) predicted positive, negative, and avoiding humor use. In addition, we tested the possible combined effects of relationship satisfaction and type of situation in predicting humor use by examining the two-way interactions between these constructs. Thus, this study is the first to incorporate an experimental manipulation of the type of situation involved, thus allowing for the simultaneous examination of the individual and interactive contributions of both the type of situation and relationship satisfaction in predicting humor use.

Hypothesis 1 (H_1). On the basis of previous research suggesting that married individuals who are more satisfied with their relationships use more positive humor and less negative humor than do those who are less satisfied with their relationships, we predicted a significant main effect of relationship satisfaction for each of our regression analyses. In particular, we expected that higher levels of romantic relationship satisfaction would be significantly related to more positive humor use, less negative humor use, and less avoiding humor use. Such a pattern would reflect the possibility that more satisfied individuals use humor in a way that is most appropriate to support and foster their romantic relationships. Thus, we expected that these individuals would engage in more positive humor use with their partners to help increase closeness and ease tension, but less negative humor use to ensure that they do not overly criticize or put down their partner. In addition, we expected that these individuals would engage in less avoiding humor use, to ensure they do not thwart the expression and sharing of true thoughts and feelings with their partner or hamper effective conflict resolution.

Hypothesis 2 (H_2). On the basis of research suggesting that individuals in romantic relationships often use humor to both increase closeness and de-escalate conflict, we hypothesized a significant main effect of type of situation. We expected that individuals would report more positive humor use in the conflict situation in comparison with the pleasant encounter. We also expected that individuals would report less negative and avoiding humor use in the conflict situation when compared with the pleasant encounter. Such a pattern would reflect the proposal that individuals in conflict situations with their romantic partners generally try to use humor to minimize relationship discomfort and conflict. This would result in a heightened use of positive humor in the conflict situation to enhance closeness and ease tension, a minimal use of negative humor to reduce the possibility of hurting one's partner, and a reduction in the use of avoiding humor to facilitate the expression of true feelings and effective conflict resolution.

Hypothesis 3 (H_3). On the basis of research suggesting that individuals who are highly satisfied with their romantic relationships are motivated to reduce conflict and maintain a healthy relationship with their partner, we predicted a significant two-way interaction between relationship satisfaction and type of situation for positive, negative, and avoiding humor use. Specifically, we expected that individuals who were high in relationship satisfaction would indicate using significantly more positive humor, less negative humor, and less avoiding humor in the conflict situation than in the pleasant encounter. This pattern would reflect a heightened emphasis by these individuals on nurturing and maintaining an amiable and satisfying relationship with their romantic partner by using humor to increase closeness and relieve tension, while also reducing the use of humor that might hurt their partner or thwart the expression of true feelings. In contrast, we did not expect that individuals low on relationship satisfaction would be as oriented toward this goal. Thus, we expected that these low-satisfaction individuals would not as readily discriminate between the two situations, resulting in equivalent levels of humor use across the two situations.

Method

Participants

Participants were 155 undergraduates, recruited through the Introductory Psychology participation pool at our university. They received course credit for their participation. To take part in this study, participants were required to be in a romantic relationship lasting at least 3 months, a standard commonly used in the romantic relationship literature (e.g., Campbell, Lackenbauer, & Muise, 2006). The mean length of the relationship for our participants was 15.6 months ($SD = 12.5$ months). Data for 1 participant was omitted due to an extremely inconsistent response pattern, leaving 154 participants (108 women, 46 men), with a mean age of 19.10 years ($SD = 1.57$ years).

Measures

Typical conflict and pleasant situations. Using procedures typically employed in the romantic relationship literature (e.g., Jackson & Ebnet, 2006), we created two separate vignettes for this study: One reflected a typical conflict situation that could be experienced with one's partner, and the other reflected a typical pleasant situation. University students report jealousy issues as one of the most frequent problems that they encounter in their romantic relationships (Knox & Wilson, 1983; Zusman & Knox, 1998). Thus, we created a conflict situation to reflect this common problem. We asked participants to imagine a situation in which their partner was upset with them because they had had lunch with an opposite-sex friend. Participants were further asked to imagine that they were discussing the issue with their partner, with each partner expressing their views on the situation.

We created the typical pleasant situation on the basis of previous research indicating that describing the events of a previous day elicits more positive affect and less negative affect for romantic couples than does discussing an area of conflict (Gottman, 1979). Thus, we asked participants to imagine a situation in which they had not had an opportunity to speak with their partner for an entire day. Participants were further asked to imagine that on the following day they and their partner had a pleasant conversation over lunch regarding the events of the previous day.

Humor use items. On the basis of a review of the ways in which humor may be used in romantic relationships, we selected and appropriately modified a number of items from previous humor scales (Alberts, 1990; DeKoning & Weiss, 2002; Graham, Papa, & Brooks, 1992; Jacobs, 1985) to tap the positive, negative, and avoiding uses of humor in romantic relationships. After reading one of the two vignettes (either the conflict or pleasant situation), participants indicated on a 7-point scale ranging from 1 (*never*) to 7 (*frequently*) how often they would use positive, negative, and avoiding humor with their partner in that situation. All items were identical for the conflict and pleasant situations, with instructions indicating, "Picturing yourself in this situation with your partner, please indicate how often you would use humor to . . ." We measured positive humor use using 8 items, such as, "make you and your partner feel closer as a couple" and "ease the tension of the situation." We measured negative humor use with 5 items, such as, "put your partner down" and "highlight your partner's weaknesses, blunders or faults." Last, we measured avoiding humor use with 11 items, such as, "avoid letting your partner know what's really on your mind," and "change the subject."

To ensure that these items actually assessed positive, negative, and avoiding humor use, we conducted two principal components analyses: one with only the participants in the conflict situation ($n = 77$), and the other with only the participants in the pleasant situation ($n = 77$). Both of these analyses were conducted with a varimax rotation, with the items being forced into three factors. The extractions for the conflict and pleasant situations each revealed the expected three factors with eigenvalues exceeding 1.0. Items with a loading of .40 or higher on a single factor were considered to load onto the factor and contribute to its interpretation. Items that had a factor loading of .40 or higher on more than one factor were considered ambiguous, and we excluded them from further consideration. To arrive at a final set of factors that were interpretable for both situations, we retained only those items that loaded onto the same factor for both the conflict and pleasant situations. By following these selection rules, we excluded three positive humor use items, one negative humor use item, and seven avoiding humor use items from the final set of scales.

On the basis of the results of the principle components analyses, we measured the use of positive humor using five items that reflected humor used to get closer to one's partner and to ease tension. We measured the use of negative humor with four items that involved using humor in a more aggressive or maladaptive fashion, such as using humor to put one's partner down. Last, we measured the use of avoiding humor with four items that involved the use of humor to avoid the situation or topic at hand, such as using humor to change the subject. Reliability levels were acceptable for each of these scales, with Cronbach's alphas of .77 for positive humor, .76 for negative humor, and .77 for avoiding humor. Furthermore, the three scales were generally distinct from one another, with positive and avoiding humor use being unrelated ($r = -.10$, ns), and positive and negative humor use showing only a very modest negative relation ($r = -.16$, $p < .05$). Negative and avoiding humor use were positively related, but at a moderate level ($r = .27$, $p < .01$).

Relationship satisfaction. We used Hendrick's (1988) seven-item Relationship Assessment Scale (RAS) to measure individuals' overall satisfaction with their relationship. Participants responded to items such as, "In general, how satisfied are you with your relationship?" and "To what extent has your relationship met your original expectations?" on a 7-point scale ranging from 1 (*not at all/poor*) to 7 (*a great deal/extremely good*). We averaged responses across items for each participant, with higher mean scores indicating greater relationship satisfaction. Prior work has indicated acceptable levels of reliability and validity for the RAS (Hendrick; Inman-Amos, Hendrick, & Hendrick, 1994). In the present study, the Cronbach's alpha for the RAS was high (.88), indicating good scale reliability.

Procedure

We tested participants in small groups of up to 10 individuals and randomly assigned them to receive a questionnaire booklet containing one of the two situations (typical conflict or pleasant encounter). We instructed participants to imagine that the described situation had happened between themselves and their partner. After reading about the situation, participants then provided ratings indicating how frequently they would use positive, negative, and avoiding humor if they were involved in such a situation with their partner. After completing the questionnaire booklet, participants also completed the RAS (Hendrick, 1988). All participants received a written debriefing form at the conclusion of the study.

Results

Means and Standard Deviations

For our entire sample of individuals in romantic relationships ($N = 154$), positive humor was reported as being used the most frequently ($M = 5.37$, $SD = 0.87$), negative humor was used the least often ($M = 2.33$, $SD = 0.90$), and avoiding humor was used moderately ($M = 3.40$, $SD = 1.24$). In addition, the participants reported being generally satisfied with their romantic relationships ($M = 5.68$, $SD = 1.03$).

Regression Analyses

We performed a separate hierarchical regression analysis for each of the three criterion variables: positive, negative, and avoiding humor use. For each analysis, we entered situation (coded as 1 = conflict situation, –1 = pleasant encounter) and the mean-centered value for romantic relationship satisfaction as the predictor variables in Step 1. We entered the two-way interaction between situation and relationship satisfaction as the predictor variable in Step 2.

The unstandardized regression coefficients for all three regression analyses are presented in Table 1. For positive humor use, the predicted significant main effect of relationship satisfaction emerged. In support of H_1, this main effect revealed that higher levels of relationship satisfaction predicted higher levels of positive humor use. H_2 was not supported, however, because the main effect of type of situation was not significant. In other words, there was no evidence that individuals reported more positive humor use in a conflict situation than in a pleasant encounter. Coupled with the further finding that the interaction term was also nonsignificant (thus failing to support H_3), this pattern suggests that the type of situation (pleasant vs. conflict) is not a relevant factor when considering positive humor use. Rather, those individuals with a high degree of romantic relationship satisfaction use more positive humor overall than do those individuals with a low degree of satisfaction, regardless of the situation.

TABLE 1. Hierarchical Regression Analyses of Positive, Negative, and Avoiding Humor Use as Predicted by Situation, Relationship Satisfaction, and the Situation × Relationship Satisfaction Interaction

Predictor variable	Criterion variable					
	Positive humor		Negative humor		Avoiding humor	
	b	SE	b	SE	b	SE
Situation	.04	.07	−.18**	.07	−.21*	.10
RAS	.19**	.07	−.20**	.07	−.19*	.10
Situation × RAS	.00	.07	−.16*	.07	−.03	.10

Note. All effects are reported as unstandardized regression coefficients. Significance levels are given for each variable at the initial point of entry in the regression equation. Situation was coded as 1 = conflict situation, −1 = pleasant encounter. RAS = relationship satisfaction (S. S. Hendrick, 1988).
*$p < .05$. **$p < .01$.

When predicting negative humor use, significant main effects emerged for both relationship satisfaction and the type of situation. Thus, in support of H_1, individuals with low levels of satisfaction reported significantly more negative humor use than did those with high levels of satisfaction. Furthermore, in support of H_2, individuals reported less negative humor use in the conflict situation than in the pleasant encounter. Last, H_3 was supported by the significant two-way interaction between type of situation and relationship satisfaction. This interaction is plotted in Figure 1 and, as predicted, shows that individuals who were high in relationship satisfaction reported using lower levels of negative humor in a conflict situation as compared with a pleasant encounter (simple slope test, $\beta = -.34, p < .001$). In contrast, individuals who were low in relationship satisfaction reported consistently high levels of negative humor use, regardless of whether they were in a conflict situation or a pleasant encounter (simple slope test, $\beta = -.02$, *ns*).

In the final regression analysis, both H_1 and H_2 were supported for avoiding humor use, as the predicted significant main effects emerged for both relationship satisfaction and type of situation. Congruent with H_1, individuals with lower levels of relationship satisfaction reported using more avoiding humor than did those with higher levels of satisfaction. In support of H_2, individuals reported using less avoiding humor in the conflict situation than in the pleasant encounter. H_3 was not supported, however, because the two-way interaction between type of situation and relationship satisfaction was not significant. Thus, there was no evidence that individuals who were high in relationship satisfaction would report using less avoiding humor in a conflict situation versus a pleasant encounter,

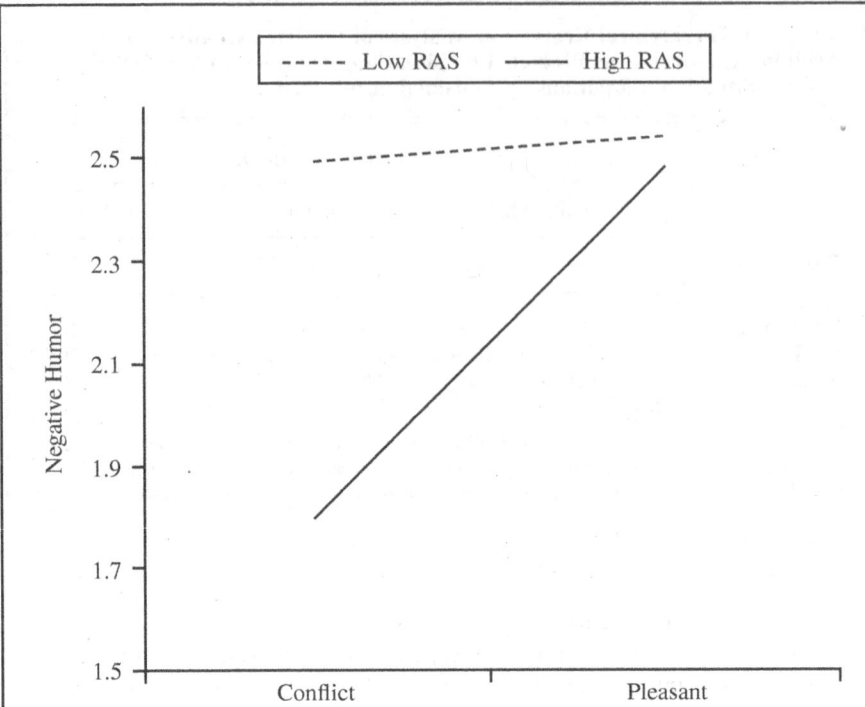

FIGURE 1. The significant two-way interaction between situation (conflict vs. pleasant event) and relationship satisfaction (measured by the Relationship Assessment Scale [RAS]; S. S. Hendrick, 1988) predicting negative humor use. Regression lines are plotted for scores that are 1 SD above and below the mean for each of the predictor variables.

whereas individuals who were low in relationship satisfaction would report equivalent levels of avoiding humor use across these two situations.

Discussion

Our results provide considerable empirical support for the proposal that humor is used in three main ways in romantic relationships (Alberts, 1990; De Koning & Weiss, 2002; Jacobs, 1985). In particular, individuals reported that they would use positive humor the most frequently with their romantic partner, avoiding humor with medium frequency, and negative humor the least frequently. This pattern supports prior work suggesting that although humor is often used positively in romantic relationships to increase closeness and ease tension, individuals do occasionally use humor to change the topic of conversation or to put their partners down. Accordingly, these findings support a multifaceted concept of humor use that encompasses both positive and negative elements (DeKoning & Weiss; Jacobs; Klein & Kuiper, 2006). Thus, it is not simply the case that humor is used only to enhance one's romantic relationship.

Our findings also support the proposal that the degree of relationship satisfaction is associated with humor use in romantic relationships. In accord with H_1, we found that individuals who reported being more satisfied with their romantic relationships also reported that they would use higher levels of positive humor with their partners and lower levels of both avoiding and negative humor. This pattern is congruent with the possibility that individuals who are more satisfied with their romantic relationships will primarily engage in the use of humor that is more beneficial for the functioning of their relationship (Alberts, 1990; De Koning & Weiss, 2002; Jacobs, 1985). Our findings extend previous work by showing this to be the case, even after taking into account two very different types of situations. In particular, regardless of whether they were in a conflict situation or a pleasant encounter, individuals who were more satisfied with their romantic relationships reported higher overall levels of positive humor use and lower levels of avoiding and negative humor use than did individuals who were less satisfied with their romantic relationships. This pattern clearly highlights the importance of relationship satisfaction as a central construct that pertains to differential patterns of positive humor use in romantic relationships.

A further novel aspect of our study is that it is among the first to include an experimental manipulation of the type of situation involved (conflict vs. pleasant encounter) when examining humor use in romantic relationships. In this regard, we found that individuals used lower levels of avoiding and negative humor in the conflict situation than in the pleasant encounter. Contrary to our expectations, however, we did not find that higher levels of positive humor were used in the conflict situation in comparison with the pleasant encounter. Overall, this pattern suggests that individuals feel more comfortable pushing the boundaries of negative humor use with their partners during typical pleasant interactions than when faced with conflict. These findings further suggest that instead of increasing the use of positive humor to further enhance closeness and ease tension with their romantic partners during conflict situations, individuals seem to reduce their use of negative and avoiding humor in these situations to try to avoid any further escalation of the conflict with their romantic partner.

The final novel aspect of our design is that it allowed for an empirical test of how relationship satisfaction and the type of situation may interact in predicting humor use in romantic relationships. We found a particularly interesting pattern for negative humor use. Specifically, individuals who were not satisfied with their romantic relationships did not readily distinguish between being in a conflict situation with their partner or engaging in a pleasant activity. In other words, they appeared oblivious to this fundamental distinction and continued to use high levels of negative humor, regardless of the situation involved. However, individuals who were more satisfied with their romantic relationships significantly reduced their use of negative humor in a conflict situation relative to their use during a pleasant encounter. We interpret this shift in humor use as part of a strategy that is used by those with high relationship satisfaction to avoid further escalation of conflict with their romantic partners. This proposal is in accord with prior studies demonstrating that the escalation of conflict situations is generally associated with lower levels of relationship satisfaction, whereas greater conflict resolution is associated with higher levels of satisfaction (Billings, 1979; Gottman, 1979; Pike & Sillars, 1985).

Limitations, Further Directions, and Conclusions

Although the present findings are interesting, they should be considered with several limitations in mind. First, the use of an undergraduate sample may have restricted the generalizability of our findings. It is possible, for example, that individuals from a different socioeconomic or cultural background, or those with a longer romantic relationship history (e.g., 10 years or more), may display different results. These possibilities could be tested in future research by involving older participants, moving to a community base, or considering cross-cultural distinctions that may pertain to humor use. Furthermore, because other fundamental personality constructs, such as agency and communion, have been shown to relate to the type of humor used (Kazarian & Martin, 2004) and to have effects on well-being (Kuiper & Borowicz-Sibenik, 2005), future researchers should also include a consideration of these additional personality dimensions.

Future researchers could also explore humor use in other types of relationships. As one illustration, Klein and Kuiper (2006) provided a detailed examination of how humor may impact relationships in middle childhood, including the use of different humor styles that may pertain to bullying. They detailed the complex nature of humor use, with some humor styles that are normally considered adaptive and positive (e.g., affiliative humor) being used indirectly in a negative fashion to further alienate a peer group against a victimized child. This more subtle use of humor may be difficult to capture in lab-based experimental or correlational research and may thus require the additional use of observational studies to document humor use in various real-life situations and relationships. Such observational work could also overcome some of the difficulties associated with an exclusive reliance on self-report. In the present study, for example, individuals may not have wanted to report high levels of negative humor use during a conflictual interaction with their romantic partner. Accordingly, examining actual conflict discussions between couples would help to clarify this pattern of humor use.

A further limitation of the present study is that it only focused on one of the individuals involved in the romantic relationship. Future researchers should examine the association between relationship satisfaction, type of situation, and humor use by both members of a romantic couple. Although such a study would necessarily introduce a greater degree of complexity, the benefit would be a more thorough examination of the ongoing and dynamic nature of humor use in romantic relationships. For example, a study using both members of a couple could examine whether one partner's degree of relationship satisfaction is linked to the other partner's pattern of humor use during an actual conflict or pleasant situation. Such a study could also track how humor use unfolds across time, with the possibility that different implications or effects of humor use are evident at various stages of an interaction with one's romantic partner.

The inclusion of both members of a romantic couple could also help to clarify the precise impact of various uses of humor on both members of the couple. In this regard, it should be noted that the present research was not designed to assess whether the particular use of humor that was intended by the individual involved in the study would be perceived as such by their partner. It is possible, for example, that humor intended to be positive in nature may actually be perceived by the partner as being avoiding in nature or even negative. Similarly, humor generated to serve a negative use may be perceived by the partner as relatively benign or perhaps even positive. Thus, research that examines the degree of concordance between romantic relationship partners regarding each of the three main uses of humor would be of particular interest. Such research might also include other individual difference constructs that may pertain to both the sensitivity and accuracy of humor use (including both generative and receptive components). As one illustration, those with a low degree of empathy may have particular difficulty in determining the intent of their partner's humor, which, in turn, may lead to further misattributions and miscommunications that then hamper their relationship.

Despite these limitations, the present study offers some important insights into the use of humor in romantic relationships. At the most general level, the findings indicate that humor is not always used positively in romantic relationships and that individuals sometimes use humor to avoid issues and say negative things to their romantic partners. In addition, not all people use humor in the same way in their romantic relationships. Instead, individuals in romantic relationships report using humor in different ways, depending on their degree of relationship satisfaction and the type of situation involved. Individuals who were more satisfied with their relationship generally used humor in ways that would benefit their relationship as a whole and were more sensitive to the situation they were in when using humor that had the potential to hurt their partner's feelings. Thus, our findings are congruent with the notion that humor is one strategy that individuals can use in romantic relationships to achieve particular relational goals such as increased bonding, reduced tension, or avoidance of a certain topic of conversation. Of particular importance, however, is that not all individuals necessarily use humor in the same way in their romantic relationships. The present work suggests that the degree of relationship satisfaction and the type of situation involved are related to the pattern of humor use in important ways.

AUTHOR NOTES

Bethany Butzer is a graduate student in social psychology at the University of Western Ontario. She conducts research on various aspects of romantic relationships, including humor use and adult attachment. **Nicholas A. Kuiper** is the director of the Clinical Psychology Graduate Program at the University of Western Ontario. He has published extensively in the areas of humor research, depression, and self-concept issues.

REFERENCES

Alberts, J. K. (1990). The use of humor in managing couples' conflict interactions. In D. D. Cahn (Ed.), *Intimates in conflict: A communication perspective* (pp. 105–120). Hillsdale, NJ: Erlbaum.

Alexander, C. S., & Becker, H. J. (1978). The use of vignettes in survey research. *Public Opinion Quarterly, 42,* 93–104.

Billings, A. (1979). Conflict resolution in distressed and nondistressed married couples. *Journal of Consulting and Clinical Psychology, 47,* 368–376.

Bippus, A. M. (2000). Making sense of humor in young romantic relationships: Understanding partners' perceptions. *Humor: International Journal of Humor Research, 13,* 395–417.

Buss, D. M. (1988). The evolution of human intrasexual competition: Tactics of mate attraction. *Journal of Personality and Social Psychology, 54,* 616–628.

Campbell, L., Lackenbauer, S. D., & Muise, A. (2006). When is being known or adored by romantic partners most beneficial? Self-perceptions, relationship length, and responses to partner's verifying and enhancing appraisals. *Personality and Social Psychology Bulletin, 32,* 1283–1294.

Cann, A., Calhoun, L. G., & Banks, J. S. (1997). On the role of humor appreciation in interpersonal attraction: It's no joking matter. *Humor: International Journal of Humor Research, 10,* 77–89.

De Koning, E., & Weiss, R. L. (2002). The relational humor inventory: Functions of humor in close relationships. *American Journal of Family Therapy, 30,* 1–18.

Goodwin, R. (1990). Sex differences among partner preferences: Are the sexes really very similar? *Sex Roles, 23,* 501–513.

Goodwin, R., & Tang, D. (1991). Preferences for friends and close relationships partners: A cross-cultural comparison. *The Journal of Social Psychology, 131,* 579–581.

Gottman, J. M. (1979). *Marital interaction: Experimental investigations.* New York: Academic Press.

Gottman, J. M. (1994). *What predicts divorce? The relationship between marital processes and marital outcomes.* Hillsdale, NJ: Erlbaum.

Graham, E. E., Papa, M. J., & Brooks, G. P. (1992). Functions of humor in conversation: Conceptualization and measurement. *Western Journal of Communication, 56,* 161–183.

Hampes, W. P. (1992). Relation between intimacy and humor. *Psychological Reports, 71,* 127–130.

Hendrick, S. S. (1988). A generic measure of relationship satisfaction. *Journal of Marriage and the Family, 50,* 93–98.

Inman-Amos, J., Hendrick, S. S., & Hendrick, C. (1994). Love attitudes: Similarities between parents and between parents and children. *Family Relations: Interdisciplinary Journal of Applied Family Studies, 43,* 456–461.

Jackson, T., & Ebnet, S. (2006). Appraisal and coping in romantic relationship narratives: Effects of shyness, gender, and connoted affect of relationship events. *Individual Differences Research, 4,* 2–15.

Jacobs, E. C. (1985). The functions of humor in marital adjustment. *Dissertation Abstracts International,* 46 (5-B), 1688. (AAT No. 8514188).

Kazarian, S., & Martin, R. (2004). Humor styles, personality and well-being among Lebanese university students. *European Journal of Personality, 18,* 209–219.

Klein, D. N., & Kuiper, N. A. (2006). Humor styles, peer relationships, and bullying in middle childhood. *Humor: The International Journal of Humor Research, 19,* 383–404.

Knox, D., & Wilson, K. (1983). Dating problems of university students. *College Student Journal, 17,* 225–228.

Krokoff, L. J. (1991). Job distress is no laughing matter in marriage, or is it? *Journal of Social and Personal Relationships, 8,* 5–25.

Kuiper, N. A., & Borowicz-Sibenik, M. (2005). A good sense of humor doesn't always help: Agency and communion as moderators of psychological well-being. *Personality and Individual Differences, 38,* 365–377.

Lauer, R. H., Lauer, J. C., & Kerr, S. T. (1990). The long-term marriage: Perceptions of stability and satisfaction. *International Journal of Aging and Human Development, 31,* 189–195.

Lefcourt, H. M., & Martin, R. A. (1986). *Humor and life stress: Antidote to adversity.* New York: Springer.

Murstein, B. I., & Brust, R. G. (1985). Humor and interpersonal attraction. *Journal of Personality Assessment, 49,* 637–640.

Pike, G. R., & Sillars, A. L. (1985). Reciprocity of marital communication. *Journal of Social and Personal Relationships, 2,* 303–324.

Schaap, C., & Jansen-Nawas, C. (1987). Marital interaction, affect, and conflict resolution. *Sexual & Marital Therapy, 2,* 35–51.

Ting-Toomey, S. (1983). An analysis of verbal communication patterns in high and low marital adjustment groups. *Human Communication Research, 9,* 306–319.

Ziv, A. (1988). Humor's role in married life. *Humor: International Journal of Humor Research, 1,* 223–229.

Ziv, A., & Gadish, O. (1989). Humor and marital satisfaction. *The Journal of Social Psychology, 129,* 759–768.

Zusman, M. E., & Knox, D. (1998). Relationship problems of casual and involved university students. *College Student Journal, 32,* 606–609.

Words as Environmental Cues: The Effect of the Word "Loving" on Compliance to a Blood Donation Request

VIRGINIE CHARLES-SIRE
NICOLAS GUÉGUEN
Université de Bretagne-Sud

ALEXANDRE PASCUAL
Université de Bordeaux 2

SÉBASTIEN MEINERI
Université de Bretagne-Sud

ABSTRACT. In a field setting, students ($N = 3600$) on different campus locations were solicited to give blood during a special one-day drive. Solicitations were made through face-to-face interactions. The solicitors wore a white T-shirt with different inscriptions: no inscription, *Loving = Helping*, *Donating = Helping*. Results showed that, when compared to the no inscription condition, the number of donors increased when the solicitor-confederates wore the T-shirt *Loving = Helping* whereas no effect was found when the confederates wore the T-shirt *Donating = Helping*. The activation spreading theory is used to explain these results. The practical application of these results for blood donation drives and other health-related fundraising events is explored.

HEALTH SERVICES DEPEND ON SAFE and readily available supplies of blood to help save lives in many countries. However, the tighter screening of blood donors in recent years has led to a decrease in the volume of blood collected. At the same time, however, the demand for whole blood and blood products is increasing at rates far exceeding the collection rates (Gillespie & Hillyer, 2002). Unfortunately, there is a worldwide shortage of active blood donors to meet the increased demand for blood (Barkworth, Hibbert, Horne, & Tagg, 2002). In light of these circumstances, researching effective methods to increase blood donations has become vital.

To help meet fundraising demands, many techniques have been highlighted in the social psychology literature (see Pratkanis, 2007, for a review). Many of these techniques use sequential requests: the foot-in-the-door technique (Freedman & Fraser, 1966), the door-in-the-face technique (Cialdini et al., 1975), the low-ball tactic (Cialdini, Cacioppo, Basset, & Miller, 1978), the lure (Joule, Gouilloux, & Weber, 1989), and the 1-in-5 prize tactic (Horvitz & Pratkanis, 2002). Some of them use ingratiation tactics such as flattery (Dunyon, Gossling, Willden, & Seiter, 2010), incidental similarity (Burger, Messian, Patel, del Prado, & Anderson, 2004), or mimicry (Van Baaren, Holland, Kawakami, & Van Knippenberg, 2004). Others use nonverbal behaviors displayed by the solicitors such as tactile contact (Kleinke, 1977), smiling (Solomon et al., 1981), or gazing (Kleinke, 1980). The goal of the following experiment was to test the effectiveness of a word-priming technique on people's receptivity to a blood donation request.

Priming and Influence Behavior

Previous research on priming has demonstrated that the activation of a concept or mental representation can exert an influence on subsequent information processing or behavior. Bargh, Chen, and Burrows (1996) found that participants primed with words related to the elderly stereotype (e.g., *traditional, retired*) walked more slowly when leaving the experiment room than those in the control group; participants primed with the concept of rudeness interrupted the experimenter more quickly and frequently than did participants primed with the concept of politeness. After exposure to sentences describing a stereotyped behavior of dependence (e.g., *can't make decisions*), participants rated as more dependent a female target who performed the identical behavior as that of a male target. After exposure to sentences describing a stereotyped behavior of aggression (e.g., *threatens other people*), participants rated a male target as more aggressive than a female target (Banaji, Hardin, & Rothman, 1993).

Moreover, impression formation was found to be unrelated to the explicit memory of primes. Priming effects can take place when techniques of subliminal priming (i.e., extremely brief exposure to stimuli) are employed. Using this method, Zemack-Rugar, Bettman, and Fitzsimons (2007) showed that individuals subliminally primed with guilt-related adjectives were more helpful than those primed with sadness-related adjectives. Regardless of the duration of exposure to the stimulus, automatic or implicit social cognition occurs when information processing is made without the person's awareness, intention, possibility of control, or effort (Bargh, 1994).

To explain how mental representations can shape social behavior, theorists have hypothesized mental structures consisting of interconnected information or attributes. The main assumption is the spreading of activation: the activation of one concept is assumed to spread along a network of meaningfully associated information. Activating the concept of gender, for example, would activate the implicit knowledge structure of gender-linked traits, stereotypes, and norms of behavior.

Surrounding Cues and Behavioral Influence

Sentences, words, and visual images are environmental cues that can affect the behavior of individuals. Berkowitz and LePage (1967) found that in the presence of a weapon, participants in a laboratory administered more electric shocks to a confederate than without the presence of the weapon. In a restaurant, Jacob, Guéguen, and Boulbry (2011) displayed various figurative cues related to the sea (a boat or the figurine of a sailor, a napkin with a picture of a boat and poetry related to the sea) or not, in the control condition. The study results showed that figurative cues related to the sea increased the patrons' consumption of fish dishes. In a second experiment, they found the same effect with the word *fish* or fish drawings displayed in several places in the dining room of the restaurant.

Other research studies have shown that pictures present in the immediate environment of an individual affect behavior. Feinberg (1986) showed that in the presence of credit card cues, individuals were more likely to give money to a charitable cause than individuals who were not exposed to the credit card cues. Similarly, McCall and Belmont (1996) found that a tip tray stamped with a credit card insignia led restaurant patrons to leave bigger tips for the waiters or waitresses than when no insignia was primed on the tip tray. Using donation boxes located in various stores, Perrine and Heather (2000) found that responses to a fundraising request to benefit an animal welfare organization increased when color pictures of puppies were displayed on the donation boxes.

From a theoretical perspective, the behavioral consequences of environmental cues are not explained by a priming effect. Marketing scientists have used the stimulus-organism-response (SOR) theoretical model to explain these behavioral effects (Donovan & Rossiter, 1982; Mehrabian & Russel, 1974). When a verbal cue is a single word, this word is the stimulus (S) which causes a participant's (or organism's) evaluation (O) followed by some behavioral response (R). Two different evaluations are possible: positive or negative. Consequently, two behavioral responses are activated: approach or avoidance. Approach behaviors are seen as positive responses to someone or to an environment, such as a desire to interact with the person or to explore the environment whereas negative responses include not wanting to interact with the person or to spend time exploring the environment. Therefore, a single word could have the property of activating a positive response, which, in return, will lead the person who is exposed to this word to initiate contact with somebody or to be motivated to perform further behavior. The words *love* or *loving*, which represents important concepts in human groupings, could be potentially effective words to use for priming or as a cue in people's environment in order to influence their behaviors.

Love and Helping Behavior

Despite advances in the field of priming, automatic social cognition, or the role of environmental cues on people's behaviors, few attempts have been made to test the influence of an automatic activation of the cognition of love on social behavior. In a natural setting experiment by Lamy, Fischer-Lokou, and Guéguen (2008), participants were interviewed in the street and asked to recall a memory involving love, or, in the control condition, a piece of music they loved. Then, they met another confederate who asked them for money. Results showed that inducing the idea of love had a significant positive effect on compliance to the request for male passersby who were asked for help (giving some money "to take the bus") by a female confederate, but not for female passersby.

These results were confirmed in another study by Fischer-Lokou, Lamy, and Guéguen (2009) in which passersby were asked for directions. Participants induced to recall a memory of love agreed to give directions and spent more time giving directions to the requester than participants in the control condition who were induced to retrieve a piece of music they loved. By using the same methodology for inducing the idea of love versus the idea of music, Lamy, Fischer-Lokou, and Guéguen (2009) observed participants' reactions toward a confederate who inadvertently dropped a stack of compact discs when they were near each other. The results demonstrated that participants were more helpful when they were induced to recall a memory involving love.

In these studies, participants were asked to recall a memory of love that was important to them before their helpfulness was tested. However, research has shown that such behavioral effects can be reached in the absence of any direct reminiscence of love or conscious awareness of love scripts, by means of an automatic activation of the concept of love. In a recent experiment by Lamy, Fischer-Lokou, and Guéguen (2010), male passersby were asked by a female confederate to indicate the direction of Saint Valentine Street or Saint Martin Street in the control group. Thirty meters ahead, the participants then encountered another female confederate who asked for help, pretending a group of four disreputable-looking male confederates had taken her mobile telephone and refused to give it back. Results showed that participants primed with the cognition of Valentine helped the female confederate recover her mobile more frequently than those primed with the cognition of Martin.

The objective of the present experiment was to study the impact of a new but more basic method that induced love cognition and to evaluate its effect on a new dependent variable associated with pro-social behavior. We decided to test the effect of the single presence of the word *loving* on people's behavior. In the aforementioned studies, possible confounding effects are associated with helping behavior. Indeed, in these experiments, it was found that the love inducing variable led men to help a female confederate more readily than a male confederate or that such a love inducing variable was not effective with female participants. It would thus appear that the love inducing method led to further interest for romantic relations more often for men than for women, which, in turn, led only men to help female confederates. When participants were asked to recall a memory of a previous love episode that had occurred in their lives, such a memory could increase the motivation for further romantic relations. In the same way, the word *Valentine*, which was used as the priming concept in Lamy et al.'s (2010) study, is clearly associated with romantic relationships given the fact that Saint Valentine's Day is an annual commemoration, held on February 14, celebrating love and affection between intimate companions. Both types of priming information are clearly associated with romantic and intimate relationships, but not with general affection toward people.

We thus decided to test the single effect of the word *loving*, without any other associations, on people's altruistic behavior. Research by Guéguen, Jacob, and Charles-Sire (in press) has shown that altruistic behavior can also be obtained by a single exposition to a physical object related to love. In 12 bakeries, a pink opaque donation box was placed near the cash register with a message soliciting donations for a humanitarian project. The moneybox had a heart shape, a round shape, or a square shape. Results showed that more donations were placed in the moneybox with the heart shape. Guéguen (in press) confirmed this effect in a tipping behavior study. In three restaurants, a bill was placed under a dish that had a heart shape, a round shape, or a square shape. Results showed that more tips were left in the bill dish with the heart shape. The author found that the heart shape had no effect on the evaluation of the employee or on the self-evaluation of the patrons' usual level of altruistic behavior, thus showing that the effect of the heart shape was probably explained by the spreading activation theory only.

Love Prime and Blood Donation

Given the positive effects of the priming word *love* on helping requests, we undertook to test the effects of exposition to this love prime on solicited blood donor behavior. Compliance-growth procedures used in previous research failed to increase blood donations. The well-known foot-in-the-door technique (i.e., immediately following small upfront requests with more costly ones) failed, in three experiments, to increase the number of blood donors (Foss & Dempsey, 1979). The researchers explained this failure by arguing that although the foot-in-the-door technique is probably effective for minimal forms of aid, it is unlikely to significantly affect willingness to comply with more substantial requests involving behaviors that are psychologically costly to perform, such as blood donation requests. Similarly, use of the door-in-the-face technique (i.e., immediately following an initial extreme request with a less costly one) increased verbal compliance with blood donation requests but failed to increase behavioral compliance (Cialdini & Ascani, 1976). Applying the survey effect technique (Morwitz, Johnson, & Schmittlein, 1993) on very large samples, Godin, Sheeran, Conner, and Germain (2008) found that previous blood donors who were first asked to complete a mail-in questionnaire about donating blood more readily donated 6 months (+6.4%) and 12 months (+6.4%) later, as opposed to previous blood donors who did not receive the questionnaire.

Thus, given the discrepancies in results obtained between these various compliance-growth procedures, and in light of the positive effect of the loving prime technique on compliance with a broad spectrum of helping behaviors, we decided to test the effect of the loving prime technique with blood donation requests. As the studies mentioned in the previous section had shown that people primed with love show more altruism, we hypothesized that blood donation solicitors wearing the inscription *Loving = Helping* on their clothes would obtain more compliance to their request.

Method

Participants

The study participants were 3,600 students (1,536 males and 2,304 females) who were solicited to donate blood in various areas on the campus of a large university on the West-Atlantic coast in France during a during a one-day blood drive.

Materials

Our collaborators who solicited students on the campus wore a white, short-sleeved T-shirt. One T-shirt had no inscription; on the second one, *Aimer = Aider* (*Loving = Helping*) was written on the front (see Figure 1); on a third T-shirt, the inscription *Donner = Aider* (*Donating = Helping*) appeared.

Procedure

Sixteen young female students ($M = 20.4$ years, $SD = 1.1$) and 16 young male students ($M = 20.6$ years, $SD = 1.3$) were recruited on a voluntary basis in a social psychology course to act as solicitors in the study during the one-day blood drive regularly organized on this campus each year. This blood-collecting event is a typical type of event organized to obtain new donors: most of the students are young and in good health, and it appears that when people give blood for the first time when they are young, the probability that they will become regular donors is increased. Each solicitor wore a t-shirt and the rest of his/her clothing appearance was the same among female and male solicitors: black trousers and a second, black, long-sleeved t-shirt under the white t-shirt.

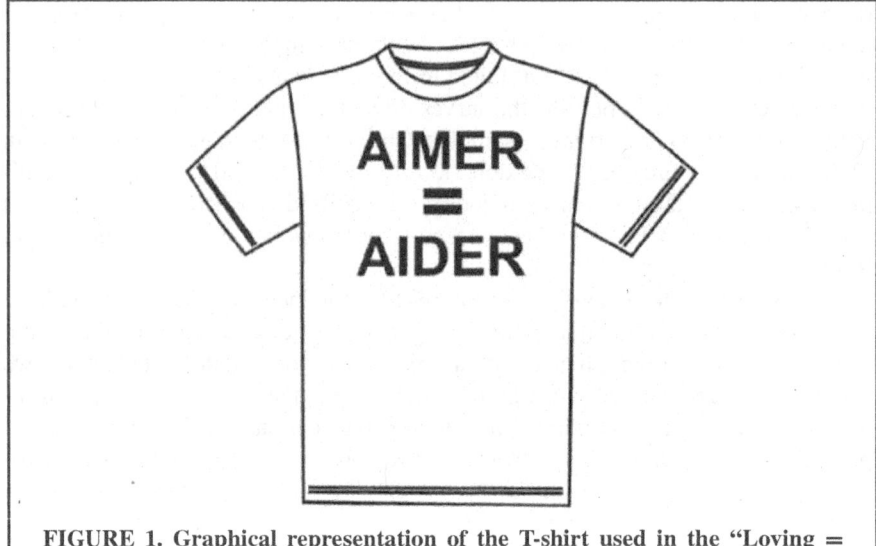

FIGURE 1. Graphical representation of the T-shirt used in the "Loving = Helping" condition.

The experiment was conducted on different campus locations in a large town of more than 300,000 inhabitant near the West Atlantic coast of France. The participants were solicited when entering different areas of the campus: libraries, cafeteria, and School buildings or when walking on the campus. As in previous years, announcements about the blood drive were posted in several places inside and outside the campus buildings.

Each solicitor was instructed to approach a student walking on the campus or entering/leaving one of the locations previously listed by saying the following:

Hello, I have been sent by the blood bank of France to make you aware of our blood drive, which is being conducted today near the cafeteria of the campus, from 10.00 a.m. to 5.30 p.m. Would you like to participate? (the solicitor noted the participant's intent). *Please take this card with you* (the solicitor offered a business card with information about the blood collection venue and collection hours) *and provide it as proof that we have spoken with you. Thanks very much and have a great day.*

In order to enable a later determination of which experimental group participants were in, the business cards offered were slightly different. There was a vertical bar on the upper right corner for the control (no inscription) group, the same vertical bar on the upper left corner for the Loving = Helping group, and a vertical bar on the bottom right corner for the Donating = Helping group. Then, later, the medical assistant who greeted potential donors as they entered the blood collection room was instructed to ask them whether they had received cards and, if so, to collect the cards from them.

Each solicitor was instructed to test 16 men and 24 women in each experimental condition. Thus, each of the 16 male and 16 female solicitors approached 120 participants (48 men and 72 women). This gender difference results from the fact that in the university where this experiment was carried out, there were 1.5 female students to every male student. The solicitor was instructed to change T-shirts after testing 8 men and 12 women. The order of the T-shirts worn by the solicitor was randomly determined. To prevent possible variations in the solicitors' behavior according to the experimental conditions, the solicitors were not informed of the experimental hypothesis. Earlier, a pre-test had been conducted in the street in order to enable the solicitors to familiarize themselves with the request and to make sure that they acted in the same way in the three experimental conditions.

Results

The dependent variables used in this experiment were the number of verbal agreements to blood donation requests during solicitor/participant interactions (i.e., verbal compliance, see Table 1) and the number of participants who actually came to the blood collection venue to offer a donation (i.e., behavioral compliance, see Table 2). A 3 (experimental conditions) × 2 (solicitor gender) × 2 (participant gender) Loglinear analysis test was performed with the number of participants who complied with the solicitors' request.

TABLE 1. Number of Participants Having Complied with the Blood Request in the Experimental Conditions According to Gender of the Participant and of the Confederate

Experimental condition	Male participants	Female participants	Total
No inscription			
Male confederates	34.7% (82/236)	43.0% (154/358)	39.7%
Female confederates	31.7% (79/249)	39.4% (148/376)	36.3%
Total	33.2%	42.5%	38.0%
"Loving = Helping"			
Male confederates	51.3% (117/228)	54.7% (191/349)	53.4%
Female confederates	49.8% (108/217)	55.2% (207/375)	53.2%
Total	50.6%	55.0%	53.3%
"Donating = Helping"			
Male confederates	40.7%% (98/241)	49.1% (183/373)	45.8%
Female confederates	42.7% (94/220)	47.4% (171/361)	45.6%
Total	41.6%	48.2%	45.6%

TABLE 2. Number of Participants Having Donated Their Blood in the Experimental Conditions According to Gender of the Participant and of the Confederate

Experimental condition	Male participants	Female participants	Total
Part 1: Versus total sample			
No inscription			
Male confederates	10.6% (25/236)	11.5% (41/358)	11.1%
Female confederates	9.2% (23/249)	11.7% (44/376)	10.7%
Total	9.9%	11.6%	10.9%
"Loving = Helping"			
Male confederates	15.8% (36/228)	16.9% (59/349)	17.1%
Female confederates	14.7% (32/217)	13.6% (51/375)	14.0%
Total	15.3%	15.2%	15.2%
"Donating = Helping"			
Male confederates	11.6% (28/241)	12.1% (45/373)	11.9%
Female confederates	13.2% (29/220)	11.6% (42/361)	12.2%
Total	12.4%	11.9%	12.1%
Part 2: Versus verbally compliant participants			
No inscription			
Male confederates	30.5% (25/82)	26.6% (41/154)	28.0%
Female confederates	29.1% (23/79)	29.7% (44/148)	29.5%
Total	29.8%	28.1%	28.7%
"Loving = Helping"			
Male confederates	30.8% (36/117)	30.9% (59/191)	30.8%
Female confederates	29.6% (32/108)	24.6% (51/207)	26.3%
Total	30.0%	27.6%	28.6%
"Donating = Helping"			
Male confederates	28.6% (28/98)	24.6% (45/183)	26.0%
Female confederates	30.9% (29/94)	24.6% (42/171)	26.8%
Total	29.7%	24.6%	26.4%

When considering verbal compliance, a main effect of the experimental conditions was found ($\chi^2(2, N = 3583) = 56.22, p < .001, r = 0.12$). Additional comparisons revealed that the no inscription response condition was statistically different from both the Loving = Helping condition (38.0% vs. 53.3%, $\chi^2(1, N = 2388) = 56.42, p < .001, r = .15$) and the Donating = Helping condition (38.0% vs. 45.6%, $\chi^2(1, N = 2414) = 14.74, p < .001, r = .08$). Comparison between the Loving = Helping condition and the Donating = Helping condition was significant (53.3% vs. 45.6%, $\chi^2(1, N = 2364) = 14.74, p < .001, r = .08$). A main effect of participant gender was found ($\chi^2(1, N = 3583) = 14.64, p < .001, r = 0.06$) revealing that women complied more frequently than men. No significant main effect of solicitor gender was found ($\chi^2(1, N = 3583) = 0.64$,

$p = .42, r = 0.01$). We found no significant interaction between participant gender and/or solicitor gender and experimental conditions ($p > .20$).

When considering behavioral compliance, a statistical analysis was performed with the total sample of participants solicited and with the subset of those who had verbally complied. The analysis of the number of total participants solicited (Table 2, Part 1). showed a main effect of the experimental conditions ($\chi^2(2, N = 3583) = 10.58, p = .005, r = 0.05$). Further comparisons revealed that the no inscription response condition was statistically different from the Loving = Helping condition (10.9% vs. 15.2%, $\chi^2(1, N = 2388) = 9.31, p = .002, r = .06$) but not significantly different than the Donating = Helping condition (10.9% vs. 12.1%, $\chi^2(1, N = 2414) = 0.88, p = .35, r = .02$). Comparison between the Loving = Helping condition and the Donating = Helping condition was significant (15.2% vs. 12.1%, $\chi^2(1, N = 2364) = 4.79, p = .03, r = .04$). Neither a main effect of participant gender ($\chi^2(1, N = 3,583) = 0.01, p = .75, r = 0.01$) nor a main effect of solicitor gender ($\chi^2(1, N = 3,583) = 0.47, p = .49, r = 0.01$) was found. We found no significant interaction between participant gender and/or solicitor gender and experimental conditions ($p > .20$).

When considering the analysis of participants who had verbally agreed with the request (Table 2, Part 2), no main effect of the experimental conditions was found ($\chi^2(2, N = 1632) = 0.93, p = .63, r = 0.02$) and further pairwise comparisons revealed no significant difference ($p > .30$). Neither a main effect of participant gender ($\chi^2(1, N = 1,632) = 1.87, p = .17, r = 0.03$) nor a main effect of solicitor gender ($\chi^2(1, N = 1,632) = 0.19, p = .66, r = 0.01$) was found. We found no significant interaction between participant gender and/or solicitor gender and experimental conditions ($p > .40$). Overall, these results suggest that the rate of behavioral compliance compared with the number of participants who verbally agreed to donate blood remained the same in the different experimental groups.

Discussion

Results from this field experiment confirm our initial hypothesis that associating words in an equation (*Love = Helping*) increased compliance with a blood donation request. First, a higher level of compliance was found when considering the data for verbal and behavioral compliance together. However, when considering only those people who initially consented to give blood (but did not actually donate), the Loving = Helping prime was not associated with higher compliance. Second, we found that the word *Loving* was linked to increased donations when compared with the control (no word) condition and was more effective than the word *Donating*. This effect is particularly interesting when considering behavioral compliance with the total number of participants solicited. In this case, it appears that the loving prime increased behavioral compliance compared to the control condition and the Donating = Helping condition, whereas the Donating = Helping condition revealed no statistical difference with the control condition. Thus, overall, these results seem to show that the loving prime had a high activation level compared to the other prime.

Such effect confirms previous research results that showed the influence of an automatic activation of the cognition of love on helping behavior (Fischer-Lokou et al., 2009; Lamy et al., 2008, 2009, 2010). In these previous studies, the activation of the love cognition was done by asking participants to think about previous romantic events in their life or through the name of a street (Saint Valentine Street). Results showed each time that the love activation increased the helping behavior only when male participants had the opportunity of offering some help to a female confederate. The love cognition had no effect when considering female participants and/or when a male confederate solicited help. In the present blood donating experiment, we did not find this gender effect. In all the conditions, we found that male and female participants complied in the same way to the blood donation request, whether a male or a female solicitor made the request. This no-gender effect could be explained by the fact that the cognition of love used in this experiment is not associated with romance or romantic relationships, but more probably with support, solidarity, and community relationships.

In France, where this experiment was carried out, blood donors receive no money. Giving blood is purely a type of human solidarity behavior. This could probably explain why the love cognition in our experiment led men and women to react in the same way to the request addressed by our male and female confederates. In the studies of Fischer-Lokou et al. (2009) and Lamy Fischer-Lokou, and Guéguen (2008, 2009, 2010), the love cognition was probably not related to support, solidarity, and community relationship, but rather to romance, romantic relationships, courtship, or, perhaps, with sex. This could be why only men reacted positively to such a priming effect when a woman asked them for help.

Studies highlighting cultural stereotypes have consistently shown that men are more eager for courtship relations or sexual intercourse than women (Hatfield, 1983; Sadalla, Kenrick, & Vershure, 1987). Such a variation in male and female behavior could explain why, in the love prime studies previously mentioned, male passersby helped female confederates more readily than female passersby did. The love cognition, in these circumstances, may have increased men's desire for romantic relationships, courtship, or sex, which, in turn, led them to help female confederates. Such cognition was probably not activated in female passersby when help was requested by a male confederate and/or was not appropriated when interacting with a female confederate. In the blood donating experiment, the love prime activated a different type of cognition, one that can be activated in the same way and at the same level with men and women, and that is why the same rate of compliance was found according to participant and/or confederate gender. In summary, the love prime was different in the previous set of studies and in this blood donating experiment, which explains the discrepant results found in helping behavior according to participant gender.

However, if the spreading activation explanation is plausible when considering the love prime, it does not explain why no effect was found in the Donating = Helping condition. Two possible explanations of this lack of significance are possible. First, this null effect could be explained by the reactance theory (Brehm & Brehm, 1981; Wicklund, 1974). This theory assumes that people feel free to do certain things. When this perceived freedom is threatened, people are motivated to restore it. In our experiment, the words *Donating = Helping* may have been perceived by the participants as a form of order to comply, which may have activated some reactance and led them to consider the request less favorably. In French, *donner* means "to donate," but the same verb is also used when people want to order someone to do something. Thus, in our experiment, this verb was perhaps interpreted as an order to give, which in turn led the solicited participants to see their freedom of behavior as threatened or restricted. This negative feeling could explain why we found a significant decrease in compliance to the request compared to that in the control condition.

Practical Applicability for Fundraising Professionals

This experiment has some practical applicability. Increasing the number of blood donations has become urgent (Barkworth et al., 2002), particularly in France where the number of donations per donor has decreased during the last decade (Danic & Lefrère, 2008). Thus, increasing the number of donors becomes important to compensate for this reduction and to increase number of blood products to treat people. Accordingly, organizations all around the world that are responsible for blood collection might be interested in testing various primes that would activate cognition associated with support, solidarity, and community relationships in their public relations, communications, or marketing campaigns.

The results found in this experiment show that one strategy might be to give the Loving = Helping T-shirt, or a variation thereof, to the thousands of volunteers who offer their time to organize blood collection events. An important increase in the total amount of blood donations could be expected. However, precautions must be taken in the choice of words printed on the T-shirt. In this experiment, we found that *Loving* was associated with an increase in the rate and the amount of donations whereas the word *Donating* was not. Testing the word prime on actual behavior beforehand is thus essential. Various pre-tests using an experimental design seem to be a good method to evaluate the efficiency of a prime. This experiment, conducted in a field setting, has demonstrated that simple and low-cost interventions can increase blood donations. A slogan such as *Loving = Helping* is easy to use in various solicitation situations and media, such as mail, electronic mail, face-to-face interactions, or on a badge worn by solicitors. This technique is easy to replicate, easy to use, and easy to adapt to other fundraising solicitations and pro-social requests.

Limitations

This study has some methodological limitations. In this experiment, we examined only students' compliance to a blood request addressed by a confederate of the same age. Previous studies conducted with the love inducing technique (Fischer-Lokou et al., 2009; Lamy et al., 2008, 2009) showed that this technique remains effective when the participants' age ranges between 20 and 60. However, these studies did not examine blood donation requests, and previous studies found that influence techniques used with blood donation requests are not always associated with an increase in the number of blood donors (Cialdini & Ascani, 1976; Foss & Dempsey, 1979).

This study was conducted in France, as were the previous studies that focused on activation of the cognition of love on helping behavior (Fischer-Lokou et al., 2009; Lamy et al., 2008, 2009). The positive effect of the word *loving* on blood donation might not be generalizable to other countries. Hence, replication in other countries is now necessary. Another limitation is that the Loving = Helping condition might have yielded more donations because the confederates changed their manner of solicitation. However, the confederates were unaware of the hypothesis made, and they had been trained in a pre-test to ensure that they acted in the same way in the three conditions.

Conclusion

In this study, we have stated that the loving concept acts as a prime that leads to the activation of further concepts associated with compassion, support, or solidarity that, in turn, lead participants to offer blood donations more readily. Such an explanation is congruent with the results of previous studies on priming (Bargh et al., 1996; Zemack-Rugar et al., 2007) which, unfortunately, never tested the word *love*, or words related to love, as primes. Our explanation, however, remains speculative, given that this study focused on end-behavior only. It appears necessary to test in further experiments whether feelings of compassion, support, or solidarity increase among groups of individuals who are exposed to a love prime.

AUTHOR NOTES

Virginie Charles-Sire is a doctoral student at the Université de Bretagne-Sud. Her current research interests are compliance gaining-procedures associated with blood donation. **Dr. Nicolas Guéguen** (Ph.D.) is a Professor of social behavior at the Université de Bretagne-Sud. His research interests are compliance gaining-procedures and nonverbal behavior. **Alexandre Pascual** is an associate professor of social psychology at the Université of Bordeaux 2. His research interests are compliance gaining-procedures associated with health and social behaviors. **Sébastien Meineri** is an associate professor of social psychology at the Université of Bretagne-Sud. His research interests are compliance gaining-procedures associated with ecology and altruism.

REFERENCES

Banaji, M. R., Hardin, C., & Rothman, A. J. (1993). Implicit stereotyping in person judgment. *Journal of Personality and Social Psychology, 65*, 272–281. doi: 10.1037/0022-3514.65.2.272

Bargh, J. A. (1994). The four horsemen of automaticity: Awareness, intention, efficiency, and control in social cognition. In R. S. Wyer, Jr. & T. K. Srull (Eds.), *Handbook of social cognition* (2nd ed., Vol. 1, pp. 1–40). Mahwah, NJ: Erlbaum.

Bargh, J. A., Chen, M., & Burrows, L. (1996). Automaticity of social behavior: Direct effects of trait construct and stereotype activation on action. *Journal of Personality and Social Psychology, 71*, 230–244.

Barkworth, L., Hibbert, S., Horne, S., & Tagg, S. (2002). Giving at risk? Examining perceived risk and blood donation behavior. *Journal of Marketing Management, 18*, 905–922. doi: 10.1037/0022-3514.71.2.230

Berkowitz, L., & LePage, A. (1967). Weapons as aggression-eliciting stimuli. *Journal of Personality and Social Psychology, 7*, 202–207.

Brehm, S. S., & Brehm, J. W. (1981). *Psychological reactance*. New York, NY: Academic Press. doi: 10.1037/h0025008

Burger, J. M., Messian, N., Patel, S., del Prado, A., & Anderson, C. (2004). What a coincidence! The effects of incidental similarity on compliance. *Personality and Social Psychology Bulletin, 30*, 35–43. doi: 10.1177/0146167203258838

Cialdini, R., & Ascani, K. (1976). Test of a concession procedure for inducing verbal, behavioral and further compliance with a request to give blood. *Journal of Applied Psychology, 61*, 295–300. doi: 10.1037/0021-9010.61.3.295

Cialdini, R. B., Cacioppo, J. T., Basset, R., & Miller, J. A. (1978). Low-ball procedure for producing compliance: Commitment then cost. *Journal of Personality and Social Psychology, 36*, 463–476. doi: 10.1145/2207676.2208698

Cialdini, R. B., Vincent, J. E., Lewis, S. K., Catalan, J., Wheeler, D., & Lee Darby, B. (1975). Reciprocal concessions procedure for inducing compliance: The door-in-the-face technique. *Journal of Personality and Social Psychology, 31*, 206–215. doi: 1975-11600-001

Danic, B., & Lefrère, J.-J. (2008). *De vous à moi, donnez votre sang* [From you to me, give you blood]. Paris, France: Medi-Text Editions.

Donovan, R. J., & Rossiter, J. R. (1982). Store atmosphere: An environmental psychology approach. *Journal of Retailing, 58*, 35–57. doi: 10.1101/gad.1502407

Dunyon, J., Gossling, V., Willden, S., & Seiter, J. S. (2010). Compliments and purchasing behavior in telephone sales interactions. *Psychological Reports, 106*, 27–30. doi: 10.2466/PR0.106.1.27-30

Feinberg, R. A. (1986). Credit cards as spending facilitating stimuli: A conditioning interpretation. *Journal of Consumer Research, 13*, 348–356. doi: 10.1086/209074

Fischer-Lokou, J., Lamy, L., & Guéguen, N. (2009). Induced cognitions of love and helpfulness to lost persons. *Social Behavior and Personality, 37*, 1213–1220. doi: 10.1007/s12144-009-9059-9

Foss, R., & Dempsey, C. (1979). Blood donation and the foot-in-the-door technique: A limiting case. *Journal of Personality & Social Psychology, 37,* 580–590. doi: 10.1037/0022-3514.37.4.580

Freedman, J. L., & Fraser, S. C. (1966). Compliance without pressure: The foot-in-the-door technique. *Journal of Personality and Social Psychology, 4,* 195–202. doi: 10.1037/h0023552

Gillespie, T. W., & Hillyer, C. D. (2002). Blood donors and factors impacting the blood donation decision. *Transfusion Medicine Reviews, 16,* 115–130. doi: 10.1053/tmrv.2002.31461

Godin, G., Sheeran, P., Conner, M., & Germain, M. (2008). Asking questions changes behavior: Mere measurement effects on frequency of blood donation. *Health Psychology, 27,* 179–184. doi: 10.1037/0278-6133.27.2.179

Guéguen, N. (in press). Helping with all your heart: The effect of cardioid dishes on tipping behavior. *Journal of Applied Social Psychology.*

Guéguen, N., Jacob, C., & Charles-Sire, V. (2011). Helping with all your heart: The effect of cardioid cues on compliance with a humanitarian aid request. *Social Marketing Quarterly, 17,* 2–11.

Hatfield, E. (1983). What do women want from love and sex? In E. R. Allgeier & N. B. McComick (Eds.), *Changing boundaries* (pp. 103–134). Palo Alto, CA: Mayfield.

Horvitz, T., & Pratkanis, A. R. (2002). A laboratory demonstration of the fraudulent telemarketers' 1-in-5 prize tactic. *Journal of Applied Social Psychology, 31,* 310–317. doi: 10.1111/j.1559-1816.2002.tb00217.x

Jacob, C., Guéguen, N., & Boulbry, G. (2011). Presence of various figurines on a restaurant table and consumer choice: Evidence for an associative link. *Journal of Foodservice Business Research, 14,* 47–52. doi: 10.1080/15378020.2011.548221

Joule, R.-V., Gouilloux, F., & Weber, F. (1989). The lure: A new compliance procedure. *The Journal of Social Psychology, 129,* 741–749. doi: 10.1080/00224545.1989.9712082

Kleinke, C. (1977). Compliance to requests made by gazing and touching experimenters in field settings. *Journal of Experimental Social Psychology, 13,* 218–223. doi: 10.1016/0022-1031(77)90044-0

Kleinke, C. (1980). Interaction between gaze and legitimacy of request on compliance in a field setting. *Journal of Nonverbal Behavior, 5,* 3–12. doi: 10.1007/BF00987050

Lamy, L., Fischer-Lokou, J., & Guéguen, N. (2008). Semantically induced memories of love and helping behavior. *Psychological Reports, 102,* 418–424. doi: 10.2466/pr0.102.2.418-424

Lamy, L., Fischer-Lokou, J., & Guéguen, N. (2009). Induced reminiscence of love and chivalrous helping. *Current Psychology, 28*(3), 202–209. doi: 10.1007/s12144-009-9059-9

Lamy, L., Fischer-Lokou, J., & Guéguen, N. (2010) Valentine Street promotes chivalrous helping. *Swiss Journal of Psychology, 69,* 169–172. doi: 10.1024/1421-0185/a000019

McCall, M., & Belmont, H. (1996). Credit card insignia and restaurant tipping: Evidence for an associative link. *Journal of Applied Psychology, 81,* 609–613. doi: 10.1037/0021-9010.81.5.609

Mehrabian, A., & Russell, J. A. (1974). *An approach to environmental psychology.* Cambridge, MA: MIT Press.

Morwitz, V. G., Johnson, E., & Schmittlein, D. (1993). Does measuring intent change behavior? *Journal of Consumer Research, 20,* 46–61. doi: 10.1086/209332

Perrine, R. M., & Heather, S. (2000). Effects of picture and even-a-penny-will-help appeals on anonymous donations to charity. *Psychological Reports, 86,* 551–559.

Pratkanis, A. R. (2007). *The science of social influence.* New York, NY: Psychological Press.

Sadalla, E. K., Kenrick, D. T., & Vershure, B. (1987). Dominance and heterosexual attraction. *Journal of Personality and Social Psychology, 52*, 730–738. doi: 10.1037/0022-3514.52.4.730

Solomon, H., Zener-Solomon, L., Arnone, M., Maur, B., Reda, R., & Roth, E. (1981). Anonymity and helping. *The Journal of Social Psychology, 113*, 37–43. doi: 10.1080/00224545.1981.9924347

Van Baaren, R. B., Holland, R. W., Kawakami, K., & Van Knippenberg, A. (2004). Mimicry and prosocial behaviour. *Psychological Science, 14*, 71–74. doi:10.1111/j.1467-9280.2005.01619.x

Wicklund, R. A. (1974). *Freedom and reactance*. Oxford, England: Lawrence Erlbaum.

Zemack-Rugar, Y., Bettman, J. R., & Fitzsimons, G. J. (2007). The effects of nonconsciously priming emotion concepts on behavior. *Journal of Personality and Social Psychology, 93*, 927–939. doi: 10.1037/0022-3514.93.6.927

PART II: LONELINESS AND INTIMATE RELATIONSHIPS

Loneliness and Marital Adjustment of Turkish Couples

AYHAN DEMIR

HÜROL FIŞILOĞLU

ABSTRACT. The purpose of the present study was to investigate the relationship between loneliness and marital adjustment in Turkish couples. Some demographic correlates of loneliness and marital adjustment such as gender, age, duration of the marriage, type of marriage, and degree of acquaintance before marriage were also examined. The UCLA Loneliness Scale (D. Russell, L. A. Peplau, & C. E. Cutrona, 1980) and the Dyadic Adjustment Scale (G. B. Spanier, 1976) were administered to 58 heterosexual married couples. The results showed that loneliness was significantly and negatively correlated with marital adjustment. For the demographic correlates, significant results were as follows: Self-selected marriages resulted in lower loneliness scores and higher marital adjustment scores than the arranged type of marriage, and marital adjustment increased parallel to an increase in the degree of acquaintance before marriage. The findings and implications are discussed in the context of practice and research.

ALL HUMAN BEINGS FEEL LONELINESS at some point in their lives (McWhirter, 1990). In addition to individual experience, societies, especially Western societies, have also been accepted as extremes, in which loneliness is a common and serious problem (Rotenberg & Morrison, 1993). This universally recognized and experienced phenomenon gained the attention of researchers in the 1970s (West, Kellner, & Moore-West, 1986). Although research on loneliness has increased in the past two decades, no consensus has been reached concerning a definition of the construct (Medora & Woodward, 1986), but various definitions have arisen. Seligman (1983) described loneliness as one of the most poorly understood of all psychological phenomena. DeJong-Gierveld (1987) considered loneliness multidimensional and defined it as a lack of opportunity to have a relationship with others on an intimate level. According to Peplau and Perlman, "Loneliness is the unpleasant experience that occurs when a person's network of social relations is significantly deficient in either quality or quantity" (1982, p. 4). In general, the most commonly accepted definition of loneliness includes the following three characteristics: (a) It results from the perceived lack of relationship in a person's social life; (b) it is a subjective experience, not equivalent with social isolation; and (c) it is unpleasant and distressing (Peplau & Perlman, 1982).

Parallel to various definitions of loneliness, one can also see different classifications. For example, Weiss (1973) had a social relation dimension in his classification of loneliness and stated that loneliness was of two types: emotional, characterized by the absence of an attachment figure, and social isolation, manifested by the absence of a social network. Young (1982) included time and situation dimensions in a classification of loneliness and defined three different loneliness types: transient, consisting of brief, occasional lonely moods; chronic, lasting 2 or more consecutive years; and situational, associated with major stressful events.

A review of the literature suggests that loneliness is correlated with a number of variables. A primary goal of these studies has been to identify the causes and consequences of loneliness. Health and psychological problems (Sadava & Thompson, 1986), alcoholism (Nerviano & Gross, 1976), suicide (Diamant & Windholz, 1981), and depression (Lobdell & Perlman, 1986) were the most frequently studied correlates of loneliness. Also, the West et al. (1986) review of the studies on loneliness showed that child abuse and neglect, bereavement, physical health problems, and stress are other possible correlates of loneliness. However, as Borys and Perlman (1985) emphasized in the case of gender, to state a simple consistent association between these variables and loneliness is difficult.

Among the numerous variables that have been correlated with loneliness, marital status also has been a focus of investigation (Bloom, Asher, & White, 1978). One reason for this focus is the view that the most common form of loneliness is to be without a partner. Barbour (1993) stated that there is a tendency to believe that being married wards off loneliness irrespective of the extent to which the marriage is satisfying, because there is always a potential companion around. Several findings have shown that loneliness is less common among married couples than single people (Essex & Nam, 1987; Gubrium, 1974; Harvey & Bahr, 1974; Kobrin & Hendershot, 1977; Parlee, 1979; Russell, 1982; Weiss, 1985).

Although most of these studies showed that loneliness is less common among married people, when unmarried people are divided into various other specific groups, the results vary somewhat by sample. Lopata (1969) found that 70% of a random sample of urban widows mentioned loneliness as a problem, and 48% of them said loneliness was the major problem they faced. The general tendency appeared to be that single (never married) people are less lonely than divorced or widowed people (Perlman & Peplau, 1984). Fortunately, there are some data to show that the loneliness of widows declines over time (Lopata, Heinemann, & Baum, 1982).

Although having a partner was found to be a positive factor modifying loneliness, the quality of family relations should also be considered, especially when basic social and emotional needs of family members have not been met and the home environment has often been marked with conflict, abuse, and neglect (Barbour, 1993). Thus, it is not merely the existence of partners but the quality of relationships that matters. According to Jones, Hobbs, and Hockenbury (1982), loneliness is not identical to solitude or any particular relational status, but such factors may be involved in the development of loneliness.

Another line of research on marital status has focused on gender. In general, it has been found that younger women report loneliness more than men, but in later life, when marital status is considered, unmarried men, whether widowed, divorced, or never married, report loneliness more than unmarried women (West et al., 1986). Perlman, Gerson, and Spinner (1978) reported that widowed men were lonelier than married men, but no differences were observed between widowed and married women. Researchers have consistently shown that married women are less lonely than unmarried women, especially unmarried women who live alone (deJong-Gierveld & Raadschelders, 1982; Rubenstein & Shaver, 1982). Tornstam (1992) found gender differences in loneliness among only specific individuals. According to the results, married women between 20 and 49 years of age reported a higher degree of loneliness than married men.

Given that the quality of the interaction in family life is so important, one single-item measurement (married vs. unmarried) alone is not adequate to cover loneliness. Parallel research on various dimensions of family and married life such as adjustment, satisfaction, growth, competence, stress, boredom, support, roles, communication, and boundaries also has to be done. For example, Perlman et al. (1978) studied marital satisfaction and found that among married women, low marital satisfaction was associated with increased loneliness. In another study, Lobdell and Perlman (1986) found that children's perceptions of their parents' marital satisfaction were correlated with their loneliness but not with parents' own reports of their marital satisfaction. In that study, the Dyadic Satisfaction subscale of the Dyadic Adjustment Scale (Spanier, 1976) was used to assess marital satisfaction.

The most comprehensive study related to measurement of family life was Ross's (1992) study. In that study of parental loneliness, Ross included 10 family dimensions such as family satisfaction and intimacy and found that loneliness was significantly and negatively correlated with intimacy in the marriage relationship. Ross's results also showed that 20% of the wives and 24% of the husbands were significantly lonely.

The literature on the relationship between married life and loneliness clearly shows that the inclusion and accurate measurement of different dimensions of family life are crucial for more conclusive results. In this context, it is important to exclude the parental dimension while evaluating the marital adjustment of husband and wife. In the conceptualization of the family, it is vital to note that husband and wife are the main parts of the system. The embeddedness of the marital subsystem within other family subsystems such as the parental subsystem suggests that marital adjustment has many consequences for those subsystems (Constantine, 1986; Minuchin, 1974).

Our specific aim in the present research was to investigate the relationship between loneliness and marital adjustment among a Turkish sample and to make a contribution to Turkish literature as well as to cross-cultural literature. In addition to those features common in most cultures, there could be culture-specific characteristics of Turkish marriages. In recent years, Turkish marriages have undergone rapid change. Arranged marriages are on the decrease; self-reported loneliness in marriages and divorce rates are increasing (Atalay, Kontaş, Beyazyt, & Madenoğlu, 1992; State Institute of Statistics, 1996). Therefore, demographic correlates of loneliness and marital adjustment such as type of marriage (arranged or self-selected), duration of marriage, degree of acquaintance before marriage, gender, and age have also been included in the study.

Method

Participants

The participants (116 individuals who were married couples; 58 women, 58 men) had also been the participants in a reliability and validity study of the Dyadic Adjustment Scale for a Turkish sample (Fişiloğlu & Demir, 1997). The mean age of the couples was 36 years, and the length of their marriages ranged from 3 months to 38 years, with a mean length of 11.7 years. Education levels ranged from primary school ($n = 14$), secondary school ($n = 39$), university ($n = 55$), to graduate school ($n = 8$). The participants were all in their first marriage; 78 individuals stated that they had chosen their spouses themselves (self-selected type of marriage). Spouses had been chosen for 24 of the participants by their families (arranged type of marriage). Fourteen participants reported that their families had introduced them to their spouses-to-be but that they themselves made the definite decision to marry (self-selection within the arrangement type of marriage). The maximum number of children per family was three.

Instruments

Two scales were used in the present study. All the participants were administered the revised UCLA Loneliness Scale (Russell, Peplau, & Cutrona, 1980) and the Dyadic Adjustment Scale (DAS; Spanier, 1976). A demographic data sheet was also developed covering the information related to gender, age, duration of marriage, type of marriage, and degree of acquaintance before marriage.

The UCLA Loneliness Scale has been widely used in loneliness research. Scores are based on 20 items with a 4-point Likert scale ranging from *never* to *often*. The scale consists of 10 positively worded statements reflecting satisfaction with social relationships and 10 negatively worded statements reflecting dissatisfaction with social relationships. The total scores range from 20 to 80, with higher scores indicating greater loneliness. Reported alpha for the UCLA was .94; test–retest reliability over 2 months was .73; concurrent validity was in the form of correlations with the Beck Depression Inventory ($r = .62$), with the Costello-Comrey Anxiety Scale ($r = .32$), and Depression Scale ($r = .55$; Russell et al., 1980).

In the present study, the Turkish version of the UCLA Loneliness Scale (Demir, 1989) was used. The reported results of Demir's (1989) reliability and validity study were as follows: the test–retest reliability over 5 weeks was .94. The alpha coefficient was .96. Concurrent validity was demonstrated with a lonely versus nonlonely person's self-report of behavior and feelings. Correlation between the UCLA Loneliness Scale and the Beck Depression Inventory was .77; correlation between the UCLA Loneliness Scale and the Multiscore Depression Inventory Social Introversion subscale was .82.

The DAS is a 32-item instrument developed by Spanier (1976) to assess the quality of the relationship perceived by married or cohabiting couples. The total score is the sum of all items, ranging from 0 to 151. Higher scores reflect a higher perception of the quality of the relationship. The DAS has a coefficient alpha of .96 for the total instrument and, for the various subscales, ranges from .73 to .94, for the same sample. The scale scores have good content and construct validity (Spanier, 1976). The reliability and validity study of the DAS for Turkish couples was done by Fişiloğlu and Demir (1997). The internal consistency was .90. The computed split-half reliability coefficient was .85 ($\alpha = .89$ for Part 1, $\alpha = .73$ for Part 2). In addition, the construct validity of the Turkish version of the DAS had a correlation with the Locke-Wallace Marital Adjustment Test ($r = .82$).

Procedure

The participants were married individuals who were recruited by purposive sampling (Kerlinger, 1986) from different cities in Turkey. The purpose was to include individuals who were in their first marriage with no more than three children and with no self-labeled problem in their marriages. Furthermore, we aimed to have a heterogeneous sample representing various education levels, lengths of marriage, and types of marriage. After verbal instructions had been given to the participants, the instruments were administered by the researchers and research assistants; participants completed and returned the instruments individually after about 30 min. Some participants completed the instruments at home, but they were discouraged from discussing their answers with each other; they returned completed instruments in envelopes provided by the researchers.

Results

To investigate the relationship between loneliness and marital adjustment, we computed a Pearson correlation coefficient in which loneliness was significantly and negatively correlated with marital adjustment ($r = -.35, p < .001$). The same correlation was calculated for the men ($r = -.35, p < .001$) and for the women ($r = -.35, p < .001$).

To determine whether there were any gender differences in loneliness and marital adjustment, we conducted t tests, which revealed that there were no significant differences between men and women in loneliness and marital adjustment. The correlation coefficients of loneliness and marital adjustment for age and duration of marriage indicated that these demographic characteristics were not related significantly to loneliness and marital adjustment.

The result of a one-way analysis of variance (ANOVA) indicated that the mean difference between marital adjustment by type of marriage (self-selected and arranged) was significant, $F(2, 111) = 5.21, p < .01$. Tukey's honestly significant difference (HSD) Multiple Comparison Test showed that the self-selected group ($M = 110.9$) differed significantly from the arranged group ($M = 99.2$). The group who self-selected their spouses had a higher degree of marital adjustment than the group whose marriages were arranged.

The result of a one-way ANOVA indicated that the mean difference on loneliness by type of marriage was significant, $F(2, 111) = 4.32, p < .025$. Tukey's HSD Multiple Comparison Test showed that the self-selected group differed ($M = 33.0$) significantly from the arranged group ($M = 38.3$). Thus, the group who self-selected their spouses had a lower degree of loneliness than the group whose marriages were arranged. The result of a one-way ANOVA also indicated that the mean difference for loneliness by degree of acquaintance before marriage was not significant.

The result of a one-way ANOVA indicated that the mean difference on marital adjustment by degree of acquaintance before marriage (a little, $n = 26$; a fair amount, $n = 22$; much, $n = 47$; very much, $n = 21$) was significant, $F(3, 111) = 7.33, p < .001$. Tukey's HSD Multiple Comparison Test showed that the group that needed "very much" adjustment ($M = 118.9$) significantly differed from the groups that needed "a little" ($M = 98.6$) and "a fair amount" ($M = 103.5$). The group that needed "much" adjustment ($M = 110.9$) also differed significantly from the group that needed "a little" ($M = 98.6$). Thus, marital adjustment increased parallel to an increase in degree of acquaintance before marriage.

Discussion

There is a great deal of information in the literature concerning loneliness and marital status. Several findings suggest that loneliness is less common among married people than among singles (Perlman & Peplau, 1984). As Barbour (1993) suggested, the general assumption is that marriage wards off loneliness, irrespective of the quality of the marriage, because there is always a possible partner around, whereas, according to Jones et al. (1982), loneliness is not identical with any particular relational status. Thus, it is the quality of the relationship that matters.

The principal focus of our investigation was the relationship between loneliness and marital adjustment. The results showed that there was an inverse relation between loneliness and marital adjustment. That is, a low level of loneliness was associated with good marital adjustment. This result could be explained and discussed in a number of ways. One possible explanation may be the role of married life. Today, in general, anxiety, fear, and questioning fundamental values are basic characteristics of life around the world. Confidence in traditional values is being challenged around the world (Boszormenyi-Nagy & Spark, 1984; Kağitcibaşi, 1996).

As O'Leary (1987) suggested, a high percentage of all clients in mental health clinics indicate that marital problems are part of their own personal difficulties, and children's problems are maintained or exacerbated by marital discord. Even physical health is influenced by marriage (Joung et al., 1997). Although establishing causality is not possible with the information obtained from this study, it could be stated that a happy married life continues to be the avenue through which people function better and feel less lonely.

Although in most studies, women reported more loneliness and dissatisfaction with their marriages than men (Beach, Sandeen, & O'Leary, 1990; Tornstam, 1992; West et al., 1986), continued exploration of the effect of gender on loneliness and marital adjustment has not produced conclusive results. Thus, the present nonsignificant gender difference on loneliness and marital adjustment should be interpreted within this context. Nevertheless, in the light of the literature and clinical application, possible differences in the perception of marriage related to gender differences could not be ruled out. For example, in a study of Turkish couples, Tezer (1992, 1994) found that women's perceptions that their husbands were the source of conflict negatively affected their marital adjustment.

Type of marriage (self-selected vs. arranged) is one of the most studied variables in Turkey (Atalay et al., 1992; Aydoğan, 1994; Erdentuğ, 1991; Hortaçsu & Oral, 1994; Imamoğlu & Yasak, 1997; Timur, 1972). The general conclusion is that within its historical development, the self-selected type of marriage has been increasing in Turkey. Possible reasons for this trend could be related to the following characteristics of the self-selected type of marriage: a higher level of self-disclosure and interaction with the partner places more emphasis on relationship motives for marriage and equality, and greater levels of comparative love (Hortaçsu & Oral, 1994). Therefore, it could be concluded that characteristics mentioned earlier may have a positive effect on the quality of the marriage both in terms of marital adjustment and the problems of loneliness.

Higher marital adjustment scores and lower loneliness scores for the self-selected type of marriage than for the arranged type of marriage could be accepted as support for a general trend in Turkey. The positive effect on marital adjustment of knowing each other before marriage also supports the result of the self-selected type of marriage. Another finding of the study was that good marital adjustment increases parallel to an increase in the degree of acquaintance before marriage. This positive effect on marital adjustment of acquaintance before marriage is also true for the arranged type of marriage. As Hortaçsu and Oral (1994) stated, arranged marriages often occur within kinship networks, so partners know each other long before the marriage. This crucial role of partners' acquaintance before marriage could be included in programs on marital adjustment.

In general, clinicians in the field of family and marital therapy have to focus on both the quality of the marriage and on loneliness. The focus on the demographic correlates of marital adjustment, especially gender and type of marriage, is important for clinicians in practice with the Turkish couples due to the fast changing cultural context of Turkey. Marriage and family therapists might consider different intervention programs. The first level of intervention could consist of preventive programs such as marital enrichment programs. The second level may be at the clinical level, where the aim is to help couples in therapy to function better.

Certain limitations of the present study should be considered in interpreting the results and in planning future research. A first limitation of the study concerns the inability to assess a causal relationship between loneliness and marital adjustment. The design of the study does not determine the cause and effect relationship and prevents any conclusive statement regarding the direction of the relationship. A second limitation of the study is the issue of generalizability of the results. The study was restricted by the availability of participants. A final limitation of the study could concern the issue of the use of a self-report measure to assess loneliness and marital adjustment. Thus, it could be argued that a possible contaminating effect of social desirability, especially for marital adjustment, might bias the results. However, though self-report methods are sometimes vulnerable to social desirability, in general, they have strong face validity (Schumm, 1990). Therefore, we used self-report measures similar to those used elsewhere in the field.

The results of this study showed an inverse relationship between loneliness and marital adjustment. This relationship must be taken into account both in research and in practice. However, the necessity still exists for further exploration to produce a more conclusive statement.

REFERENCES

Atalay, B., Kontaş, M., Beyazit, S., & Madenoğlu, K. (1992). *Türk aile yapisinin araştirmasi* [Investigation of Turkish family structure]. Ankara, Turkey: DPT Matbaasi.

Aydoğan, F. (1994). *Van'da kirsal kesiminden kente gelen ailelerin evlenmeye ilişkin tutum ve davranişlarindaki değişmeler* [The changes of attitude and behaviors of migrants who moved from rural area to urban area]. Aile Kurultayi, Ankara, Turkey: T. C. Başbakanlik Aile Araştirma Kurumu Başkanliği.

Barbour, A. (1993). Research report: Dyadic loneliness in marriage. *Journal of Group Psychotherapy, Psychodrama, and Sociometry, 46,* 70–72.

Beach, S. R. H., Sandeen, E. E., & O'Leary, K. D. (1990). *Depression in marriage.* New York: The Guilford Press.

Bloom, B. L., Asher, J. J., & White, S. W. (1978). Marital disruption as a stressor: A review and analysis. *Psychological Bulletin, 85,* 867–894.

Borys, S., & Perlman, D. (1985). Gender differences in loneliness. *Personality and Social Psychology Bulletin, 11,* 63–74.

Boszormenyi-Nagy, B. I., & Spark, M. G. (1984). *Invisible loyalties: Reciprocity in intergenerational family therapy.* New York: Brunner/Mazel.

Constantine, L. L. (1986). *Family paradigms: The practice of theory in family therapy.* New York: Guilford Press.

deJong-Gierveld, J. (1987). Developing and testing a model of loneliness. *Journal of Personality and Social Psychology, 53,* 119–128.

deJong-Gierveld, J., & Raadschelders, J. (1982). Types of loneliness. In L. A Peplau & D. Perlman (Eds.), *Loneliness: A sourcebook of current theory, research, and therapy* (pp. 105–119). New York: Wiley-Interscience.

Demir, A. (1989). UCLA yalnizlyk ölçeğinin geçerlik ve güvenirliği [The validity and reliability of UCLA Loneliness Scale]. *Psikoloji Dergisi, 7,* 23, 14–18.

Diamant, L., & Windholz, G. (1981). Loneliness in college students: Some therapeutic consideration. *Journal of Student Personnel, 22,* 515–579.

Erdentuğ, N. (1991). Türkiyenin Karadeniz bölgesinde evlenme görenekleri ve törenleri [The marriage ceremony and rules of Black Sea region of Turkey]. In B. Dikeçligil & A. Çiğdem (Eds.), *Aile Yazilari: Evlilik Kurumu ve Ilişkileri* (pp. 319–327). Ankara, Turkey: T. C. Başbakanlyk Aile Araştirma Kurumu Başkanliği Yayinlari.

Essex, M. J., & Nam, J. (1987). Marital status and loneliness among older women: The differential importance of close family and friends. *Journal of Marriage and the Family, 49,* 93–106.

Fişiloğlu, H., & Demir, A. (1997). *Applicability of the Dyadic Adjustment Scale for measurement of marital quality with Turkish couples.* Manuscript submitted for publication.

Gubrium, J. F. (1974). Marital desolation and the evaluation of everyday life in old age. *Journal of Marriage and the Family, 36,* 107–113.

Harvey, C. D., & Bahr, H. M. (1974). Widowhood, morale and affiliation. *Journal of Marriage and the Family, 36,* 97–106.

Hortaçsu, N., & Oral, A. (1994). Comparison of couple- and family-initiated marriages in Turkey. *The Journal of Social Psychology, 134,* 229–239.

Imamoğlu, O., & Yasak, Y. (1997). Dimensions of marital relationships as perceived by Turkish husbands and wives. *Genetic, Social, and General Psychology Monographs, 123,* 211–232.

Jones, W. H., Hobbs, S. A., & Hockenbury, D. (1982). Loneliness and social skill deficits. *Journal of Personality and Social Psychology, 42,* 682–689.

Joung, I. M. A., Stronks, K., Mheen, V. D., Poppel, F. W. A., Meer J. B. W., & Mackenbach, J. P. (1997). The contribution of intermediary factors to marital status differences in self-reported health. *Journal of Marriage and the Family, 59,* 467–490.

Kağitcibaşi, Ç. (1996). *Family and human development across cultures: A view from the other side.* Hillsdale, NJ: Erlbaum.

Kobrin, E. F., & Hendershot, E.G. (1977). Do family ties reduce mortality? Evidence from the United States, 1966-1968. *Journal of Marriage and the Family, 39,* 737-745.

Lobdell, J., & Perlman, D. (1986). The intergenerational transmission of loneliness: A study of college females and their parents. *Journal of Marriage and the Family, 48,* 589-595.

Lopata, H. Z. (1969). Loneliness: Forms and components. *Social Problems, 17,* 248-261.

Lopata, H. Z., Heinemann, G. D., & Baum, J. (1982). Loneliness: Antecedents and coping strategies in the lives of widows. In L. A. Peplau & D. Perlman (Eds.), *Loneliness: A sourcebook of current theory, research, and therapy* (pp. 310-326). New York: Wiley-Interscience.

McWhirter, B. T. (1990). Loneliness: A review of current literature, with implications for counseling and research. *Journal of Counseling and Development, 68,* 417-422.

Medora, N., & Woodward, J. C. (1986). Loneliness among adolescent college students at the midwestern university. *Adolescence, 21,* 391-402.

Minuchin, S. (1974). *Families and family therapy.* Cambridge, MA: Harvard University Press.

Nerviano, N. J., & Gross, W. F. (1976). Loneliness and locus of control for alcoholic males: Validity against Murrey need and Catell trait dimension. *Journal of Clinical Psychology, 32,* 479-484.

O'Leary, K. D. (1987). The emergence of marital assessment. In K. D. O'Leary (Ed.), *Assessment of marital discord: An integration for research and clinical practice* (pp. 1-12). Hillsdale, NJ: Erlbaum.

Parlee, M. B. (1979). The friendship bond. *Psychology Today, 113,* 43-54.

Peplau, L. A., & Perlman, D. (1982). Perspectives on loneliness. In L. A. Peplau & D. Perlman (Eds.), *Loneliness: A sourcebook of current theory, research, and therapy* (pp. 1-18). New York: Wiley-Interscience.

Perlman, D., Gerson, A. C., & Spinner, B. (1978). Loneliness among senior citizens: An empirical report. *Essence, 2,* 239-249.

Perlman, D., & Peplau, L. A. (1984). Loneliness research: A survey of empirical findings. In L. A. Peplau & S. E. Goldston (Eds.), *Preventing the harmful consequences of severe and persistent loneliness* (pp. 13-46). Washington, DC: U.S. Government Printing Office.

Ross, R. F. (1992). A preliminary investigation of parental loneliness. *Dissertation Abstracts International, 58,* 8.

Rotenberg, K. J., & Morrison, J. (1993). Loneliness and college achievement: Do loneliness scale scores predict college drop-out? *Psychological Reports, 73,* 1283-1288.

Rubenstein, C., & Shaver, P. (1982). The experience of loneliness. In L. A Peplau & D. Perlman (Eds.), *Loneliness: A sourcebook of current theory, research, and therapy* (p. 213). New York: Wiley-Interscience.

Russell, D. (1982). The measurement of loneliness. In L. A. Peplau & D. Perlman (Eds.), *Loneliness: A sourcebook of current theory, research, and therapy* (pp. 81-104). New York: Wiley-Interscience.

Russell, D., Peplau, L. A., & Cutrona, C. E. (1980). The revised UCLA Loneliness Scale: Concurrent and discriminant validity evidence. *Journal of Personality and Social Psychology, 39,* 472-480.

Sadava, S. W., & Thompson, M. M. (1986). Loneliness, social drinking and vulnerability to alcohol problems. *Canadian Journal of Behavioral Sciences, 18,* 133-139.

Schumm, W. R. (1990). Evolution of the family field: Measurement principles and techniques. In J. Touliatos, B. F. Perlmutter, & M. A. Stratus (Eds.), *Handbook of family measurement techniques* (pp. 23-36). Newbury Park, CA: Sage.

Seligman, A. G. (1983). The presentation of loneliness as a separate diagnostic category and its disengagement from depression. *Psychotherapy in Private Practice, 1,* 33-37.

Spanier, G. B. (1976). Measuring dyadic adjustment: A new scale for assessing the quality of marriage and similar dyads. *Journal of Marriage and the Family, 38*, 15-28.

State Institute of Statistics. (1996). *Divorce statistics*. Ankara, Turkey: State Institute of Statistics, Printing Division.

Tezer, E. (1992, July). *The relationship between marital conflict and marital satisfaction*. Paper presented at the meeting of the Person Centered Approach, Isle of Terschelling, The Netherlands.

Tezer, E. (1994). *Evli eşler arasindaki çatişmalar ile çeşitli demografik değişkenlerin evlilik doyumuna etkisi: Kadin eşin bir işte çaliştiği ve çalişmadiği eşler üzerine bir araştirma* [The effects of marital conflict and certain demographic characteristics on marital satisfaction: A study on couples of working and non-working wives]. *Psikiyatri, Psikoloji ve Psikofarmakoloji Dergisi, 2*, 209-217.

Timur, S. (1972). *Türkiye'de aile yapisi* [Family structure in Turkey]. Ankara, Turkey: Hacettepe Universitesi Yayinlari.

Tornstam, L. (1992). Loneliness in marriage. *Journal of Social and Personal Relationships, 9*, 197-217.

Weiss, R. S. (1973). *Loneliness: The experience of emotional and social isolation*. Cambridge, MA: MIT Press.

Weiss, R. S. (1985). Loneliness: What we know about it and what we might do about it. In L. A. Peplau & E. S. Goldston (Eds.), *Preventing the harmful consequences of severe and persistent loneliness* (pp. 3-12). Washington, DC: U. S. Government Printing Office.

West, D. A., Kellner, R., & Moore-West, M. (1986). The effects of loneliness: A review of the literature. *Comprehensive Psychiatry, 27*, 351-363.

Young, J. E. (1982). Loneliness, depression and cognitive therapy: Theory and application. In L. A. Peplau & D. Perlman (Eds.), *Loneliness: A sourcebook of current theory, research, and therapy* (pp. 379-405). New York: Wiley-Interscience.

How Does Culture Influence the Degree of Romantic Loneliness and Closeness?

SEAN SEEPERSAD
California State University, Fresno

MI-KYUNG CHOI
Ewha Womans University

NANA SHIN
Auburn University

ABSTRACT. A culture promoting a strong desire for romantic relationships can greatly influence feelings of romantic loneliness and of closeness. In this study, the authors hypothesized that when not in a romantic relationship, U.S. young adults experience greater degrees of romantic loneliness because of a high desire for romantic relationships, compared with Korean young adults. The authors also predicted that when in a romantic relationship, U.S. young adults experience greater closeness to their romantic partner than do Korean young adults. Results revealed that in a sample of 227 U.S. and Korean students, U.S. students reported significantly higher levels of romantic loneliness than did Koreans when not in a romantic relationship and significantly lower levels of romantic loneliness when in a stable romantic relationship. U.S. students also reported a greater degree of closeness in romantic relationships than did Korean students. The results suggest that Western cultures' strong emphasis on the importance of romantic relationships may unduly amplify individuals' levels of loneliness.

ONE COMMONLY HELD SOCIETAL BELIEF is that loneliness is caused by a lack of a romantic partner and is cured by being in a romantic relationship. Weiss (1989), for example, documented this belief in his research and commented that romantic relationships seemed to be an antiloneliness pill for single parents in America. Other researchers have shown the lack of romantic partners or intimate relationships to be an important perceived causal factor for one's present feelings of loneliness (Rokach & Brock, 1998; Rubenstein & Shaver, 1982). However, this belief linking loneliness to romantic relationships may be a Western concept. Goodwin (1999) proposed that Western cultures such as North America place great importance on romantic love, probably as a solution to disconnection experienced in these individualistic cultures. In some sense, romantic relationships may be viewed as the opposite of loneliness: the ideal intimate relationship. Thus, this belief may have a negative effect on lonely individuals in Western cultures. It is possible that in Western cultures, which heighten the desire for romantic relationships, the absence of romantic relationships can, on one hand, unnecessarily amplify feelings of loneliness compared with non-Western cultures. On the other hand, individuals from Western cultures who are already in romantic relationships may experience a greater degree of closeness compared with individuals in non-Western cultures because of the greater importance place on romantic love.

Culture as an Influence on Romantic Loneliness

In one of the more influential models of loneliness, Peplau and Perlman (1982) described loneliness as a discrepancy between desired and achieved levels of social interaction. This model is particularly useful because it focuses on the subjective nature of loneliness and helps to explain why individuals may experience different levels of loneliness in similar situations. For example, two people may be alone, but one person may experience loneliness because he or she desires company, and the other person may not experience loneliness because he or she is studying for an exam and wishes to be alone. The model can also be useful in explaining varying levels of loneliness in romantic situations (defined as *romantic loneliness* by DiTommaso & Spinner, 1993) among cultures that promote different levels of desire for romantic relationships. Western cultures promote strong levels of desire for romantic relationships compared with non-Western cultures (Goodwin, 1999; Medora, Larson, Hortaçsu, & Dave, 2002). Therefore, when a person from a Western culture is not in a romantic relationship, he or she may experience a high level of loneliness because of the intense desire to be in a romantic relationship. Conversely, a person from a non-Western culture may have less of a desire to be in a romantic relationship and thus less feelings of loneliness.

If romantic relationships are more highly desired in Western cultures than in non-Western cultures, then it is also possible that Westerners experience a greater degree of closeness to their romantic partners than do their non-Western counterparts. A close relationship would include such features as "a sense of connectedness, shared understandings, mutual responsiveness, mutual dependence, self-disclosure, or intersubjectivity" (Aron & Mashek, 2004, p. 417). Medora et al. (2002) found that American college students were more likely to believe in unrealistic and idealized romantic notions such as love at first sight and the ideal mate than were Turkish or Indian college students. It is possible that Westerners experience a greater degree of closeness in romantic relationships because of the combination of (a) having a greater desire for romantic relationships and therefore investing more into these relationships and (b) having unrealistic and idealized romantic notions that can amplify the effect of being in a romantic relationship. Previous researchers have not directly addressed the issue of cross-cultural differences of closeness in romantic relationships.

Korea provides a good contrast to the United States in terms of cultural emphasis on the desire for romantic relationships among adolescents and young adults. According to Youn (2001), Korean parents of adolescents are usually disappointed or worried if their child meets members of the opposite sex because there is a belief in Korean society that adolescents who meet members of the opposite sex will become failures in their adult lives. Goodwin (1999) also pointed out that unlike Western cultures, which rely heavily on romantic relationships as a source of psychological intimacy, non-Western collectivistic cultures such as Korea have other strong sources of intimacy, such as parents and siblings. In fact, the importance of love for choosing a marital partner is more prevalent in Western countries such as the United States, England, and Australia than it is in non-Western countries such as Japan and India (Levine, Sato, Hashimoto, & Verma, 1995). Whereas individuals in Western countries such as the United States view romantic relationships as possibly the most important and central source of love and intimacy (and thus as very needed and desired), individuals in non-Western countries such as Korea may not view romantic relationships with the same degree of importance as a source of love and psychological intimacy.

Hypotheses

In this study, we explored the association between romantic relationships, the degree of closeness within these relationships, and romantic loneliness within a Western country (United States) and a non-Western country (Korea) to test the following two hypotheses. First, we hypothesized that U.S. participants who have romantic relationships would experience less romantic loneliness than would Korean participants, but that U.S. participants who do not have romantic relationships would experience greater romantic loneliness than would Korean participants. Second, we hypothesized that U.S. participants who have romantic relationships would report a greater degree of closeness to their romantic partners than would Korean participants.

Method

Participants and Procedure

Participants were 271 students taking introductory social science courses in U.S. and Korean public universities who volunteered to take part in the study. Of the participants, 170 were from the United States, and 101 were from Korea. The majority of participants in both the U.S. and the Korean samples were female

(87% and 95%, respectively), with the Korean sample having a significantly greater proportion of women than the U.S. sample, $t(269) = -2.13$, $p = .03$. All participants reported not being married. Participants' ages ranged from 18 to 25 years. The mean age of the U.S. sample ($M = 19.67$ years, $SD = 1.28$ years) was slightly lower than that of the Korean sample ($M = 22.44$ years, $SD = 1.38$ years). A t test showed this age difference to be significant, $t(269) = -16.68$, $p < .01$. We did not collect any other demographic data.

To detect changes in the romantic partners of participants over time, we administered the questionnaire separately in the two countries at two points in time: once at the beginning of each country's respective spring semester (Time 1 [T1]) and again at the end of their respective spring semester (Time 2 [T2]). The length of time (approximately 13 weeks) between the two data collection points was approximately the same in both countries.

Further analysis revealed that majority of both U.S. and Korean participants either were in the same romantic relationship at both T1 and T2 or reported not being in a romantic relationship at either T1 or T2. These participants constituted 83–84% of both samples. Forty-eight percent of participants in both countries reported not being in a romantic relationship at either time point, whereas 35% of the U.S. participants and 36% of the Korean participants reported being in the same relationship at both time points. The proportions of participants either in a romantic relationship or not in a romantic relationship were not significantly different between the two samples. Because of the small number of participants who had a change in their romantic relationships from T1 to T2, we did not include these participants in the analyses.

Measures

We used two measures to assess participants' levels of romantic loneliness and their romantic social network. A translator translated the questionnaire into Korean, and a second translator then independently back-translated it into English to ensure that the Korean questionnaire was approximately the same as the English questionnaire.

Romantic loneliness. We measured romantic loneliness using one of the subscales of the short version of the Social and Emotional Loneliness Scale for Adults (SELSA; DiTommaso & Spinner, 1993). It consists of five items such as "I have an unmet need for a close romantic relationship." Participants responded on a 7-point Likert scale with answers ranging from 1 (*strongly disagree*) to 7 (*strongly agree*). The scale showed good reliability with Cronbach's αs of .85 and .86 at T1 and T2, respectively.

Romantic social network. We adapted this measure from that of Williams and Solano (1983). The measure consisted of two parts. The first part asked respondents to give the initials of their romantic partner. If respondents had the same initials for their romantic partner at both T1 and T2, this indicated a stable romantic partner. The absence of initials at both T1 and T2 indicated no romantic relationship over the period. Thus, we used this measure to determine relationship status (i.e., whether respondents had either a stable romantic relationship or no romantic relationship from T1 to T2). The second part of the measure, also adapted from that of Williams and Solano, asked participants who reported having a romantic partner to indicate how close they are to their romantic partner on a 7-point Likert scale ranging from 1 (*not at all close*) to 7 (*very close*).

Results

Association Between Relationship Status and Romantic Loneliness Across the United States and Korea

We conducted a multivariate analysis of variance (MANOVA) to test the hypothesis that culture influences the degree of romantic loneliness experienced. Participants' romantic loneliness at T1 and T2 was the repeated measure, and we entered it as the dependent variable into the MANOVA. We entered country and relationship status as independent variables. The analysis controlled for age and gender. There were no significant within-subject effects. However, the between-subjects results revealed that (a) relationship status had a significant main effect, $F(1, 186) = 377.18$, $p < .01$; (b) country did not have a significant main effect; and (c) the interaction between country and relationship status was significant, $F(1, 186) = 186.06$, $p < .01$. A follow-up post hoc test revealed that romantic loneliness was significantly greater for both U.S., $t(128) = 25.26$, $p < .01$, and Korean, $t(83) = 3.94$, $p < .01$, students who were not in a romantic relationship compared with those who were in a romantic relationship.

Figure 1 shows the interaction effect of romantic loneliness averaged across T1 and T2. U.S. students who were not in a romantic relationship reported higher romantic loneliness than did Korean students who were not in a romantic relationship. However, U.S. students who were in the same stable, romantic relationship reported lower levels of loneliness than did their Korean counterparts.

Degree of Closeness for U.S. and Korean Participants in a Stable Romantic Relationship

We conducted a MANOVA to determine whether U.S. students in romantic relationships reported greater levels of closeness within these relationships. The MANOVA compared the levels of closeness in romantic relationships at T1 and T2 for U.S. and Korean students, while controlling for age and gender. The results showed no significant within-subject effects, suggesting that the levels of closeness did not significantly change from T1 to T2. However, the between-

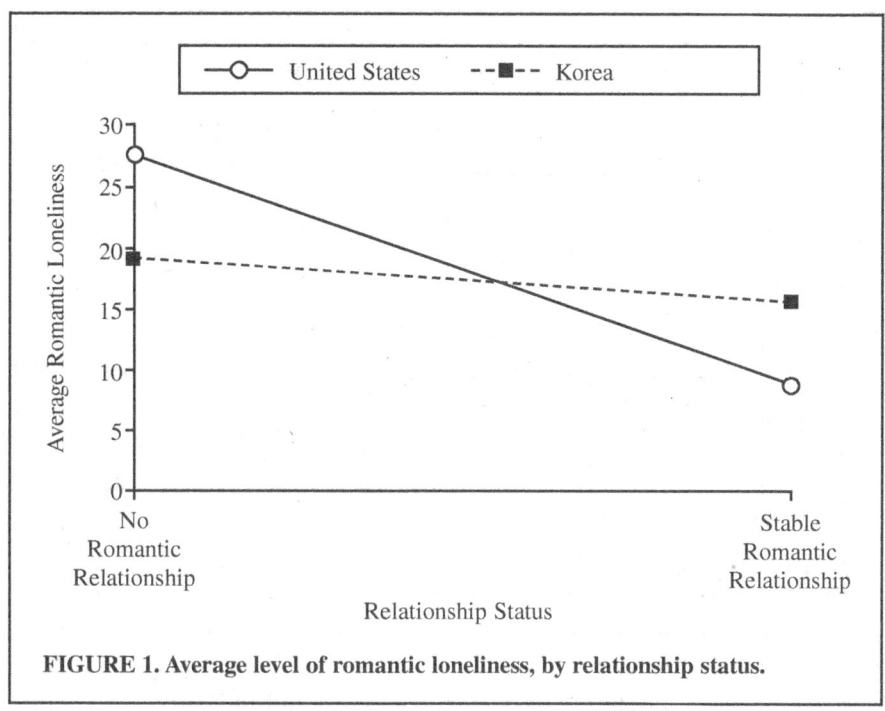

FIGURE 1. Average level of romantic loneliness, by relationship status.

subjects results showed a significant difference between the levels of closeness for U.S. and Korean students, $F(1, 92) = 5.76$, $p = .02$. Across T1 and T2, U.S. students reported significantly greater levels of closeness than did Korean students (see Figure 2).

Discussion

The results of this study provide evidence for our hypotheses that culture influences both the level of romantic loneliness that individuals experience and the degree of closeness that they experience. The results suggest that romantic relationships have significantly greater influence on romantic loneliness for U.S. students than for Korean students. U.S. students reported significantly stronger feelings of romantic loneliness when a romantic partner was absent and significantly weaker feelings of romantic loneliness when a romantic partner was present in comparison with Korean students. It is interesting to note that in both countries, having a romantic relationship is related to decreased loneliness. However, although having a romantic relationship can reduce feelings of loneliness in both countries, the process seems amplified among U.S. participants.

The findings also revealed that U.S. students reported significantly higher levels of closeness in their romantic relationships than did Korean students.

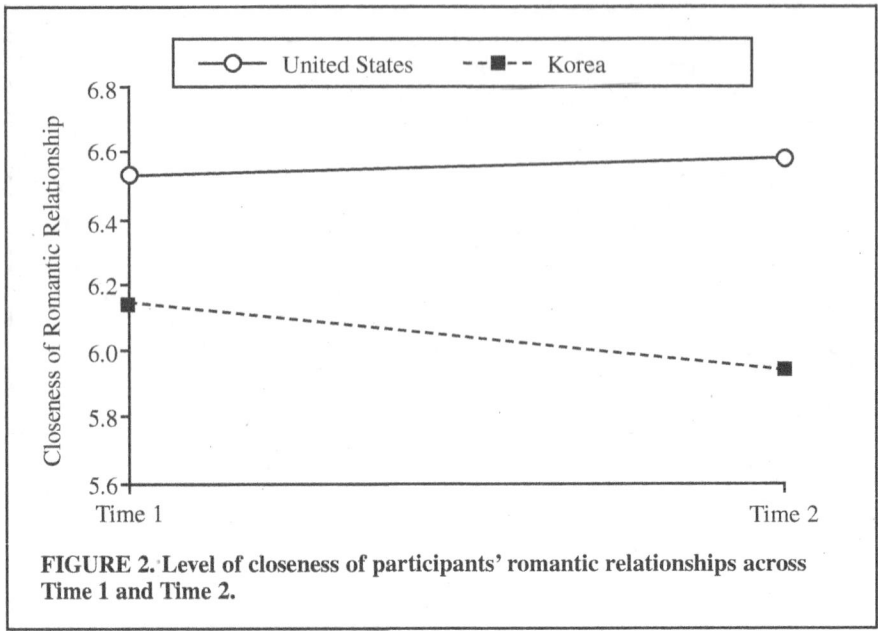

FIGURE 2. Level of closeness of participants' romantic relationships across Time 1 and Time 2.

These higher levels could be an indication of individuals' placing greater importance on these relationships in the United States than in Korea.

This research is an important first step in thinking about how loneliness, romantic relationships, and culture interact. Previous researchers investigating loneliness have focused on how it varies cross-culturally without considering the possible influence of romantic relationships. Future researchers should investigate if the findings remain the same when contrasting different Western and non-Western countries.

This study had two main limitations. First, the sample was primarily female. It is possible that there are gender differences in how much importance men and women ascribe to romantic relationships cross-culturally, which would thus affect their levels of romantic loneliness. Second, there was a small amount of error associated with determining whether a respondent had a stable romantic relationship or no romantic relationship. It is possible that a respondent may have switched romantic partners from T1 to T2, but if both romantic partners had the same initials, we would have incorrectly coded this scenario as a stable romantic relationship. It is similarly possible that a person had a romantic relationship between T1 and T2 but not when the data were collected, resulting in our incorrectly coding the person as having no romantic relationship. However, we determined these errors to be acceptable because of the small possibility that either scenario occurred.

In conclusion, in Western culture, in which romantic relationships are heavily emphasized, lonely individuals often assume that the reason for their loneliness is the lack of a romantic partner. The results of the present study suggest that it is not only the absence of a romantic partner that causes such strong feelings of loneliness but also the social expectation of having a romantic partner.

AUTHOR NOTES

Sean Seepersad is an assistant professor in the Department of Child, Family, and Consumer Sciences at California State University, Fresno. His research interests include loneliness among adolescents and young adults and its association with attachment styles, coping, and social skills. **Mi-Kyung Choi** is an assistant professor at Ewha Womans University, Korea. Her research interests include cross-cultural relationships among young adults. **Nana Shin** is a University Postdoctoral Research Fellow at Auburn University. Her research interests include young children's social and emotional competence during the preschool period and how children's experiences in the family system relate and influence their emergent relationships over time.

REFERENCES

Aron, A. P., & Mashek, D. J. (2004). Conclusion. In D. J. Mashek & A. Aron (Eds.), *Handbook of closeness and intimacy* (pp. 415–428). Mahwah, NJ: Erlbaum.

DiTommaso, E., & Spinner, B. (1993). The development and initial validation of a measure of social and emotional loneliness (SELSA). *Personality and Individual Differences, 14,* 127–134.

Goodwin, R. (1999). *Personal relationships across cultures.* New York: Routledge.

Levine, R., Sato, S., Hashimoto, T., & Verma, I. (1995). Love and marriage in eleven cultures. *Journal of Cross-Cultural Psychology, 26,* 554–571.

Medora, N. P., Larson, J. H., Hortaçsu, N., & Dave, P. (2002). Perceived attitudes towards romanticism: A cross-cultural study of American, Asian-Indian, and Turkish young adults. *Journal of Comparative Family Studies, 33,* 155–179.

Peplau, L. A., & Perlman, D. (1982). Perspectives on loneliness. In L. A. Peplau & D. Perlman (Eds.), *Loneliness: A sourcebook of current theory, research and therapy* (pp. 1–18). New York: Wiley.

Rokach, A., & Brock, H. (1998). Coping with loneliness. *The Journal of Psychology, 132,* 107–128.

Rubenstein, C. M., & Shaver, P. (1982). The experience of loneliness. In L. A. Peplau & D. Perlman (Eds.), *Loneliness: A sourcebook of current theory, research and therapy* (pp. 206–223). New York: Wiley.

Weiss, R. S. (1989). Reflections on the present state of loneliness research. In M. Hojat & R. Crandall (Eds.), *Loneliness: Theory, research, and applications* (pp. 1–16). Newbury Park, CA: Sage.

Williams, J. G., & Solano, C. H. (1983). The social reality of feeling lonely: Friendship and reciprocation. *Personality and Social Psychology Bulletin, 9,* 237–242.

Youn, G. (2001). Perceptions of peer sexual activities in Korean adolescents. *Journal of Sex Research, 38,* 352–360.

Longing, Love and Loneliness

AMI ROKACH

Loneliness carries a significant social stigma. In our culture, lack of friendship and social ties is socially undesirable. Lonely people have, often, very negative self-perceptions, and great difficulty to establish social ties, which often suggests that the alienated person may have personal inadequacies, or socially undesirable attributes (Lau & Gruen, 1992). "Lonely people are perceived as less psychologically adjusted, less achieving, and less intellectually competent in relating to others" (Lau & Gruen, 1992, p. 187). Research has demonstrated that the seriousness of the social stigma of loneliness is very much affected by the gender of the lonely. Loneliness, just like for instance depression, tends to be regarded by the public as unmasculine and consequently more undesirable for men (Lau, 1989). Furthermore, men may hesitate to admit that they are lonely because of those very same negative connotations (Borys & Perlman, 1989). A recent study about the prevalence of social isolation, in the dawn of the twenty first century, revealed that Americans are far more isolated than they previously were. The social network seems, now, to include less and less people: it is the family, or our spouse, or no one at all. Unfortunately, a growing number of people appear to have no one in whom they can confide, resulting in an increasingly fragmented society, where social ties, that were such an integral part of daily life in past generations, are weakening or disappearing all together (McPherson, Smith-Lovin & Brashears, 2006).

The twenty first century has been marked, up to now, at least, as the technological century. While in the 1950s television was the "hottest", newest, and most advanced technological development for home entertainment, today we are flooded by computers, iPhones, Tablets, the Internet, and the ability to be in contact with, practically, the whole world in an instance. T.S. Elliot (cited in Putnam, 2000), wisely I might add, declared many decades ago when television just started that "it is a medium of entertainment which permits millions of people to listen to the same joke at the same time, yet remain lonesome" (p. 217). It is truer than ever today. People can now work from home, and children may spend hours "connecting" with others online, thus eliminating the need for face-to-face interaction. Lewis et al., (2000) poignantly observed it about children, but it most probably is accurate about adults as well. "A child's electronic stewards (such as) televisions, videos, and computer games – are the emotional equivalents of bran; they occupy attention and mental space without nourishing" (p. 198). People thus, depend more and more on technology and less and less on each other. It is a way of coping with social alienation. Many lonely, alienated people flick on the television set for "company," surfing from channel to channel. Putnam (2000) made an interesting observation and suggested that the correlation between channel surfing and social surfing (engaging in wider, occasional social relations) is more than just metaphorical. Television watching has become the Ativan of the lonely, alienated, and socially disconnected individuals. The Internet has become an integral and important (sometimes central) part of our lives. The vast majority of North Americans get much of their information from the Internet (Jones & Prinz, 2005).

It is clear that virtual connection and friendships are growing in popularity and in some instances replacing real ones. Cell phones have become an essential part of life in the Western Hemisphere. Interestingly, and possibly contrary to our expectations, research found that many lonely individuals prefer online social interaction as they perceive them to be less threatening than actual meetings (Caplan, 2003, 2005; Subrahmanyam & Lin, 2007).

Technology was geared to help us establish relationships. It so happens that the very same technology that has allowed people to strengthen their contact with distant family members and friends, and to develop friendship with people around the world, is actually replacing the necessary day-to-day human interactions (Sleek, 1998). In fact Kraut, Patterson, Lundmark, Kiesler, Mukopadhyay & Scherlis (1998) reported that increased use of the Internet leads to shrinking social support and happiness, and results in depression and increased loneliness. Ornish (1998) echoed those findings by observing that "at their best, e-mail and chat rooms can be another way of staying in touch and keeping up with loved ones who may be thousands of miles away in real space but instantly available in cyberspace. All too often, however, technology provides a way of numbing loneliness without experiencing real intimacy" (p. 100-101).

The need to belong

People are social animals. There is a basic human need to belong, to be part of an intimate and caring relationship with a partner who is close, and deeply concerned about us (Miller, 2012). In order to fulfill that need, we are driven to establish close contact with others, and participate in intimate relationships. Research has demonstrated that people who are closely related to others or have an intimate partner, live happier, longer, healthier, and more fulfilling lives (Koball, Moiduddin, Henderson, Goesling & Besculides, 2010). More poignant indications can be seen in the observation that people holding their lover's hand felt supported and their brain's response to a threatening situation was reduced (Coan, Schaefer & Davidson, 2006) and even pain was reported to be less potent when one was, as little as looking at a *photograph* of one's loved one. And contrary to that, people who have less than the needed quantity and quality of intimacy in their lives, risk a variety of health problems, loneliness and mortality (Cohen, 2004; Berkman & Glass, 2000). Happy contented partnerships lead to greater well-being than unhappy ones do, and yet many people feel more fulfilled even in an unhappy relationship than they do when they are completely alone, preferring a bad relationship to utter loneliness (Miller, 2012). Segrin (1998) observed that those with unsatisfying ties have a higher probability than those in intimate and satisfying relationships, to experience depression, alcoholism and eating disorders. Lack of intimacy may be both the cause and the enhancer of emotional problems (Miller, 2012).

What is that sense of belonging that man wants so much to have?

In the past, especially for the generation who matured in the "great depression," one's work was seen as the valued means of self-fulfilment: "bread winning" through a career or a job for men, and the creation of a home and family base for women. Ours, is a different time. We believe in the importance and uniqueness, of relating to others, believing that we know how to conquer the barriers against closeness that we ourselves have erected. At present, self-esteem can essentially be affirmed by relationships. As Gordon (1976) so poignantly observed about 35 years ago, "To be alone is to be different, to be different is to be alone, and to be in the interior of this fatal circle is to be lonely. To be lonely is to have failed" (p.15). We seem to be living in a "Noah's Ark" society where everything goes two by two, and if you are lonely you are out of place. However, while we yearn for close, intimate relationships, the social conditions we create are not conducive to the development of such relations. Our present lifestyle, which was developed in the last 25 years, creates and reinforces separateness and isolation, making loneliness even more difficult to cope with.

There is substantial evidence suggesting that perceived social support can buffer the negative impact of stress on psychological distress, depression and anxiety (Kawachi & Berkman, 2001). Additionally, social support may alleviate stress by ways of providing a solution to the problem we are facing, or it may facilitate healthful behaviours such as exercise, personal hygiene, proper nutrition, and rest (House, 1981). In general, people who are part of a social network are, naturally, subjected to social controls and peer pressures that influence normative health behaviours (Cohen, 2004). By abiding by those normative social expectations one may get a sense of identity, predictability, stability, belonging, and self-worth (Cohen, 2004; Thoit, 1983; Willis, 1985). A person commonly feels that she belongs when she feels valued, needed, and important to a group of people with whom she feels that she is part of (Friedman, 2007). Research indicates that *social isolation*, and the concomitant loneliness it may cause, is itself a stressor which contributes to one's decreased sense of control, lower self-esteem, suppressed immune function, and interferes with practiced health behaviours (Cacioppo et al., 2002; Uchino et al., 1996). Romantic relationships, as mentioned earlier in this book, can ward off loneliness, and add to our feeling of worth, belonging, and value.

The nature of intimacy

Intimacy is a complex concept and is composed of *knowledge, caring, interdependence, mutuality, trust and commitment*. (Ben-Ari & Lavee, 2007; Miller, 2012; Prager & Robert, 2004). An intimate relationship indicates that the partners have extensive personal, confidential and private *knowledge* about each other. That rich information may include their histories, feelings and desires which they would commonly not reveal to other people. Intimate partners do not just <u>know</u> but <u>care</u> about each other, feeling affectionate towards their partner, to a greater extent than they would to someone else. Intimate partners' lives are intertwined and they affect each other continually. The extent to which they need and influence each other, is frequent, it impacts meaningfully on the other, and they do so in many areas of their lives (Berscheid et al., 2004; Miller, 2012). Intimate couples often exhibit *mutuality*, thinking of themselves as "us" (Fitzsimons & Kay, 2004) and in addition, intimacy means *trust* where the partners know that it is safe to open up and that their partner will be supportive of them (Reis et al.,

2004). And finally, being in such a unique and protective relationship, intimate partners are *committed* to their relationship, they expect them to go on indefinitely and to reach that goal, they are ready to invest time, effort and resources at their disposal. Miller (2012) asserts that "none of these components is absolutely required for intimacy to occur, and each may exist when the others are absent" (p. 3).

While many complain, after years of togetherness, that "love went out the window," some couples – and we may want to learn from them – do continue to feel passionately in love, although that love changes over time (Walster & Walster, 1978). People in mutually nurturing relationships report higher general life satisfaction than reported by those who do not get that caring and nurturance (Baumeister, Wottman & Stillwell, 1993). Interestingly, and as with other basic needs, such as food for example, once people feel that they belong, say in a romantic union, they are less likely to search for another partner (DeWall, Baumeister & Vohs, 2008). In fact, contend Baumeister & Leary (1995) intimate relationships are so important to humans, that there may be an "internal gauge" which they termed the "Socio-meter" and which helps us constantly monitors the environment for clues to changes in our inclusionary status. For it is so important to us, that as we become aware of it, we may endeavour to improve it (see also Leary & Springer, 2001). Both, loneliness and belonging, share the subjective perception of connectedness to others. Mellor et al., (2008) found that those who reported a higher need to belong experienced decreased loneliness when they were satisfied with their social network. Unsatisfied belongingness needs, may thus lead to social isolation, and loneliness. It is, generally, seen as the discrepancy between the need to belong and the degree in which that need is satisfied which is crucial in ushering the experience of loneliness. Olds & Schwartz (2009), utilizing the evolutionary perspective to belongingness, asserted that those who are socially connected, live longer, have more robust immune systems, and are better equipped to respond to stress. Medical research, indicates that social connection is good and important to our health, or more succinctly, "Human beings, both as a species and as individuals, survive only through attachment to one another ... we are designed to become attached to one another" (Olds & Schwartz, 2009, p. 57)

Weiss (1974) asserted that social relations, and particularly intimate ones, are a rich source of:

> 1. Attachment – which can be seen in good relationships that may provide us with security and commitment.
> 2. Social integration – which may be felt when companionship and shared activities are part of our social relations.
> 3. Opportunity for nurturance – is being fostered by relationships that provide us with a sense of being needed, and possibly for nurturing someone else.
> 4. Reassurance of worth –may be the consequence of a relationship which provides us with a sense of competence and of being valued, and
> 5. Guidance – when relationships allow us to receive trustworthy advice and suggestions.

Romantic relationships

Establishing and maintaining close, intimate relationships has been recognized as a fundamental human motivation (Baumeister & Leary, 1995; McCarthy, Ginsberg & Cintron, 2008). Marriage is seen in our culture as the most intimate adult bonding, providing affection, love, and support (Laurenceau, Feldman, Barrett & Rovine, 2005; Strong, DeValut & Cohen, 2011). Long term, committed intimate relationships are essential to physical and emotional well-being (Cohen, Gottlieb & Underwood, 2000; Lynch, 2000). Intimate relationships have been shown to buffer people from the pathogenic effects of stress (Prager, 1995). It was documented that people who are in intimate relationships experience faster recoveries from illness than those who do not have intimate relationships (see also Flora & Segrin, 2000). Intimacy is first and foremost a reciprocal interactive experience and as Kouneski & Olson (2004) asserted intimacy is the cornerstone of love relationships. It is described as a close relationship which commonly is seen to include sex, but which even more importantly includes emotional closeness "having someone to talk to, to share our selves, to give and receive love, affection, personal validation, trust, and self-disclosure" (Strong et al., 2011; Hook et al., 2003).Strong et al., (2011) suggested that intimate relationships may positively affect our self-esteem, and were shown to be related to happiness, contentment, and a sense of well-being. Intimacy can be expressed by sharing with one's partner, being open, honest and trusting of each other. Intimacy (as can also be gauged from the articles published in this book) has been rated as more important in relationship satisfaction than autonomy, individuality, freedom, agreement or sexual satisfaction (Hassebrauck & Fehr, 2002). Attachment theory starts from the premise that in childhood, parents or primary caregivers are the most important figures with whom a child bonds (Bowlby, 1969). Similarly, attachment and caregiving are central, interrelated components of love relationships (Feeny & Noller, 1996).Bowlby (1973), the originator of attachment theory, emphasized emotional accessibility and responsiveness in all attachment relationships. Johnson (2002) even suggested that seeking and maintaining contact with significant others is an innate, primary motivating principle in humans and she perceives dependency as an innate part of being human rather than a childhood trait that we outgrow. Secure attachment, it was suggested, provides a secure base from which individuals can explore and experience their world (Mikulincer, 1997). The emotional engagement and the trust that this engagement holds, are crucial.Romantic relationships, love, and sex are significantly affected by the three parameters named by Mikulincer & Shaver (2009) attachment to one's partner, caregiving behaviour which they both display, and their sexual relationships. They maintained that these three ingredients "are important for understanding romantic love, because the system's smooth functioning brings relationship partners together, increases physical and emotional closeness, and heightens feelings of love and gratitude toward the partner as well as feelings of being loved and esteemed by the partner" (p. 49).

On love

"I used to feel loved because I was special. Now, I feel special because I am loved and because I can love" (Ornish, 1998, p. 91)

What is love? That is a question that is probably as old as humanity. Writers, philosophers, poets and the sculptors have attempted to describe and capture its meaning for centuries, but it is only relatively recently that social scientists have shown interest in researching and writing about love (Fehr, 2006). Rubin (1970, 1973) who was the first psychologist to write extensively about love, suggested that love has three components: intimacy, need/attachment, and caring. Berscheid & Hatfield's (1974) model of love was the next major contribution to the study of love. They differentiated between _companionate_ [characterized by friendly affection and brings about caring, trust, honesty and respect] (Hatfield & Walster, 1978; Brehm, 1992) and _passionate_ love, often characterized by emotional extremes, physiological arousal and sexual attraction (Fehr, 2006).

Lee (1973) and Hendrick & Hendrick (1986) and have drawn a typology of six different love styles, described below. They include Agape (altruistic love), Storge (friendship-based love), ludus (game-playing love), Mania (obsessive, dependent love), pragma (practical love), and Eros (romantic, passionate love) (Fehr, 2006). Sternberg (1986) proposed the triangular theory of love, with passion, intimacy, and commitment as its dimensions. Eight different kinds of love result from the various combinations of these three elements. Fehr (1988) wanted to find out what ordinary people think of love. She explored it and found that people listed honesty, trust, caring, dependency, sexual passion, and physical attraction as representing love to them. Fehr concluded that laypersons perceive love to encompass, both, companionate and passionate loves. She observed that companionate love was regarded as central to love, whereas passionate kinds of love were considered peripheral (see also Fehr, 2006).

To conclude, here is an eloquent definition of love that was offered by Gottschall & Nordlund (2006) who exclaimed that "To love someone romantically is … to experience a strong desire for union with someone who is deemed entirely unique. It is to idealize this person, to think constantly about him or her, and to discover that one's own life priorities have changed dramatically. It is to care deeply for the person's well being, and to feel pain or emptiness when he or she is absent" (p. 450).

Love and loneliness

A love relationship, where we expect to be cared for, could under some circumstances be terribly lonely (Rokach, 1988, 1989). Love and loneliness, by definition, are not supposed to go together, but many times they do. How can someone who is loved feel lonely?!

Relationships are never smooth sailing into the horizon. Couples encounter disappointments, anger, unfulfilled wishes, and love from our partner which may not provide us with what we need. Thus, although love–loneliness connection may be an oxymoron, it is not infrequently that people are in love, and feel lonely; longing for more, waiting to be embraced and understood, and being unable to evade the loneliness that they experience when the love they receive is not what they need.

Gordon & McKinney (2010) maintained that much of what they referred to as "torrential romance,", is related to the lovers' attempt to sustain the intensity of the relationship by introducing some sort of crisis exemplified by anger outbursts, marked withdrawal, etc. If lovers actually do so in order to keep the flame alive, then they may end up withdrawing emotionally from one another, feel hurt, alienated, and lonely. Shaver & Hazan (1987) maintained that with time, romantic love and sexual attraction wanes, attachment anxieties may lead to conflict or mutual withdrawal, familiarity replaces novelty, and lovers either find themselves securely attached and caring deeply about each other, or experiencing such distress as boredom, disappointments or loneliness.

The wear and tear of love

Love and relationships can be harmed and damaged, not only by the process of time, which Hazan & Shaver discussed, but also due to various pitfalls such as hurt feelings, jealousy, lying, and betrayal (De Paulo et al., 2009; Vangelisti, 2009). We want to be loved by our intimate partners, and, we hope that our relational value – the degree to which our partner considers our intimate relationship valuable, important, and close – is high. It is painful and maybe even devastating to find out that our partner perceives it lower than we would like it to be perceived by him or her. Should such relational devaluation occur, that is, that we are no longer thought of as positively as before, we experience pain, anger, hurt, and loneliness (DeWall et al., 2010; Miller, 2012; see also DeWall, 2009).People, even in close, intimate relationship may experience ostracism, when their partner gives them the "cold shoulder," and ignores them. Ostracism is utilized commonly to punish the other; it can be very painful, as it threatens our basic social needs (Sommer et al., 2001; Williams, 2007). The "silent treatment" not only threatens our need to belong, but may also damage our feelings or self-worth, and reduce our perceived control over the interactions. Usually the ostracized partner does not know what to further expect. When their belongingness is threatened and when their feelings of alienation intensify, people may either work hard to regain their partner's regard, or start looking elsewhere (Miller, 2012; Williams, 2007).Romantic relationships are dynamic. Partners change over time, and their relationship does as well. Research suggests that romantic relationships tend to evolve, over time, from passionate to companionate love, or may even be replaced by other feelings which are not as intimate and binding as love is (Keller, 2000). It must be noted that if both romantic partners change in concert with one another, then they are on the same trajectory and are together on the same life journey. However, if their personal growth is bidirectional, meaning that they grow at different rates and in different directions, they may end up feeling isolated from the one they love, feel left behind, resentful, and lonely. Thus, love that changes may transform the relationship, and potentially leave one or both partners, lonely.

REFERENCES

Baumeister, R.F., Wotman, S.R., & Stillwell, A.M. (1993). Unrequited love: On heartbreak, anger, guilt, and scriptlessness, and humiliation. *Journal of Personality and Social Psychology*, *64*, 377–394.

Baumeister, R.F., & Leary, M.R. (1995). The need to belong: Desire for interpersonal attachments as a fundamental human motivation. *Psychological Bulletin, 117*(3), 497–529.

Ben-Ari, A., & Lavee, Y. (2007). Dyadic closeness in marriage: From the inside story to a conceptual model. *Journal of Social and Personal Relationships, 24*, 627–644.

Berkman, L.F., & Glass, T.A. (2000). Social integration,social networks, social support and health. In L.F. Berkman & I. Kawachi, (Eds.), *Social epidemiology* (pp. 137–174). New York: Oxford University Press.

Berscheid, E, Snyder, M., & Omoto, A.M. (2004). Measuring closeness: The Relationship Closeness Inventory (RCI) revisited. In D.J. Mashek & A. Aron, (Eds.), *Handbook of closeness and intimacy* (pp. 81–101). Mahwah, NJ: Erlbaum.

Berscheid, E., & Walster (Hatfield) E. (1974). A little bit about love. In T.L. Huston, (Ed.), *Foundations of interpersonal attraction* (pp. 355–381). NY: Academic Press.

Borys, S., & Perlman, D. (1985). Gender differences in loneliness. *Personality and Social Psychology Bulletin, 11*, 63–74.

Bowlby, J. (1969). Attachment and loss. *Vol.1: Attachment.* New York: Basic Books.

Bowlby, J. (1973). Affection bonds: their nature and origin. In R.S. Weiss, (Ed.), *Loneliness: The experience of social and emotional isolation* (pp. 38–52). Cambridge Mass: The MIT Press.

Brehm, S.S. (1992). Intimate relationships. 2nd Ed. NY: McGraw-Hill. *Loneliness: The experience of social and emotional isolation* (pp. 38-52).Cambridge Mass: The MIT Press.

Cacioppo, J.T., Hawkley, L.C., Crawford, E., Ernst, J.M., Burleson, M.H., Kowalewski, R.B., Malarkey, W.B., Cauter, E.V., & Berntson, G.G. (2002). Loneliness and health: Potential mechanisms. *Psychosomatic Medicine, 64*, 407–417.

Caplan, S.E. (2003). Preference for online social interaction: A theory of problematic Internet use and psychosocial well-being. *Communication Research, 30*(6), 625–648.

Caplan, S.E. (2005). A social skill account of problematic internet use. *Journal of Communication, 55*(4), 721–736.

Coan, J.A., Schaefer, H.S., & Davidson, R.J. (2006). Lending a hand: Social regulation of the neural response to threat. *Psychological Science, 17*, 1032–1039.

Cohen, S. (2004). Social relationships and health. *American Psychologist.* Special Issue: Awards Issue 2004, *59*, 676–684.

Cohen, S., Gottlieb, B.H., & Underwood, L.G. (2000). Social relationships and health: Challenges for measurement and interventions. *Advances in Mind Body Medicine, 17*(2), 129–141.

DePaulo, B.M., Morris, W.L., & Sternglanz, R.W. (2009). When the truth hurts: Deception in the name of kindness. In A.L. Vangelisti, (Ed.), *Feeling hurt in close relationships* (pp. 167–190). New York: Cambridge University Press.

DeWall, C.N. (2009). The pain of exclusion: Using insights from neuroscience to understand emotional and behavioral responses to social exclusions. In M.J. Harris, (Ed.), *Bullying, rejection, and peer victimization: A social cognitive neuroscience perspective* (pp. 201–224). New York: Springer.

DeWall, C.N., Baumeister, R.F., & Vohs, K.D. (2008). Satiated with belongingness? Effects of acceptance, rejection and task framing on self-regulatory performance. *Journal of Personality and Social Psychology, 95*, 1367–1382.

DeWall, C.N., MacDonald, G., Webster, G.D., Masten, C.L., Baumeister, R.F., Powell, C., & Eisenberger, N.I. (2010). Acetaminophen reduces social pain: Behavioral and neural evidence. *Psychological Science, 21*, 931–937.

Feeney, J.A., & Noller, P. (1996). *Adult Attachment.* London: Sage Publications.

Fehr, B. (1988). Prototype analysis of the concept of love and commitment. *Journal of Personality and Social Psychology, 55*, 557–579.

Fehr, B. (2006). A prototype approach to studying love. In R.J. Sternberg & K. Weis,(Eds.), *The new psychology of love* (pp. 225–246). New Haven, CT: Yale University Press.

Fitzsimons, G.M., & Kay, A.C. (2004). Language and interpersonal cognition: Causal effects of variations in pronoun usage on perceptions of closeness. *Personality and Social Psychology Bulletin, 30*(5), 547–557.

Flora, J., & Segrin, C. (2000). Relationship development in dating couples: Implications for relational satisfaction and loneliness. *Journal of Social and Personal Relationships, 17*(6), 811–825.

Friedman, R.L. (2007). *Widening the therapeutic lens: Sense of belonging as an integral dimension of the human experience.* A Dissertation submitted to the Wright Institute Graduate School.

Gordon, J., & McKinney, A. (2010). Love and lust: A phenomenological investigation. *Journal of the British Society for Phenomenology, 41*(1), 8–32.

Gordon, S. (1976). *Lonely in America.* NY: Simon & Schuster.

Gottschall, J., & Nordlund, M. (2006). Romantic love: A literary universal? *Philosophy and Literature, 30,* 450–470.

Hassebrauck, M., & Fehr, B. (2002). Dimensions of relationship quality. *Personal Relationships, 9,* 253–270.

Hatfield, E., & Walster, G.W. (1978). *A new look at love.* Lanham, MD: University Press.

Hendrick, C., & Hendrick, S.S. (1986). A theory and method of love. *Journal of Personality and Social Psychology, 50,* 392–402.

Hook, M., Gerstein, L., Detterich, L., & Gridley, B. (2003). How close are we? Measuring intimacy and examining gender differences. *Journal of Counselling and Development, 81,* 462–472.

House, J.A. (1981). *Work stress and social support.* Reading, MA: Addison-Wesley.

Johnson, S.M. (2002). *Emotionally focused couple therapy with trauma survivors: strengthening attachment bonds.* New York, NY: Guilford Press.

Jones, T. L., & Prinz, R. J. (2005). Potential roles of parental self-efficacy in parent and child adjustment: A review. *Clinical Psychology Review, 25,* 341–363.

Kawachi, I., & Berkman, L. (2001). Social ties and mental health. *Journal of Urban Health, 78*(3), 458–467.

Keller, S. (2000). How do I love thee? Let me count the properties. *American Philosophical Quarterly, 37*(2), 163–173.

Koball, H.l., Moiduddin, E., Henderson, J., Goesling, B., & Besculides, M.(2010). What do we know about the link between marriage and health? *Journal of Family Issues, 31,* 1019–1040.

Kouneski, E., & Olson, D.H. (2004). A practical look at intimacy: ENRICH couple typology. In D.J. Mashek & A. Aron, (Eds.), *Handbook of closeness and intimacy* (pp. 117–133). Mahwah, New Jersey: Lawrence Erlbaum Associates Publishers.

Kraut, R., Patterson, M., Lundmark, V., Kiesler, S.,Mukopadhyay, T., & Scherlis, W. (1998). Internet paradox: A social technology that reduces social involvement and psychological well-being? *American Psychologist, 53*(9), 1017–1031.

Lau, S. (1989). Sex role orientation and domains of self-esteem. *Sex Roles, 21,*415–422.

Lau, S., & Gruen, G.E. (1992). The social stigma of loneliness: Effect of target person's and perceiver's sex. *Personality and Social Psychology Bulletin, 18*(2), 182–189.

Laurenceau, J.P., Feldman Barrett, L., & Rovine, M.J. (2005). The interpersonal process model of intimacy in marriage: A daily-diary and multilevel modeling approach. *Journal of Family Psychology, 19*(2), 314–323.

Leary, M.R., & Springer, C.A. (2001). Hurt feelings: The neglected emotion. In R. Kowalski, (Ed.), *Aversive behaviours and interpersonal transgressions* (pp. 151–175). Washington, DC: American Psychological Association.

Lee, J.A. (1973). *The colors of love: An exploration of the ways of loving.* Don Mills, ON: New Press.

Lewis, T., Amini, F., & Lannon, R. (2000). *A general theory of love.* New York: Random House.

Lynch. J.J. (2000). *A cry unheard: New insights into the medical consequences of loneliness.* Baltimore, MD: Bancroft Press.

McCarthy, B., Ginsberg, R.L., & Cintron, J.A. (2008). Primary prevention the first two years of marriage. *Journal of Family Psychotherapy, 19*(2), 143–156.

McPherson, M., Smith-Lovin, L., & Brashears, M.E. (2006). Social isolation in America: Changes in core discussion networks over two decades. *American Sociological Review, 71*(3), 353–375.

Mellor, D., Stokes, M., Firth, L., Hayashi, Y., & Cummins, R. (2008). Need for belonging, relationship satisfaction, loneliness, and life satisfaction. *Personality and Individual Differences, 45,* 213–218.

Mikulincer, M. (1997). Adult attachment style and information processing: Individual differences in curiosity and cognitive closure. *Journal of Personality and Social Psychology, 72*(5), 1217–1230.

Mikulincer, M., & Shaver, P.R. (2009). An attachment and behavioural systems perspective on social support. *Journal of Social and Personal Relationships, 26*(1), 7–19.

Miller, R. S. (2012). *Intimate relationships* (6th International ed.). New York, NY: McGraw Hill.

Olds, J., & Schwartz, R.S. (2009). *The lonely American: Drifting apart in the twenty-first century.* Boston, MA: Beacon Press.

Ornish, D. (1998) *Love and survival: the scientific basis for the healing power of intimacy.* New York: HarperCollins.

Prager, K.J. (1995). *The psychology of intimacy.* New York: The Guildford Press.

Prager, K.J., & Robert, L.J. (2004). Deep intimate connection: self and intimacy in couple relationships. In D.J. Mashek & A. Aron, (Eds.), *Handbook of closeness and intimacy* (pp. 43–60). Mahwah, New Jersey: Lawrence Erlbaum Associates, Publishers.

Putnam, R.D. (2000). *Bowling Alone: The collapse and revival of American community.* New York: Simon & Schuster.

Reis, H.T., Clark, M.S., & Holmes, J.G. (2004). Perceived partner responsiveness as an organizing construct in the study of intimacy and closeness. In D.J. Mashek & A. Aron, (Eds.), *Handbook of closeness and intimacy* (pp. 201–225). Mahwah, NJ: Erlbaum.

Rokach, A. (1988). The experience of loneliness: A tri-level model. *Journal of Psychology, 122,* 531–544.

Rokach, A. (1989). Antecedents of loneliness: A factorial analysis. *The Journal of Psychology, 123*(4), 369–384.

Rubin, Z. (1970). Measurement of romantic love. *Journal of Personality and Social Psychology, 16,* 265–273.

Rubin, Z. (1973). *Liking and loving.* NY: Holt, Reinhart & Winston.

Segrin, C. (1998). Disrupted interpersonal relationships and mental health problems. In Spitzberg, B.H., & Cupach, W.R., (Eds), *The dark side of close relationships* (pp. 327–365). Mahwah, NJ: Erlbaum.

Sleek, S. (1998). Isolation increases with Internet use. *APA Monitor, 29*(9), 1, 30 & 31.

Sommer, K.L., Williams, K.D., Ciarocco, N.J., & Baumeister, R.F. (2001).When silence speaks louder than words: Explorations into the intrapsychic and interpersonal consequences of social ostracism. *Basic and Applied Social Psychology, 23,* 225–243.

Sternberg, J.R. (1986). A triangular theory of love. *Psychological Review, 93,* 119–135.

Strong, B., DeValut, C., & Cohen, T.F. (2011). *The marriage and family experience: intimate relationships in a changing society* (11th ed.) Belmont,CA: Wadsworth.

Subrahmanyam, K., & Lin, G. (2007). Adolescents on the net: Internet use and well being. *Adolescence, 42,* 659–677.

Thoits, P.A. (1983). Main and Interactive Effects of Social Support: Response to LaRocco. *Journal of Health and Social Behavior, 24,* 92–95.

Uchino, B.N., Cacioppo, J.T., & Kiecolt-Glaser, J.K. (1996). The relationship between social support and physiological processes: A review with emphasis on underlying mechanisms and implications for health. *Psychological Bulletin, 119,* 488–531.

Vangelisti, A.L. (Ed.). (2009). *Feeling hurt in close relationships.* New York: Cambridge University Press.

Walster, E., & Walster, G.W. (1978). *A new look at love.* Reading, MA: Addison Wesley.

Weiss, R.S. (1974). The provisions of social relationships. In Z. Rubin, (Ed.), *Doing onto others.* Englewood Cliffs, N.J.: Prentice-Hall.

Williams, K.D. (2007). Ostracism. *Annual Review of Psychology, 58,* 425–452.

Willis, T.A. (1985). *Supportive functions of interpersonal relationships.* San Diego, CA,US: Academic Press, San Diego, CA.

Index

Note:
Page numbers in **bold** type refer to figures
Page numbers in *italic* type refer to tables

Aboud, F.E.: and Glasberg, R. 11
adolescents: co-rumination 32; conflict resolution strategies 32–3, *33*; encouragement 32; friendship quality 42–3; interactional processes 35, 41–3; intimate exchange 32; negative friendship quality *39*; positive friendship quality *38*; romantic relationships 26–44; study correlations *37*
Agape 97
age differences: longing in children 9–20
Alberts, J.K. 101
anger 11

Bargh, J.A.: Chen, M. and Burrows, L. 117
Baumeister, R.F.: and Leary, M.R. 157
Beck Depression Inventory 139
behaviour 63; helping and love 119–28
behavioural influence 118–19
belonging: need 155–6
Bennett, M. 12
Bern's Sex Role Inventory 14
Berscheid, E.: and Hatfield, E. 159
Bettman, J.R.: Zemack-Rugar, Y. and Fitzsimons, G.J. 117
blood donation: participants *123*, *124*; request compliance and 'loving' word 116–29
Boulbry, G.: Guéguen, N. and Jacob, C. 118
Bowlby, J. 158
Brody, R.L.: and Hall, J.A. 13
Burrows, L.: Chen, M. and Bargh, J.A. 117
Butzer, B.: and Kuiper, N.A. 4, 100–14
Buysse, A.: *et al* 3, 58–81

Carnochan, P.: Shaver, P.R. and Fisher, K.W. 10–11
Charles-Sire, V.: *et al* 4, 116–29
Chen, M.: Bargh, J.A. and Burrows, L. 117
children: longing study (Sweden) 9–20, *16*, *17*, *18*, *19*
Choi Mi-Kyung: Shin, N. and Seepersad, S. 4, 146–53
Clark, M.S.: and Mills, J.S. 91
closeness: culture and loneliness 146–53

co-rumination 28, 32
conflict: relationships 84–9, 106; resolution strategies 29, 32–3, *33*; and satisfaction in romantic relationships 84–9; vs pleasant situations and humor use 103–4
Conflict Resolution Style Inventory 85
Couchoud, E.A.: Zoller, D. and Denham, S.A. 13
couples 135–42; empathy and social support provision 58–81
Cramer, D. 3, 84–9
culture: loneliness and closeness 146–53

Davies, M.F. 91–8
Davis, M.H.: *et al* 3, 58–81; and Oathout, H.A. 60
De Koning, E.: and Weiss, R.L. 101
Demir, A. 135–42
Denham, S.A.: Zoller, D. and Couchoud, E.A. 13
desire 10
Devoldre, I.: *et al* 3, 58–81
Distel, M.A. 1
Doherty, W.J. 2

embarrassment 12
emotion 10–11, 12–13; studies 14
empathy 59–60; research 60–2; and social support for couples 58–81; study 63; study descriptive statistics *65*, *70*; study multiple regression analyses *66*, *70*, *73-7*
encouragement 28–9, 32
Eros 92, 97

Feinberg, R.A. 118
Fisher, A.: Timmers, M. and Manstead, A.S. 13
Fisher, K.W.: Shaver, P.R. and Carnochan, P. 10–11
Fişiloğlu, H. 135–42
Fitzsimons, G.J.: Zemack-Rugar, Y. and Bettman, J.R. 117

INDEX

friendship quality: negative *39*; positive *38*; and romantic relationships 26–44
future time orientation in romantic relationships (FTORR) 48–56

Garner, P.W.: Robertson, S. and Smith, G. 13
gender 29–30; differences in child longing 9–20; roles 98; stereotypes 49
Gerson, A.C.: Perlman, D. and Spinner, B. 137
Glasberg, R.: and Aboud, F.E. 11
Gordon, J. 156; and McKinney, A. 159
Gottman, J.: *et al* 86, 89
Gottschall, J.: and Nordlund, M. 2
Guéguen, N.: *et al* 4, 116–29; Jacob, C. and Boulbry, G. 118

Hall, J.A.: and Brody, R.L. 13
Harris, P.L. 11
Harter, S.: and Whitesell, N.R. 11
Hatfield, E.: and Berscheid, E. 159
Hazan, C.: and Shaver, P. 159–60
Heather, S.: and Perrine, R.M. 118
Heinhold, A.M.: Kerr, S.L. and Palladino, L. 13–14
Hendrick, S.S.: Relationship Assessment Scale 87
Holm, O. 9–20
Hortaçsu, N.: and Oral, A. 142
humor: in relationships 100–14; use in conflict v pleasant situations 103–4

interactional processes 28–30, *35*, 41–3; co-rumination 28; conflict resolution strategies 29; encouragement 28–9; gender 29–30; intimate exchange 28
Interpersonal Reactivity Index 63
intimacy 156–8
intimate exchange 28; measure 32

Jacob, C.: Guéguen, N.; and Boulbry, G. 118
Johnson, S.M. 158

Kalnok, M.: and Malatesta, C.Z. 13
Kerr, S.L.: Heinhold, A.M. and Palladino, L. 13–14
Klein, D.N.: and Kuiper, N.A. 112
Korea 5; parents 148
Kouneski, E.: and Olson, D.H. 158
Kuiper, N.A.: and Butzer, B. 4, 100–14; and Klein, D.N. 112

Leary, M.R.: and Baumeister, R.F. 157
Lee, J.A. 92
Lewis, T.: *et al* 154
loneliness 136, 156; culture 146–53; relationship status **151**

longing: aspects 9–20; definition 10
love 2; helping behaviour 119–28; social desirability 93–5
love styles: Agape 97; endorsement 91–8; Eros 92, 97; impression management 95–7, *96*; Ludus 97; social desirability *94*
Loving = Helping condition **122**
Ludus 97

McKinney, A.: and Gordon, J. 159
Malatesta, C.Z.: and Kalnok, M. 13
Manstead, A.S.: Timmers, M. and Fisher, A. 13
marital adjustment: for Turkish couples 135–42
marriage 141, 158
Meineri, S.: *et al* 4, 116–29
Mellor, D.: *et al* 157
Mills, D. 92
Mills, J.S.: and Clark, M.S. 91

Nordlund, M.: and Gottschall, J. 2
North America: loneliness 1

Oathout, H.A.: and Davis, M.H. 60
Olds, J.: and Schwartz, R.S. 157
O'Leary, K.D. 141
Olson, D.H.: and Kouneski, E. 158
Öner, B. 49
Oral, A.: and Hortaçsu, N. 142
Ornish, D. 2, 155, 158

Palladino, L.: Kerr, S.L. and Heinhold, A.M. 13–14
parents 13–14; Korean 148
Pascual, A.: *et al* 4, 116–29
Peplau, L.A.: and Perlman, D. 147
Perlman, D.: *et al* 137; Gerson, A.C. and Spinner, B. 137; and Peplau, L.A. 147
Perrine, R.M.: and Heather, S. 118
psychology 1
Putnam, R. 154–5

relationships: closeness level **152**; cognitive representations 27–8; conflict 84–9, 106; humor hierarchical regression analyses *109*; humor in 100–14; humor and satisfaction 102–3; pleasant situations 106; quality 64; satisfaction 84–9
Ridgeway, D.: and Russell, J.A. 11–12
Robertson, S.: Garner, P.W. and Smith, G. 13
Rokach, A. 1–5, 154–60
romantic involvement 34
romantic relationships 26–44; future time orientation in (FTORR) 48–56; satisfaction and conflict 84–9
Ross, R. 137

INDEX

Rubin, Z. 159
Russell, J.A.: and Ridgeway, D. 11–12

Sakalli-Ugurlu, N. 48–56
satisfaction: and conflict in romantic relationships 84–9; and humor 102–3
Schwartz, R.S.: and Olds, J. 157
Sedikides, C.: and Sprecher, S. 14
Seepersad, S.: Choi Mi-Kyung and Shin, N. 4, 146–53
Sex Role Inventory: Bern's 14
Shaver, P.: and Hazan, C. 159–60
Shaver, P.R.: Fisher, K.W. and Carnochan, P. 10–11
Shin, N.: Seepersad, S. and Choi Mi-Kyung 4, 146–53
Smith, G.: Robertson, S. and Garner, P.W. 13
social desirability: responding and love styles 91–8, *94*
social relations 157
social support 58–9; behaviour 63; empathy 59–60; and empathy for couples 58–81
Social Support Interaction Coding System (SSICS) 63
Spectrum, The 2
Spinner, B.: Perlman, D. and Gerson, A.C. 137
Sprecher, S.: and Sedikides, C. 14
stereotypes: gender 49
Sternberg, R.J. 91–2, 159
Storge 92
Strong, B.: *et al* 158
Sweden: children longing study 9–20, *16*, *17*, *18*, *19*

technology 155
Thomas, J.J. 3, 26–44
Timmers, M.: Fisher, A. and Manstead, A.S. 13
Turkey: couples and marital adjustment 135–42; women 54

UCLA Loneliness Scale 139
United States of America (USA) 5

Verhofstadt, L.L.: *et al* 3, 58–81

Walster, E.: and Walster, G.W. 92
Weiss, R.L.: and De Koning, E. 101
Weiss, R.S. 136, 157
Whitesell, N.R.: and Harter, S. 11
Wolfe, T. 1
women 54
words: as environmental cues 116–29

yearning 10
Youn, G. 148
Young, J.E. 136

Zemack-Rugar, Y.: Bettman, J.R. and Fitzsimons, G.J. 117
Zoller, D.: Denham, S.A. and Couchoud, E.A. 13